Epiphany in the Modern Novel

Epiphany
in the Modern Novel

by Morris Beja

University of Washington Press
Seattle

Published by the University of Washington Press 1971
Library of Congress Catalog Card Number 71-117725

Printed in Great Britain

To Nancy

Βεβαίως

Acknowledgments

I am grateful to the following publishers and copyright holders for specific permission to quote from the relevant materials : the Society of Authors on behalf of the Trustees of the Estate of James Joyce, for *Stephen Hero* (copyright 1944 by New Directions Publishing Corporation); the Viking Press, Inc., and Jonathan Cape Ltd., for James Joyce, *A Portrait of the Artist as a Young Man*; Random House, Inc., for James Joyce, *Ulysses*, and William Faulkner, in particular *Absalom, Absalom!*, *Light in August*, and *The Sound and the Fury*; Charles Scribner's Sons, for Thomas Wolfe, *Look Homeward, Angel* and *Of Time and the River*; Harper and Row, Publishers, Inc., for Thomas Wolfe, *The Web and the Rock* and *You Can't Go Home Again*; Leonard Woolf, and the Berg Collection of the New York Public Library, for the manuscript of Virginia Woolf's *The Waves*; Harcourt Brace Jovanovich, Inc., and Quentin Bell, Angelica Garnett, and the Hogarth Press Ltd., for Virginia Woolf, in particular *Mrs. Dalloway*, *To the Lighthouse*, and *A Writer's Diary*.

Early versions of some of the materials in this book appeared in the *Critical Quarterly*, *Renascence*, and *Modern Fiction Studies* (copyright © 1965 by the Purdue Research Foundation), and I am grateful for permission to reprint those materials. I would especially like to thank A. E. Dyson of the *Critical Quarterly* for his kindness and interest.

Actually, this book and I owe many debts to many people. At Cornell University, I am especially grateful to Walter J. Slatoff, who guided my earliest endeavors, and to M. H. Abrams, whose ideas on Romantic literature first gave me the impulse to pursue my topic and whose encouragement helped me keep at it. Robert H. Elias and James McConkey helped shape and improve the early versions of my study, and George H. Healey, Curator of Rare Books, aided me at various stages in my research.

The list of still other mentors, friends, and colleagues who have at various times read all or major portions of my manuscript is comforting, at least to me : Howard Babb, Jonathan Baumbach, Bernard Benstock, Robert M. Estrich, Gordon K. Grigsby, Julian Markels, John M. Muste, Claude M. Simpson, Herbert J. Stern,

Harold E. Toliver, and Francis L. Utley have all made valuable suggestions and comments. Albert J. Kuhn, chairman of the English Department, has helped encourage Ohio State University to provide a research grant; I would like to thank him for that and for much else. I am also taking this opportunity to put in print my gratitude to the Fulbright program for the chance to tinker at my project while spending a year as lecturer at the University of Thessaloniki, Greece, 1965-66. During that year, two friends at home—Barry E. Gross and Richard T. Martin—performed in respect to this study many thankless tasks for which I would nevertheless like to thank them.

Some of my gratitude is of an even more personal kind : to Thomas R. Dragnette, whom I never met, who was killed in the Korean War, and whose library his mother gave to me at a time when I had few books of my own; to my family, especially my mother and father; to Andrew and Eleni, for being around; above all, to my wife Nancy, to whom I dedicate this book—grateful that through it all she has remained my envoy from the fair courts of life.

Morris Beja

Ohio State University
March, 1970

Contents

Epiphany in the Modern Novel

He believed that it was for the man of letters to record these epiphanies with extreme care, seeing that they themselves are the most delicate and evanescent of moments.

James Joyce, *Stephen Hero*

I

Introduction

> By a different conformation of its senses a Creature might be made to apprehend any given Portion of space, as greater, or less in any Proportion, than it appears to us. This we are assured of from Optics. I doubt not also but by a *different conformation* of yᵉ Brain a Creature might be made to apprehend any given portion of time as longer or shorter in any proportion than it appears to us. Glasses can make an *inch* seem a *mile*. I leave it to future ages to invent a method for making a *minute* seem a *year*.
>
> Laurence Sterne[1]

As a matter of fact, men had "invented" such a method long before Sterne wrote these remarks; if we can take their word for it, mystics had gone even further and experienced eternity within the pulsation of an artery. And men have also written of more mundane experiences, mere spots of time when they felt as if they had not only transcended time but also reached some sort of new awareness. In James Joyce's *Stephen Hero*, written early in our century, Stephen describes one such experience and calls it "epiphany"—a word he uses to refer to sudden illuminations produced by apparently trivial, even seemingly arbitrary, causes. Of course, Stephen merely provides a new name for an old experience, but his timing is appropriate : the kind of moment of insight he talks about has played an important and new role in modern literature. It has long received attention in poetry and autobiography, but in the novel it was largely subordinated or even ignored until the end of the nineteenth century.

Phenomena like epiphany are difficult to define precisely, and I have no illusions about the possibility of arriving at a universally

---

[1] "*Fragment Inédit*," in Paul Stapfer, *Laurence Sterne* (Paris, 1870). Quoted in Alan Dugald McKillop, *The Early Masters of English Fiction*, p. 197.

acceptable definition—although I recognize how disingenuous that may sound at the start of a book on the subject. Yet I do feel that the very attempt at definition would be valuable, and that an examination of this particular type of moment of illumination can increase our general understanding of modern fiction, its concerns, and its techniques. This book, which concentrates on three major figures in addition to Joyce—Virginia Woolf, Thomas Wolfe, and William Faulkner—attempts to show that, even if Joyce had never lived and Stephen had never roamed the streets of Dublin, what they both called "epiphany" would still have been a profoundly important presence in the contemporary novel. Nevertheless, Joyce did provide us with a convenient and suggestive word; and although my chapter on him will examine in detail his own special views on epiphany, we ought to try at the outset to arrive at a general working definition. And as long as we are going to use Joyce's term, the starting point for any attempt at defining it ought logically to be the all too brief passage in which he tells us that by an epiphany Stephen "meant a sudden spiritual manifestation, whether in the vulgarity of speech or of gesture or in a memorable phase of the mind itself. He believed that it was for the man of letters to record these epiphanies with extreme care, seeing that they themselves are the most delicate and evanescent of moments."[2]

Stephen describes the manifestation as "sudden"—a mere moment, indeed the "most delicate and evanescent" of moments. Like the mystical experience or the conversion—neither of which can be identified with it—the epiphany may be prepared for over long periods of time; but when the experience does come, it is not gradual but immediate.

The sudden manifestation, Stephen also says, is a "spiritual" one. The sort of experience dealt with under the concept of epiphany can easily be interpreted religiously, and until the past few centuries moments of revelation were almost invariably regarded as just what the phrase implies: moments in which an external divine force reveals the truth. But although "epiphany" is a theological term, it is not necessarily a religious concept. It can also be re-

---

[2] *Stephen Hero*, p. 211. Stephen here describes epiphany as both a "manifestation" and a "moment"; he also generally feels free to use the term to refer to the whole experience or incident that causes the revelation. Moreover, Joyce called the manuscripts in which he recorded such experiences "epiphanies." I shall assume the same freedom.

garded as perfectly natural, if unusual, and this has become the increasing tendency, until in modern literature writers who regard it as deriving from divine grace—Gerard Manley Hopkins, T. S. Eliot—are conspicuous exceptions. Joyce, as we shall see, is not, and his use of the word "spiritual" is figurative.

An epiphany is a sudden spiritual "manifestation"—a showing forth, an illumination, a revelation. Stephen, during the conversation with Cranly in *Stephen Hero*, expresses the belief that this manifestation may be produced by any one of a number of things : an ordinary concrete object, a work of art, a snatch of talk overheard on the street, a gesture—or some "memorable phase of the mind itself." In Joyce's case, the most important revelations derived from phases of the mind are the dream-epiphanies he recorded in his own manuscripts. But under the same general heading we can also include those revelations that arise from memory. There are two major types : what I call the "retrospective" epiphany, and that of "the past recaptured." The retrospective epiphany is one in which an event arouses no special impression when it occurs, but produces a sudden sensation of new awareness when it is recalled at some future time. I shall discuss such moments of delayed revelation when we come to both Joyce and Thomas Wolfe. Discussion of experiences involving the actual recapture of the past, as opposed to its mere recollection, is best postponed until the section on Marcel Proust in my second chapter.

We can already see, therefore, that in themselves the statements in *Stephen Hero* are helpful but not all sufficient. For fuller clarification of the nature of epiphany we cannot restrict ourselves to them : neither the general development and use of epiphany in fiction, nor its development and use in Joyce's own works, have precisely followed the lines, vague and general as they are, laid down in that early fragment. So without setting up a rival theory, we must still enlarge upon Stephen's exposition in order to encompass aspects of epiphany implicit in Joyce's practice, as well as that of other modern novelists, although these aspects are not explicitly dealt with in *Stephen Hero*. In this way we can, I think, establish criteria for distinguishing from epiphany other types of moments of vision and intensity.

First, we should not confuse epiphany with revelations which, however sudden, are simply results of direct statement. The classical scene of recognition, or anagnorisis, yields a powerful and sudden

illumination—but one whose quality usually differs from the illumination of epiphany. Whatever effect the discoveries at the end of
Oedipus Rex, Othello, or *Tom Jones* may have on the passions of
a character or reader, these discoveries are themselves rational, not
"spiritual." They arise logically from direct statement or evidence
rather than dramatically from indirect suggestion. Even remarks
treated in a much lower key will often provide information too
directly for us to speak of epiphany. When Proust's Swann demands
to know whether Odette has ever had homosexual affairs, he makes
her nervous with all his questions. "How on earth can I tell?" she
answers furiously. "Perhaps I have, ever so long ago, when I didn't
know what I was doing, perhaps two or three times." Completely
unprepared for such an answer, Swann perceives the nature of his
beloved as never before, his heart lacerated by "those words, 'two
or three times' "; but this revelation, although produced suddenly
by "nothing more than a few words" (*Swann's Way*, 1:278), does
not really convey the impression of those other, more privileged
moments in Proust when we have the sense of what Joyce called
epiphany. Swann has come upon his new knowledge in too rational,
straightforward a manner.

Of course, an epiphany does sometimes originate in a direct
statement. Yet the revelation produced is then somehow irrelevant
to that statement; we have something along the lines of the Zen
koan, which is a question so apparently absurd (what is the sound
of one hand clapping?) that it produces enlightenment with what
Aldous Huxley has called the irrelevance of the Marx Brothers
(*Doors of Perception*, p. 19). This irrelevance is connected to a
more general notion which might be called the Criterion of Incongruity: that when the cause of an illumination is clearly important, there is no epiphany unless the revelation is not strictly
relevant to whatever produces it.

Another way of saying much the same thing would be to use the
term Criterion of Insignificance. It is "a trivial incident," a "triviality," that makes Stephen think of collecting epiphanies. Joyce once
told his brother, "It is my idea of the significance of trivial things
that I want to give the two or three unfortunate wretches who may
eventually read me."[3] The insignificance of anything that produces
an epiphany is of course purely relative. The incident is important

---

[3] Quoted from Stanislaus Joyce's diary, in Richard Ellmann, *James Joyce*,
p. 169.

in so far as it provides a revelation, but it would seem minor to someone else, and perhaps at any other time to the person experiencing it. In this quality lies one of the principal roots of the increasing use of epiphany in modern literature. For as men have found themselves putting less and less trust in the truths and absolutes of the past, they have more and more come to stress the *trivia* of existence. They have sought meaning in what they could see, all around them, in the apparently inconsequential objects and events of everyday life. It is true that an interest in trivial detail has always been important in literature, but today it has taken on such a special character and become so central that Erich Auerbach is undoubtedly correct when he regards concern with "minor, unimpressive, random events" as one of the hallmarks of twentieth-century literature (*Mimesis*, p. 546). He examines it in Virginia Woolf but also mentions Proust, Knut Hamsun, Thomas Mann, André Gide, and Joyce. There are, of course, other major figures he might have named in this connection; one of the most important is Joseph Conrad. In *Lord Jim*, Marlow—who is so sensitive to the "light of glamor created in the shock of trifles"—tells of his conversation with a French officer : "I kept him company; and suddenly, but not abruptly . . . he pronounced, '*Mon Dieu*! how the time passes!' Nothing could have been more commonplace than this remark; but its utterance coincided for me with a moment of vision . . . there can be but few of us who had never known one of these rare moments of awakening when we see, hear, understand ever so much —everything—in a flash—before we fall back again into our agreeable somnolence" (pp. 225, 143).

"Nothing could have been more commonplace than this remark." Nor more irrelevant, perhaps. But no one, I imagine, would deny the relevance of Marlow's own comments to epiphany. However, that is not quite the same thing as saying that an epiphany can arise *only* from an insignificant or irrelevant object or event. Certainly Joyce never says it, explicitly; but without exception the epiphanies he himself recorded all imply it. And in other writers, when one comes across some glorious, earth-shaking moment of revelation, one is not really tempted to speak of epiphany, or at least I am not. I would very much hesitate to call Dante's vision at the end of the *Paradiso* an epiphany; he sees God in all His magnificence, not the mere babe in a manger of the Epiphany.

If I had to commit myself to a brief definition of epiphany, then,

I would call it a *sudden spiritual manifestation, whether from some object, scene, event, or memorable phase of the mind—the manifestation being out of proportion to the significance or strictly logical relevance of whatever produces it.*

This book examines the part such sudden spiritual manifestations play in the modern novel. My first chapter provides some idea of the tradition and present context against which contemporary authors use epiphany; it surveys not only types of moments of intense new awareness and how they have figured in Western literature, but also concepts of time and aesthetic perception relevant to my subject. This discussion is followed by a chapter on each of four major novelists, whom I have chosen both because they are significant in themselves and because, in part by the very diversity of their use of epiphany, they are representative of many novelists whom I only mention or discuss briefly, and of others whose names never appear in my pages at all. Together, then, these four chapters form an attempt to demonstrate ways in which epiphany has been employed in modern fiction, and ends it has served; individually, each is a critical essay on a single figure—carrying forward my general themes and arguments, but also analyzing the uses each writer has made of moments of revelation in his own technique and works, and discussing the extent to which such moments are essential to his views of art and experience.

Throughout, the idea I want to stress is that the role of epiphany in the modern novel has been both immensely important and unique to our time. These two qualities are most conspicuously reflected in the astonishing frequency with which sudden moments of intuitive insight appear in twentieth-century fiction, a frequency unmatched and even unapproached in the fiction of the past. But perhaps still more noteworthy is the fact that a sense of epiphany, or something very close to it, is vital to the artistic concepts and aims of many of our most significant novelists. It is, indeed, at the very core of their view of their function as artists. Like Joyce's Stephen, they have "believed that it was for the man of letters to record these epiphanies with extreme care, seeing that they themselves are the most delicate and evanescent of moments." To Henry James, for example, the "imaginative" mind is the one able to convert "the very pulses of the air into revelations."[4] Virginia Woolf suggests that the best way to understand "what a novelist is doing" is to try to imitate him : "Recall, then, some event that has left a distinct impression on you—how at the corner of the street, perhaps, you passed two people talking. A tree shook; an electric light danced; the tone of the talk was comic, but also tragic; a whole vision, an entire conception, seemed contained in that moment." Faced with this impression, the artist tries "to reconstruct it in words"[5]—to "fix," in Joyce's phrase, "the most elusive of his moods" (*Stephen Hero*, p. 32). To Thomas Wolfe, "the reason that the artist lives and works and has his being" is his "intolerable desire to fix eternally in the patterns of an indestructible form a single moment of man's living, a single moment of life's beauty, passion, and unutterable eloquence, that passes, flames and goes . . ." (*Of Time and the River*, pp. 550-51). As if in explicit agreement, F. Scott Fitzgerald writes that what he, Wolfe, and Hemingway as well have in common is the attempt in their fiction "to recapture the exact feel of a moment in time and space"—an attempt which, as we shall see, he is correct in associating with "what Wordsworth was trying to do. . . ."[6] William Faulkner, too, believes that the "craft" of the novelist is "to arrest for a believable moment" the experience of life.[7] And when Marcel Proust tells us in *Within a Budding Grove* that one of Elstir's paintings is a masterpiece because "he had succeeded in transcribing, in fixing for all time upon the painted sheet . . . the throb of one happy moment" (1 :676), he defines his own ultimate aim. We shall see that this aim appears in other modern novelists, too, and that many of them feel, as well, that the work of art attains its greatest power when the artist does not merely record, but produces in his audience a sense of new and sudden vision.

When I say that the importance and centrality of epiphany are new in modern fiction, and peculiar to it, I am not trying to imply that earlier novelists did not include in their works the specific kind of moment of perception I am examining. That would, of course, simply not be true. But my point is that although some novelists— notably Dickens, George Eliot, and Hardy—wrote novels that con-

[4] "The Art of Fiction," in *The House of Fiction*, pp. 31-32.
[5] "How Should One Read a Book?" in *The Common Reader: Second Series*, pp. 259-60.
[6] *The Letters of F. Scott Fitzgerald*, p. 251.
[7] *New York Times*, 3 July 1961, p. 6.

tain such moments, those novels do not rely on epiphany as an essential technique, and their authors did not themselves value it as a keystone of their art. They can no more be said to have written "epiphanic" novels than the writer who at one point in his book refers to a traffic light can thereby be called a Symbolist. With the qualified, relative exceptions of a few isolated figures such as Sterne, Flaubert, Dostoyevsky, and Pater, novelists before James and Conrad, say, did not use moments of revelation to the same extent, or with the same emphasis—and certainly not with the same distinct effect—as many modern novelists do.

Nor do I mean to imply that every novelist writing in the twentieth century turns out books swarming with sudden spiritual manifestations. But it is interesting that those who do (such as Joyce, Proust, Virginia Woolf, Dorothy Richardson, Wolfe, Faulkner, Lawrence Durrell, John Barth) are often those who have been especially associated with "modern" trends in literature, and who have adopted techniques that did not appear in eighteenth- and nineteenth-century novels. Contrast these writers (if I may ignore, for convenience, all those whose use of epiphany is noticeable but not especially striking or essential, and who therefore come somewhere in between) with some of their contemporaries who do not make significant use of epiphany—H. G. Wells, Arnold Bennett, Theodore Dreiser, Sinclair Lewis, C. P. Snow, James Gould Cozzens—novelists whose technique, if not the ends they make it serve, is largely traditional. My point could also apply to the development of the modern short story. As Irene Hendry Chayes early suggested,[8] the stories in *Dubliners*, as well as those by Chekhov, Katherine Mansfield, Virginia Woolf, Sherwood Anderson, Hemingway, and many contributors to the *New Yorker*, are clearly different from those by earlier writers; and just as clearly the chief differences are related in method and objectives to epiphany.

Of course, these correspondences are not accidental, and throughout this book—and particularly in my first chapter—I try to explore some of the reasons *why* epiphany has taken on so much new importance, and to suggest some of the characteristics of the modern world, its temper, and its literature that have contributed toward making our fiction so full of what Conrad calls "moments of awakening." In this century epiphanies have tended to be attached

[8] Irene Hendry [Chayes], "Joyce's Epiphanies," *Sewanee Review* 54 (Summer 1946): 452, 454.

to certain recurrent attitudes toward the meaning of experience, toward the nature of reality, and even toward the means of salvation—or, at least, of enlightenment. We cannot refer to any single generalization as the common denominator accounting for the new importance in fiction of special moments of intensity, for this subject is a vast and complex one. But we can, while recognizing the uniqueness of each writer's treatment of such moments, propose various possibilities—common if not ubiquitous denominators—which will help us understand and in some degree even account for the general emphasis and attention these moments have received.

We shall be reminded, for example, that despite the general disillusion with religion during the past few generations, a continuing need—perhaps even an intensified one—has been felt for meaningful, unifying, "spiritual" emotions or experiences that would provide men with answers to some of their burning questions. No longer confident, however, of a divine answer, men have wanted their own; no longer willing to wait for Truth until God calls them to it, they have sought for it today, on earth, here and now. There has been a general secularization of what once was inevitably regarded —and, of course, still often is—as the divinely inspired moment of new knowledge. Besides the uneasy disillusion with religion, or at any rate with orthodox religions, another influence on the quality of the moments of illumination recorded in modern fiction has been the equally great loss of faith in reason. The conviction that enlightenment is no more likely to come from rationalism and logic than it is from God makes the need for instantaneous, intuitive illumination seem all the more critical. If the literary epiphany is now usually represented so as to seem irreligious, and occasionally even antireligious, it is, as well, almost invariably seen as irrational, and very often even antirational.

In the particular area of prose fiction, we shall come across a number of more specific trends which have also furthered the importance of epiphany. One worth mentioning here, since it is probably the most significant of all, is the fascination of twentieth-century novelists with psychology and the subjective processes of the mind. This interest in the pattern or lack of pattern of consciousness has been enhanced by the old but newly emphasized discovery that character can often be more profoundly and powerfully revealed by our mental reactions to so-called trivia than by our external reactions to demonstrably important events.

But this is only one example of how epiphany has been a part of the chief preoccupations of modern fiction. These preoccupations are, in turn, manifestations of the increased awareness of the novel as an art form capable of confronting the most complex experiences and the most subtle themes. A corollary of this new respect has been the invasion of the novel by the characteristics, techniques, and standards of poetry. The concerns of poetry as well: and this is a major point, for the novelists whom we shall see displaying great interest in apparently insignificant objects and trivial events do so less in the naturalistic tradition of Defoe and Richardson than in the spiritual tradition of Marvell and Hopkins and the Romantic tradition of Blake and Wordsworth.

Just as epiphany is associated with the dominant themes of modern fiction, so is it one of its most useful and central techniques. Of course, as a technique stressing the disconnected moment, it has limitations too, and some of its tendencies—toward choppiness, toward interruption of the flow of a narrative, as well as toward an occasional overemphasis on things that in the end seem insignificant no matter how we approach them—must be carefully controlled. Or made purposeful, as in what Northrop Frye calls the tachistocopical method of *The Waste Land* (*The Modern Century*, p. 66).

For more important are the positive functions the epiphany can perform. One of the most important of all is its use as a structural device. It may, for example, mark climaxes in a narrative, as it especially does in the novels of Joyce and Virginia Woolf. Or, through the sudden recapture or recollection of the past, it may introduce a flashback that reveals some necessary background or even becomes a lengthy and almost independent episode, as, say, in Faulkner, Mrs. Woolf, and Alain Robbe-Grillet. This technique also appears in many modern plays. Indeed, the structure of a drama like Arthur Miller's *Death of a Salesman* is based on it. Willy Loman relives various moments of his past through the slightest suggestions; portrayed in flashbacks, they seem to his disturbed mind as if they are actually in the present. Such constant disruption of chronology has been even more common in motion pictures, which have so profoundly influenced the fiction of our time. Recently, this technique has become especially persistent; in France, the early "New Wave" films—most notably Alain Resnais' *Hiroshima, Mon Amour* and *Last Year at Marienbad*—leaned on it heavily. An epiphany will also often serve as a unifying or integrating device, instantaneously bringing together many of the main threads of a novel; all the novelists I am discussing use it for this end, with varying success.

Another reason for the favor epiphany has found with the modern writer is that it enables him to overcome some of the barriers he has forced himself to accept. He has, notably, felt chained by "point of view" and his reluctance to abandon a façade of "objectivity." A novelist can remain, like the God of the creation, beyond his handiwork, paring his fingernails—and at the same time get his views across by allowing his characters moments of revelation in which they transcend themselves and see into the truth of things. In some ways Bloom and Mrs. Dalloway may not be very bright, but when they have moments of insight, that insight serves their creators well.

Thus the epiphany, in one sense a frozen tableau, can nevertheless be a valuable instrument for drama, presenting in a scene or event what might otherwise have to be explained or summarized. Joyce once told a friend that he wanted his reader "to understand always through suggestion rather than direct statement."[9] Many other modern novelists, in their similar desire to shun the obvious, have avoided broad narrative summary in favor of indirection and the recording of individual, apparently trivial dramatic scenes. A number of these writers have come to realize that their aim—not exposition, but art—is best served, not by statement and explanation, but by drama and revelation.

[9] Quoted in Frank Budgen, *James Joyce and the Making of Ulysses*, p. 21.

2

The Tradition

Time travels in divers paces with divers persons. I'll tell
you who Time ambles withal, who Time trots withal,
who Time gallops withal, and who he stands still withal.
                                    As You Like It, act 3, sc. 2

I. THE PRESENT OF THINGS PAST

. . . The motion by which one measures time is circular,
is in a closed circle; and might almost equally well be
described as rest, as cessation of movement—for the there
repeats itself constantly in the here, the past in the
present.
                    Thomas Mann, *The Magic Mountain*, p. 344

The experience Joyce chose to call epiphany has taken on new
significance in the modern novel, but it did not come out of a
vacuum or arise through spontaneous generation; consequently, it is
helpful to set it against some of its literary, philosophical, and
religious background, in a roughly chronological discussion and
from a perspective that is, inevitably, highly selective.

The epiphany is one type of moment of illumination, and the
main tradition of such moments begins on the road to Damascus
with Paul; for, in the West, the moment of vision is a Christian
phenomenon, with only a few real antecedents in classical or
Hebraic literature. The prophets, for example, had visions of God
and visitations from Heaven, but not the same sort of sudden enlightenment that has since been called the conversion experience,
or the sense of union with God that we call "mystical." As Teufelsdröckh points out, "the Old World knew nothing of Conversion,"
which is a "new-attained progress in the Moral Development of
man" : "what to Plato was but a hallucination, and to Socrates a
chimera, is now clear and certain to your Zinzendorfs, your Wesleys,

24

and the poorest of their Pietists and Methodists."[1] Until relatively recent times, in both East and West, the moment of revelation was invariably considered to be of divine origin. The very word "revelation" presupposes a revealing force bestowing the new vision upon recipients—though not necessarily passive recipients.

The outstanding example of such a divine revelation is the one arising from the mystical experience. Even when understood in its strict sense, it seems at first to have much in common with epiphany: both are sudden and intense moments of exhilaration or pain, and both involve a new sense of awareness. Of the eight characteristics of Satori, or Enlightenment, discussed by D. T. Suzuki, four also describe epiphany : the experience is irrational; it involves "intuitive insight"; it is authoritative (it cannot be refuted by "logical argument"); and it is "a momentary experience." The other characteristics are not necessarily involved in epiphany, though they may be : Enlightenment is affirmative; it provides a sense of "the Beyond, the Absolute, or God"; it has an "impersonal tone"; and it produces a "feeling of exaltation."[2] Actually, however, these similarities are almost superficial and incidental, and the differences are much more significant. The mystical state is not merely "impersonal"— one of its main traits is the necessity for the denial and even the annihilation of the self. In epiphany, on the contrary, the revelation is often very personal, involving a distinct awareness of the self rather than denial of it; the emphasis is frequently on the personality of the subject, not on the object revealed. And what is revealed is not necessarily "the Beyond," the divine ground of all being, or the Godhead, as it must be in the mystical experience. Moreover, it is not only by their fruits that you shall know them. The means differ even more markedly, for while physical sensations are usually prominent in epiphany, the mystic must escape from and mortify the senses in order to attain his goal.

The epiphany is actually more reminiscent of the conversion, which also (though one often hears otherwise) is not necessarily mystical. Many of the figures who have left famous accounts of this experience—Paul, Augustine, John Bunyan, Jonathan Edwards,

---

[1] Thomas Carlyle, *Sartor Resartus*, p. 149 (II, x). According to another, later, Germanic thinker, the psychologist Otto Rank, the Christian era did introduce to humanity a new psychological type— "the inspirational" (*Beyond Psychology*, pp. 141-42).

[2] See D. T. Suzuki, *Zen Buddhism*, pp. 103-8.

Thomas Carlyle—are no more genuine mystics, despite their frequently being called so, than are other writers who have undergone "conversions" but to whom the term cannot even be loosely attached —such as John Stuart Mill, John Henry Newman, and André Gide. William James goes so far as to say that conversion is "a normal adolescent phenomenon" and even points out that there is such a thing as the "non-religious" or "counter-conversion," in which one passes "from orthodoxy to infidelity" (*Varieties of Religious Experience*, pp. 199, 176). In either case, the experience follows basically the same pattern. A person has been going through a period of deep despair and doubt. Throughout his change, he feels that he is passive and being acted upon. And though the experience may be prepared for, in the end it almost invariably comes suddenly. (Quoting John Wesley's conclusion from hearing the accounts of his followers "that sanctification is commonly, if not always, an instantaneous work," James adds that this is, "if not the healthier-minded, yet on the whole the profounder spiritual instinct" [pp. 227-28].) There is frequently a sense of rebirth, both because the world seems new and because there has been an intense struggle, a conflict like that of the Buddha under the Bodhi-tree. But after the despair and the struggle there is the reward of a profound stability and peace, and the Nay-sayer becomes a Yea-sayer, no longer indifferent.

The account in Saint Augustine's *Confessions* indicates that his experience closely followed what has since come to seem the archetypal pattern of the conversion. There were, first, the gradual approaches toward truth—the momentary "flash of one trembling glance" revealing "THAT WHICH IS" only to be pushed back by his falling upon his "wonted habits" (p. 138 [VII]). Finally, he was thrown into the very depths of despair when a visitor told him of two soldiers who had been given faith suddenly upon reading the life of Saint Anthony. In tears at comparing his own state with theirs, Augustine rushed into the garden, where he heard a voice chanting, "Take up and read."

> I seized, opened, and in silence read that section on which my eyes first fell : Not in rioting and drunkenness, not in chambering and wantonness, not in strife and envying; but put ye on the Lord Jesus Christ, and make not provision for the flesh, in concupiscence. No further would I read; nor needed I : for instantly

at the end of this sentence, by a light as it were of serenity in-
fused into my heart, all the darkness of doubt vanished away.
[P. 167 (VIII)]

In the *Confessions*, the very form of which is that of a monologue
spoken to God, Augustine never lets us forget that his experience
arose not so much out of himself as from an external force, to whom
he owes everything : this feeling, although it seems especially strong
in him (it has even been claimed that the concept of grace was "his
personal contribution to Christian thought"[3]), is one of the most
characteristic elements of the traditional spiritual conversion.

Augustine is also a key figure to consider in any discussion of the
development of modern views toward time. While the Greeks had
concentrated for the most part on its physical aspects—time as
motion, say—Augustine is a precursor of many later writers in his
psychological emphasis. For, although he regards time as an objective phenomenon, he nevertheless says that it is measured within
the minds and souls of men. His discussion is meant largely as an
answer to the skeptics' question of why, if the idea of man has
existed in God from eternity, man himself has not existed from
eternity. The answer is that he has, for, as T. S. Eliot later expresses
it, "all time is eternally present."[4] Augustine recognizes "that
neither things to come nor past are"—but he also rejects the concept
of the three times of past, present, and future. Rather " 'there be
three times : a present of things past, a present of things present,
and a present of things future.' For these three do exist in some
sort, in the soul, but otherwise do I not see them; present of things
past, memory; present of things present, sight; present of things
future, expectation" (*Confessions*, p. 258 [XI]).

This notion of the psychological coexistence of all time—a
medieval commonplace—has had a renewed importance in modern
literature. The juxtaposition of past and present forms the very
basis of Ezra Pound's *Cantos*, and Pound explicitly states that "all
ages are contemporaneous."[5] It is important in *Ulysses* and *Fin-*

[3] Benjamin B. Warfield, "Augustine," in *Encyclopaedia of Religion and
Ethics*, 2:223.
[4] "Burnt Norton," in *The Complete Poems and Plays*, p. 117.
[5] Ezra Pound, *The Spirit of Romance*, quoted in Wyndham Lewis, *Time
and Western Man*, p. 7.

negans Wake and pervades many other works as well. Thomas Wolfe begins his career, on the first page of *Look Homeward, Angel,* with the statement that "every moment is a window on all time." The main purpose of the historical pageant on England in Virginia Woolf's *Between the Acts* is probably to show that all things remain the same, and that Mrs. Swithin is right not to "believe in history" (p. 203)—which is, after all, a nightmare from which we are trying to awake. William Faulkner has also spoken of his "theory that time is a fluid condition which has no existence except in the momentary avatars of individual people. There is no such thing as *was*—only *is*."[6] And one of the narrative voices of John Barth's "Title" rejects the notion that "what's past is past. On the contrary, what's forever past is eternally present."[7] The most thorough literary exponent of this "theory" is of course Proust, who ends *The Past Recaptured* by saying that he plans in his novel (that is, the vast work he has just finished) to describe men "as occupying in Time a place far more considerable than the so restricted one allotted them in space, a place, on the contrary, extending boundlessly since, giant-like, reaching far back into the years, they touch simultaneously epochs of their lives—with countless intervening days between—so widely separated from one another in Time" (2 : 1124).

Proust, who lays special stress on moments when we find the ability to "recapture" the past in all its reality, is also foreshadowed by Augustine's long discussion of memory, one of the rare instances in which the saint uses all his literary powers in praise of a quality in man. Augustine, too, seems to have recognized something of what Proust means by those states of mind in which we do not so much recall as re-create : we could not speak of such emotions as grief or fear, he says, "did we not find in our memory, not only the sounds of the names according to the images impressed by the senses of the body, but notions of the very things themselves . . ." (*Confessions*, p. 210 [X]). The value thus ascribed to memory is in large part symptomatic of the increasing concern in medieval thinkers over the apparent paradox of change in a universe of per-

---

[6] Quoted in Jean Stein, "William Faulkner," in *Writers at Work: The "Paris Review" Interviews*, p. 141.

[7] *Lost in the Funhouse*, p. 106. But Samuel Beckett's Molloy says: "I speak in the present tense, it is so easy to speak in the present tense, when speaking of the past. It is the mythological present, don't mind it" (*Molloy*, p. 34).

manence. Memory is able to resolve this paradox, for it is the presence of things past in the memory of man that manifests the continuity of existence under God.

Much later, some of these concepts reappear, in a vastly different context, when John Locke gives memory, together with the sense experiences it retains, primacy in his philosophy. And a full familiarity with "the sagacious *Locke*" (*Tristram Shandy*, p. 9 [1 :4]) makes Walter Shandy determined to control all the memories his son will ever have, and therefore his very soul. Conscious as he is of the inscriptions to be put on Tristram's *tabula rasa*, he is especially concerned with the boy's governor; it is while he gives his reasons for keeping a careful watch on the governor that we realize how close Shandy's thinking is to epiphany : "There are a thousand unnoticed openings . . . which let a penetrating eye at once into a man's soul; and I maintain . . . that a man of sense does not lay down his hat in coming into a room—or take it up in going out of it, but something escapes, which discovers him" (pp. 414-15 [6 :5]). As it turns out, his son is occasionally fortunate in the impressions to which he is exposed; in the most famous moment of perception in the novel, the ten-year-old Tristram sees his uncle Toby free a fly that has been pestering him and say, "This world surely is wide enough to hold both thee and me." Whatever the reason ("by what secret magic"), and however out of proportion the result may be to the cause ("I often think that I owe one half of my philanthropy to that one accidental impression"), Tristram knows full well "that the lesson of universal good-will then taught and imprinted by my uncle *Toby*, has never since been worn out of my mind" (pp. 113-14 [2 :12]). As in Augustine, Sterne's concept of memory is closely tied to his attitude toward time. (And his handling of time in his fiction—as well as his interest in it and timelessness and eternity, in the fleetingness of the moment and its preservation, in temporal and spatial form—makes him seem one of our most contemporary novelists and has been the principal source of his influence on modern literature, especially on Virginia Woolf and James Joyce.)

Augustine, however, had not let his emphasis on its psychology lead him to regard time as purely subjective, as does Sterne—or, in the same century, Immanuel Kant, to whom "time" and "space" are terms applicable only to human experience. In this notion, as in the concepts of aesthetics to which it is allied, the "Idealist" Kant shows

the strong influence of the Empirical theory that we only know
sensible phenomena. Kant does not believe that these phenomena
are all that exist; beyond them are the things in themselves—but
they are unknowable. He thus emphasizes a division between subject and object during the act of perception which makes full intuitive knowledge impossible. Philosophers since Kant, whether
they have accepted or rejected his views, have tended to see largely
in his terms the problem of how much knowledge of the objective
world reason and intuition can respectively give.

The philosophy of Arthur Schopenhauer, who adapted Kant's
aesthetics to the needs of Romanticism, does away with the dualism
between subject and object, for even the world is will and idea.
Though influenced by Locke and Kant, Schopenhauer reacts against
both the Empirical and the Idealist ways of looking at things. He believes, first, that "the senses afford us mere *sensation*, which is far
from being *perception*" (*The World as Will and Idea*, 2 : 185). They
can reveal, that is, the phenomenon, but not the thing in itself, just
as Kant had claimed; but it is in his proposal of a faculty beyond
the senses that Schopenhauer makes "the most peculiar and important step" in his philosophy, "the transition from the phenomenon to the thing in itself, which Kant gave up as impossible"
(2 : 399). The phenomenon corresponds to the Idea, while the will
is the thing in itself, which lies outside time. His discussion of this
point becomes very complicated, but basically he is reacting, like
most of the writers and thinkers to whom I refer in this chapter,
against "reason." We cannot arrive at truth through knowledge,
"for knowledge always comes to things from without, and therefore
must forever remain outside them." The "comprehension of the
inner nature of things," however, "would only be reached if we
could find *ourselves* in the inside of things, so that their inner nature
would be known to us directly" (2 : 175). Instead of knowledge,
Schopenhauer propounds something very much like Henri Bergson's "intuition." We enter into the object perceived; in fact, "we
ourselves also belong to the inner nature that is to be known, *we
ourselves are the thing in itself* . . ." (2 : 405). Nevertheless, in the
end we cannot accomplish this identification perfectly, and Kant is
therefore correct in so far as "the thing in itself is only not absolutely
and from the foundation knowable . . ." (2 : 407).

To Schopenhauer, as to Bergson, a reaction against reason in
favor of intuition partially involves a reaction against science in

favor of art. In many ways, his comments on art are strikingly similar to those of young Stephen Dedalus : he grades works according to their degree of impersonality, from the lyric through the ballad and epic and finally to "the drama, which is the most objective and, in more than one respect, the completest and most difficult form of poetry"; but even lyric poetry may deliver us from "desire and its stain," just as to Stephen art must be free of desire and loathing. Art generally belongs to the man of genius, but in the lyric form men otherwise undistinguished may also occasionally produce masterpieces, for its achievement is "to seize the mood of a moment and embody it in a song" (1 :321-23). The most lasting works of art are often those that arise from the inspiration of the most delicate and evanescent of moments.

> . . . Certainly the work which is done at a stroke . . . the work which is completed in the inspiration of its first conception, and as it were unconsciously dashed off, like the melody which comes entirely without reflection, and quite as if by inspiration, and finally, also the lyrical poem proper, the mere song, in which the deeply felt mood of the present, and the impression of the surroundings, as if involuntary, pours itself forth in words, whose metre and rhyme come about of their own accord—. . . all these, I say, have the greatest advantage of being purely the work of the ecstasy of the moment, the inspiration, the free movement of genius, without any admixture of intention and reflection; hence they are through and through delightful and enjoyable, without shell and kernel, and their effect is much more inevitable than that of the greatest works of art, of slower and more deliberate execution. [3 :180-81]

These comments are far from original; in fact, by stressing inspiration they represent what M. H. Abrams has shown to be "the oldest, most widespread, and most persistent account of poetic invention." As described by Abrams in *The Mirror and the Lamp: Romantic Theory and the Critical Tradition*, inspiration usually has four characteristics : "the composition is sudden, effortless, and unanticipated" by the poet; it is "involuntary and automatic," independent of the poet's will; "the poet feels intense excitement"; the complete work is as unfamiliar to the poet "as though it had been written by someone else." Although the writers who have described this process have differed most on its source, "the earliest and most tenacious theory adduced to explain these phenomena attributed the poem to the dictation of a supernatural visitant" (p. 189). It is here that we see how Schopenhauer has made the transition to the Romantic tradition; he does not even imply an external force or divine grace, and in fact he says only that the work comes "quite as if" by inspiration.

This change in attitude is only part of a much broader trend in regard to aesthetic perception and moments of revelation. Men had become less preoccupied with God and more interested in man, less amazed by supernatural visitants than by the power of the poet, less concerned with the object perceived than with the perceptive subject, less appreciative of grace and more fascinated by the imagination. We are gradually coming from the moment of divine revelation of Augustine to the secular "epiphany"—the great new interest in which, as a matter of fact, dates from the Romantic movement. That movement is itself a result of many of the trends I am talking about, but it has in turn been responsible for much of their vigor and importance. Indeed the epiphany, at least as it usually appears in literature from now on, seems essentially a "Romantic" phenomenon.

The most influential Romantic statement on inspiration is probably Wordsworth's "Preface" to the *Lyrical Ballads*, an essay packed with phrases showing an awareness of the poetic value of moments of illumination : "a state of vivid sensation"; "to choose incidents and situations from common life . . . and . . . to throw over them a certain colouring of imagination, whereby ordinary things should be presented to the mind in an unusual aspect"; "all good poetry is the spontaneous overflow of powerful feelings." Wordsworth's stress in these comments is clearly on the artist, not on a divine source; it is also on the subject, not the object : "the feeling . . . gives importance to the action and situation, and not the action and situation to the feeling." Wordsworth therefore exemplifies a transition between the emphasis of previous ages on an external force and the modern concentration on the subjective elements of experience, as in, say, Wallace Stevens. When Walter Pater says that Wordsworth "appeared to himself as but the passive recipient of external influences" (*Appreciations*, p. 55), he fails to see how far Wordsworth actually departs from previous ways of looking at the world—"the mighty world / Of eye, and ear,—both what they half create / And what perceive . . ." ("Tintern Abbey," lines 104-7). (Compare Wallace Stevens : "there never was a world for her / Except the

one she sang and, singing, made.""[8]) Of course Wordsworth is far
from regarding his moments of illumination as completely secular;
earlier in "Tintern Abbey" he has spoken of them as occasions when
we have "a sense sublime / Of something far more deeply inter-
fused" (lines 95-96); and sometimes he even hints, as in "Resolution
and Independence," that his experience may have come to him "by
peculiar grace, / A leading from above, a something given" (lines
50-51). However, when he comes in *The Prelude* to his exposition
of what almost amounts to a theory of epiphany, he leaves no doubt
that the mind is lord and master :

> There are in our existence spots of time
> That with distinct pre-eminence retain
> A renovating virtue . . .
> A virtue, by which pleasure is enhanced,
> That penetrates, enables us to mount,
> When high, more high, and lifts us up when fallen.
> This efficacious spirit chiefly lurks
> Among those passages of life that give
> Profoundest knowledge to what point, and how,
> The mind is lord and master—outward sense
> The obedient servant of her will. Such moments
> Are scattered everywhere, taking their date
> From our first childhood. [12. 208-25]

We can see from this and other passages that until the modern
period the major figure in English literature to have made extensive
use of epiphany is not a novelist, but a poet, and a Romantic poet,
two facts which are not merely coincidental. It is, then, no wonder
that Joyce once gave "highest palms" in English literature to Wordsworth, together with Shakespeare and Shelley.[9] Many of Wordsworth's best-known poems—"Resolution and Independence," "Stepping Westward," "I Wandered Lonely as a Cloud," "The Solitary
Reaper"—are records of epiphanies, and R. D. Havens is wrong
when he remarks that the spots of time "yielded strength but not
wisdom" (*The Mind of a Poet*, p. 231). The passage I have quoted
tells us that they give "profoundest knowledge"; elsewhere in *The
Prelude* Wordsworth speaks of "the power of truth / Coming in
revelation" (2. 392-93); the "blessed mood" described in "Tintern

[8] "The Idea of Order at Key West," in *The Collected Poems*, p. 130.
[9] *Letters of James Joyce*, 2:90. Compare p. 91: "I think Wordsworth of all
English *men of letters* best deserves your word 'genius' " (my italics).

B

Abbey" enables us to "see into the life of things" (lines 37, 49). And in "The Tables Turned" he says:

> One impulse from a vernal wood
> May teach you more of man,
> Of moral evil and of good,
> Than all the sages can. [Lines 21-24]

And notice what the impulse reveals: man, evil, good—not the divine ground of all being, for despite some ambiguous passages like the one about the Simplon Pass, with all its apocalyptic imagery, Wordsworth was not a mystic and the experiences he describes are not mystical. A true Romantic, he was too concerned with self to wish to annihilate it.

Wordsworth's view of experience foreshadows not only Joyce, but Proust as well. Like Proust, Wordsworth puts great emphasis on time, the past, and memory, and in the "Preface" he makes the point that the poet's emotion is not so much recollected as re-captured: it "does itself actually exist in the mind." When the daffodils flash upon his inward eye, he is happy not because he remembers an image that had once been pleasant, but because he regains his past feelings. His constant meditation on his memories also leads him to give to many of his childhood experiences mean-ings they did not originally have, to make them what I call "retro-spective" epiphanies.

In foreshadowing Proust, Wordsworth echoes the arch Romantic of them all, Jean Jacques Rousseau. As in the confessional auto-biographies of Augustine and Wordsworth, and the fictional ones of Proust and Thomas Wolfe, Rousseau in his *Confessions* finds great significance in his total ability to recapture lost sensations, in those moments when we go back to the past and "the whole returns again; I call to mind the time, place, tone, look, gesture, circum-stance; nothing escapes me" (*Confessions*, 1:130 [III]). However, Rousseau's distinct preference for recollected over present reality did not prevent him from also experiencing those spots of time when, "entirely given up to the present moment," one does "not remember anything"—the sacred moments which, in fact, often seem altogether timeless, "where time counts for nothing, where the present lasts forever" (*Reveries of a Solitary*, pp. 48, 113 [II, V]). Such was Rousseau's sensation after his accident at Ménil-montant, when in "a delicious moment" he felt newly born, with no before or after. That experience of "ravishing charm," like so many recorded by Wordsworth, contained a peculiar blend of the mystical and the Romantic, the impersonal and the subjective : during it Rousseau had "no distinct notion" of his "individuality"— yet he says, nevertheless, that "it seemed to me that I filled with my light existence all the objects which I perceived" (pp. 48-49 [II]).

Another English Romantic poet to make a great deal out of spots of time is Shelley, who in a number of poems records occasions when he became, in Wordsworth's phrase, "a dedicated Spirit."[10] And it is from Shelley's remarks in the "Defence of Poetry" on the transitoriness of poetic inspiration that Joyce drew his image of the "fading coal" to refer to the state of the mind during the "mysterious instant" of *claritas*— that is, the moment of epiphany (*Portrait*, p. 213).

Shelley also serves as an example of how the Romantics took up the interest in the relativity of time that had so fascinated Sterne, who had not doubted that man "might be made to apprehend any given portion of time as longer or shorter in any proportion than it appears to us." Romanticism, as Georges Poulet shows, desired to give "the moment all the profundity, all the infinity of duration of which man feels capable" (*Studies in Human Time*, p. 26). Thus Blake speaks in "Auguries of Innocence" of holding "Infinity in the palm of your hand / And Eternity in an hour" (lines 3-4), while time, Shelley himself writes,

> . . . is our consciousness of the succession of ideas in our mind. . . . If a mind be conscious of an hundred ideas during one minute by the clock, and of two hundred during another, the latter of these spaces would actually occupy so much greater extent in the mind as two exceed one in quantity. If, therefore, the human mind by any future improvement of its sensibility should become conscious of an infinite number of ideas in a minute, that minute would be eternity.[11]

The Romantics had thus long anticipated Proust's realization in *The Past Recaptured* that "the subjective chronometers allotted to men are not all regulated to keep the same time . . ." (2 : 1079), Henry James's reference to moments "which I can make as long or

---

[10] *The Prelude*, 4 : 337; see Shelley's "Hymn to Intellectual Beauty," stanza 6; "To Mary ——— ———," stanza 4.

[11] Note to *Queen Mab*, in *The Complete Poetical Works of Shelley*, p. 607.

as short, for intensity, as I like . . ." (*The Sense of the Past*, p. 235), and Virginia Woolf's sense of "the unlimited time of the mind" (*The Waves*, p. 194). As we shall see, however, these are only a few of the many writers who have gone on to pursue this topic exhaustively.

Similar notions were soon expressed in America by Ralph Waldo Emerson, who believed that "all history is sacred; that the universe is represented in an atom, in a moment of time."[12] We can see in all of Emerson's work, and in fact in the whole Transcendentalist movement, many signs of the importance of moments when we transcend time and come upon a new vision, moments which seem so profound that we "ascribe more reality to them than to all other experiences": "With each divine impulse the mind rends the thin rinds of the visible and finite, and comes out into eternity, and inspires and expires its air" (1 :251, 258). Every fact, every datum of existence, no matter how "dull" and "despised," he writes in his journal, "is an Epiphany of God" (*Journal*, 4 :488). Influenced by the Romantics, Transcendentalism made changes in the traditional attitudes toward revelatory experiences, changes in line with the general developments I have mentioned. David Bowers describes how a number of Transcendentalists, although they by no means denied the possibility of religious insight, nevertheless tended to transform the "inner light" of the Quakers into "a wholly natural organ. Instead of being dependent, as in the early orthodoxies, upon divine Grace—upon a kind of flooding of the mind by light from without—the power of the inner light was now grounded in the nature of the mind itself, becoming merely one mental faculty among others. . . ."[13]

Walt Whitman, who was greatly influenced by Emerson, combined the body and the soul, the sexual and the celestial, in the unorthodox moments of transcendence he included in his poetry. To Whitman, "the great thing is to be inspired as one divinely possessed,"[14] and though with him one is never quite sure who possesses whom, he records semimystical trance states and revelations in

---

[12] "The Over-Soul," in *Essays: First and Second Series*, 1 : 278.
[13] "Democratic Vistas," in *Literary History of the United States*, p. 349. In Emerson, however, as in Wordsworth, there are also opposite tendencies. "All writing," he says in "Experience," "comes by the grace of God, and all doing and having" (*Essays*, 1 : 71). Yet for him the nature of God is itself largely internal and subjective, and in any case he generally emphasizes grace much less than previous philosophers had.
[14] Quoted in F. O. Matthiessen, *American Renaissance*, p. 539.

many of his short poems, in "Out of the Cradle Endlessly Rocking," and in the fifth section of "Song of Myself."

Such sexual ecstasy contrasts sharply, in England, with Tennyson's "trance" in the ninety-fifth lyric of *In Memoriam*, when the "living soul" of Hallam was "flash'd" on his, and he "came on that which is." Other Victorians have also left records of such experiences, and of those that can be called "conversions" one of the most eminent is John Henry Newman's at the age of fifteen, a profoundly religious one involving a conviction that he "was elected to eternal glory" (*Apologia pro Vita Sua*, p. 108). Though he went through periods of uncertainty of choice, Newman never went through atheistic or agnostic doubt. Following more closely the traditional, more troubled pattern of events and emotions as recorded by Augustine, Bunyan and Jonathan Edwards, and yet also more characteristic of its own time, was the experience of Carlyle and Teufelsdröckh. They went through the usual sequences from the Everlasting No through the Centre of Indifference to arrive at last at the Everlasting Yea, where they "awoke to a new Heaven and a new Earth. The first preliminary moral Act, Annihilation of Self . . . had been happily accomplished . . ." (*Sartor Resartus*, p. 141 [II, viii]). Carlyle's mysticism here is not convincing, and in the end few people have succeeded so little in abandoning the awareness of self; nevertheless, there is no question that his experience was genuinely religious, and his conversion belongs to a tradition that, though it is by no means over, has been overshadowed by a newer, secular one—in which, interestingly, the experience has continued to follow pretty much the same pattern.

John Stuart Mill's *Autobiography*, for example, records a conversion involving no sense of grace or religious feelings whatsoever. Just as significantly, it can be considered a conversion to the Romantic view of life : Mill went from a cold rationalism to a sudden new awareness of the importance of the feelings. Despite its secular character, the phases of this Romantic conversion appeared in the regular order. Mill began it in a state of despair, "the state, I should think, in which converts to Methodism usually are, when smitten by their first 'conviction of sin.' "

. . . I did not think I could possibly bear it beyond a year. When, however, not more than half that duration of time had elapsed, a small ray of light broke in upon my gloom. I was reading, accidentally, Marmontel's "Memoires," and came to the passage which relates his father's death, the distressed position of the family, and the sudden inspiration by which he, then a mere boy, felt and made them feel that he would be everything to them— would supply the place of all that they had lost. A vivid conception of the scene and its feelings came over me, and I was moved to tears. From this moment my burden grew lighter. The oppression of the thought that all feeling was dead within me, was gone. I was no longer hopeless : I was not a stock or a stone. [*Autobiography*, pp. 133, 140-41]

Only after this incident was Mill able, among other things, to appreciate the poetry of Wordsworth, who came to have a profound effect on him (pp. 147-48 [V]).

The tendency to adapt a spiritual pattern and terminology to a secular experience is even more evident in Walter Pater. Although the contrasts between Pater and, say, Newman are of course immense, they are never more so than when the emphasis of Marius the Epicurean on moments of intensity is given a spiritual interpretation : "Such manner of life might come even to seem a kind of religion—an inward, visionary, mystic piety or religion, by virtue of its effort to live days 'lovely and pleasant' in themselves, here and now, and with an all-sufficiency of well-being in the immediate sense of the object contemplated, independently of any faith . . ." (*Marius the Epicurean*, p. 100). What had in earlier men served their religion, in Pater becomes his religion—but only figuratively, for the experiences he describes are clearly secular and above all aesthetic. In his impressionistic view of criticism, "the first step towards seeing one's object as it really is, is to know one's own impression as it really is," and vague studies of "what beauty is in itself" are "as unprofitable as metaphysical questions elsewhere" (*The Renaissance*, pp. viii-ix). In his "Conclusion" to *The Renaissance*, he pays special attention to the impression that comes to us in a moment of peculiar sensitivity, a sensation so "limited by time" that it is "gone while we try to apprehend it, of which it may ever be more truly said that it has ceased to be than that it is," yet in which "what is real in our life" reveals itself. Such impressions are so intense that their worth lies not in what they can lead to, but in themselves : "not the fruit of experience, but experience itself, is the end" (pp. 235-36). Meaningful as these moments may be, therefore, Pater emphasizes the sensations they involve much more than any inherent revelation; yet he goes far beyond even Joyce in the value he ascribes to them, for Stephen merely says that it is the function of the artist to record epiphanies. Pater demands that he cultivate them, crowd his life with them, "for art comes to you proposing frankly to give nothing but the highest quality to your moments as they pass, and simply for those moments' sake" (p. 239). It is in this demand that he differs most from Joyce, who stresses the spontaneity of his sudden spiritual manifestations. (Stuart Gilbert goes too far when he says that Pater's "sharp impressions, exquisite moments, are identical with what Joyce called 'epiphanies' " [*James Joyce's Ulysses*, p. 87]; but certainly Hugh Kenner's claim that the characterization of Stephen "parodies" Pater fails to recognize a genuine influence [*Dublin's Joyce*, p. 17]. "Jim says," Stanislaus Joyce wrote in 1904, "that his ambition in life is to burn with a hard and gem-like ecstasy" [*Dublin Diary*, p. 43].)

Pater's ideas are embodied in *Marius the Epicurean*, an important work in the history of epiphany and one of the earliest novels to make extensive use of it, as well as a novel that had a great influence on early twentieth-century literature. Marius, like Pater an empiricist as well as an epicurean, believes that "our knowledge is limited to what we feel"; and his realization that "the little point of this present moment alone really is, between a past which has just ceased to be and a future which may never come" (pp. 94-95), leads him to resolve to fill his life with exquisite sensations, and to concentrate only on the present. Yet Marius' "poetic temper"—that is, his tendency to live "in reminiscence"—leads him to an acknowledged inconsistency, "a desire, after all, to retain 'what was so transitive.' Could he but arrest for others also, certain clauses of experience, as the imaginative memory presented them to himself!" (pp. 104-5). Such, we have seen in my Introduction, is what a number of modern novelists regard the function of the artist to be. Marius, strictly speaking not an artist, does not arrest the moment "for others also," but he does have a convenient notebook in which he records, apparently at random, tableau-like scenes which remind us of Stephen Dedalus' plan for a collection of epiphanies: a group of men leading a fine but hurt race horse to slaughter ("And I had come across the incident just when it would figure to me as the very symbol of our poor humanity . . ."); children from an orphanage counting themselves to see that no one is missing; a child waiting at a brick furnace for his father, seeing, "as it were, in that moment, all the long tale of days, of early awakings, of his own coming life of drudgery at work like this"; a man carrying his little son, who has been injured by a fall of brickwork. All these incidents somehow show Marius that he has "failed in love." "I would," he writes, "that a stronger love might arise in my heart!" (pp. 284-86). This self-realization prepares him for Christianity, for his ultimate sacrifice of his life to save his friend Cornelius, and for his own salvation.

In the work of Fyodor Dostoyevsky, men instantaneously flit between ecstasy and doubt, again and again finding themselves on high peaks of salvation that perilously expose them to sudden plunges into the abyss of damnation. "There are moments," Kirilov says in *The Possessed*, "when time suddenly stops and becomes eternal." During these brief seconds, "you suddenly feel the presence of eternal harmony in all its perfection." Such a sensation is by its nature immediately lost; it is "not of this earth," and "man, as he is constituted on earth, can't endure it. He must be either physically transformed or die."[15] Kirilov's reiterations that "to endure ten seconds of it, we would have to undergo a physical transformation" cause the matter-of-fact Shatov to warn him, "Watch out, Kirilov, I've heard that's how epilepsy begins. An epileptic described to me exactly what it feels like just before a fit. It's just like what you said: five seconds, and he felt it was impossible to endure it any longer" (p. 610 [III, 5]). In fact, Dostoyevsky's own attitudes toward time and illumination seem to have been deeply affected by his attacks of epilepsy (as, perhaps, were those of his contemporary, Flaubert, although Flaubert's fits were less certainly epileptic).

Epilepsy has been looked upon in many societies as a "holy" disease, and Dostoyevsky's accounts of the last moments before its attack describe the gamut of emotions traditionally associated with the conversion. The fit comes, he has Prince Myshkin reflect in *The Idiot*, while its victim is in a state of profound doubt and despair—"suddenly in the midst of sadness, spiritual darkness and oppression." Abruptly, there is "a flash of light" in the epileptic's brain, "and with extraordinary impetus all his vital forces suddenly" begin "working at their highest tension." His soul is "flooded with intense

[15] Pp. 223, 609 (II, 1; III, 5). Compare Franz Kafka on Moses' "dying vision" of the Promised Land: "a life like this could last forever and still be nothing but a moment. Moses fails to enter Canaan not because his life is too short but because it is a human life" (*The Diaries: 1914-1923*, pp. 195-96).

inner light," and he experiences an illumination—a sense "of com-
pleteness, of proportion, of reconciliation, and of ecstatic devotional
merging in the highest synthesis of life" (pp. 213-14, 222 [II, 5]).
The revelation involves "an extraordinary quickening of self-
consciousness," a "direct sensation of existence in the most intense
degree." An existence so intense is necessarily unrelated to time :
"at that moment," Myshkin says, "I seem somehow to understand
the extraordinary saying that *there shall be no more time.*" A non-
temporal state, as Kirilov suggests, is an "eternal" one; and of the
moment he is trying to describe Myshkin says that "probably . . .
this is the very second which was not long enough for the water to
be spilt out of Mahomet's pitcher, though the epileptic prophet had
time to gaze at all the habitations of Allah" (pp. 214-15). Like the
conversion also, the prelude to an attack of epilepsy produces a deep
sense of peace : "all his uneasiness, all his doubts, all his anxieties
were relieved at once; they were all merged in a lofty calm, full of
serene, harmonious joy and hope" (p. 213). It is this aspect of the
revelation that makes it so valuable. To Myshkin, "for the infinite
happiness he had felt in it, that second really might well be worth
the whole of life" (p. 214)—and Dostoyevsky himself is quoted as
having remarked, of the "bliss" preceding his own attacks, "I would
not exchange it for all the happiness that life could grant me !"[16]
Unfortunately, the final unendurable instant is not one of bliss but
of horror : the "sufferer"—that is the word now—breaks out in "a
terrible, indescribable scream that is unlike anything else" (*Idiot*,
p. 222); then come the convulsions. Inevitably—as in the case of
spiritual crises with no overt physiological bases—a reaction sets in
after the attack. In Myshkin's life, "stupefaction, spiritual darkness,
idiocy stood before him conspicuously as the consequence of these
'higher moments' " (p. 214). Thomas Mann, in a fascinating essay,
"Dostoyevsky—Within Limits," speaks of this reaction as the "hangover" (p. 438).

Mann, whose own fictional works often deal with the relationship
between physiology and spiritual vision, with "genius as disease,
disease as genius," believes that this hangover is "even more in-
dicative of the nature of the disease than the transport that heralds
the attack." In examining Dostoyevsky's accounts of his experience,
Mann stresses its physiological sources. Within that broadly skeptical

[16] Quoted in Robert Payne, *Dostoyevsky*, p. 188.

though admiring approach, his specific emphases seem still more characteristically modern; for Mann, Dostoyevsky's revelation is a kind of sublimated orgasm, a "transformed manifestation of the sexual act, a mystical debauch."[17]

To look at it from this angle is of course only one way of stressing the physical nature of the phenomenon Dostoyevsky writes about—and thereby, usually, of minimizing or totally rejecting its religious significance : suspicion is somehow attached to any spiritual enlightenment dependent upon the mere body. This need not be so, to be sure, and in fact is not so in a number of religions, including that begun by the man Dostoyevsky calls the "epileptic prophet." Islam makes a major distinction between Mahomet's words while he was in a physical trance state (these constitute the Koran) and those he uttered without having undergone a physiological change (words considered *less* sacred). But in the West the attitude of the twentieth century is, typically, Mann's—or the more extreme contemporary views of John Osborne's *Luther*, or William Styron's *Set This House on Fire*, in which Cass dismisses a moment of "vision and insight" he has experienced as "the purest hokum, pleasant maybe, pleasant as hell, really, but phony," since it came to him while he was "sick from booze and abuse of the flesh and semi-starvation" and was merely "chemically induced."[18] Similar expressions of mistrust have also appeared in the controversies centering on LSD. Even Dostoyevsky's Myshkin hastens to distinguish his experience from "abnormal and unreal visions of some sort . . . as from hashish, opium, or wine, destroying the reason and distorting the soul"—although this suspicion is also, of course, not universally shared.[19]

---

[17] Pp. 435, 438-39. In *The Magic Mountain*, Dr. Krokowski takes a similar position, rejecting the interpretation of "pre-analytic times" that the epileptic fit is a "prophetic visitation"; he treats it, instead, "half poetically, half in ruthlessly scientific terminology, as the equivalent of love and an orgasm of the brain" (pp. 299-300). Although both passages are clearly influenced by and allude to Freud, the remarks in *The Magic Mountain* predate "Dostoevsky and Parricide" (1928), where Freud records with satisfaction that "the earliest physicians described coition as a minor epilepsy . . ." (p. 180).

[18] P. 267. Compare Styron's *The Confessions of Nat Turner*, in which Nat's visions come only after he has made himself weak and feverish through days of fasting.

[19] *The Idiot*, p. 214. On the whole subject of artificially induced visions and their literary significance, see M. H. Abrams, *The Milk of Paradise*, and Aldous Huxley, *The Doors of Perception*.

The real question, as Mann sees, is "after all and above all . . . *who* is diseased, *who* mad, *who* epileptic" ("Dostoyevsky," p. 443). Is it an Aschenbach or a Hans Castorp, a Myshkin or a Smerdyakov? Like Whitman, Dostoyevsky sees no reason why an experience may not be both of the body and of the soul, why a known physiological source for an illumination should in any way rule out a sacred source as well. Although the precise religious significance of Dostoyevsky's moments of revelation remains ambiguous ("It's life that matters, nothing but life—the process of discovering, the everlasting and perpetual process, not the discovery itself, at all"; *Idiot*, p. 375 [III, 5]), he is a reminder that, despite a general secular trend, not every nineteenth-century writer concerned with moments of intense new understanding disregarded God as their possible source.

In England, Gerard Manley Hopkins is the chief Victorian figure of whom it can be said both that he stands in direct contrast to the increasingly secular outlook and that his work is pervaded with moments of sudden insight. Hopkins is a man outside his times in other ways as well—whether because he was ahead of them or behind them (or both) it is hard to say. He believes that illuminations come to man from God through what he calls "inscape" and "instress," two terms which he never actually defines; but, though they are vague, their importance to him is obvious, and he constantly refers to them in both his poetry and prose. To him, inscape is "the very soul of art," and "poetry is in fact speech only employed to carry the inscape of speech for the inscape's sake—and therefore the inscape must be dwelt on."[20] Inscape may be identified as "the dearest freshness" which, Hopkins says in "God's Grandeur," lives "deep down things"; perhaps the clearest statement of what he means is in his sonnet, "As Kingfishers Catch Fire":

> . . . like each tucked string tells, each hung bell's
> Bow swung finds tongue to fling out broad its name;
> Each mortal thing does one thing and the same :
> Deals out that being indoors each one dwells;
> Selves—goes itself; *myself* it speaks and spells,
> Crying *Whát I dó is me: for that I came.*
>
> [*Poems and Prose*, pp. 27, 51]

---

[20] *The Correspondence of Gerard Manley Hopkins and Richard Watson Dixon*, p. 135; *The Journals and Papers*, p. 289.

Of the many attempts by critics toward a definition of inscape, the most widely accepted seems to be that of W. A. M. Peters, who calls it "the outward reflection of the inner nature of a thing" (*Hopkins*, p. 248). To this we need only add that Hopkins stresses the individuality of the inner nature thus reflected, for inscape also corresponds to the "distinctive self" he speaks of in his comments on Saint Ignatius Loyola (*Note-Books*, p. 312). Like epiphany, inscape may involve not only concrete objects, but also works of art, events, scenes, gestures, even personal characteristics; for all these things are charged with the grandeur of God and will flame out like shook foil : "all the world is full of inscape" (*Journals*, p. 230), and "all things therefore are charged with love, are charged with God and if we know how to touch them give off sparks and take fire, yield drops and flow, ring and tell of him" (*Note-Books*, p. 342).

Epiphany is not the same as inscape, but can perhaps be roughly identified with the other essential aspect of Hopkins' aesthetics—instress, a word even more difficult to define. W. H. Gardner points out that in its first known use, in the comments on Parmenides, instress seems to mean "a supernatural force which binds in, bounds the finite One" (*Hopkins*, 1 : 11). But we cannot limit ourselves to this definition, as shown in "The Wreck of the Deutschland" :

> His mystery must be instressed, stressed;
> For I greet him the days I meet him, and bless when I
> understand. [*Poems and Prose*, p. 14]

These lines imply more than merely a binding supernatural force, and the related "stressed" means much more than "emphasized"; instress, as Gardner claims, is therefore also "often the *sensation* of inscape—a quasi-mystical illumination, a sudden perception of that deeper pattern, order and unity which gives meaning to external forms" (p. xxi). If this definition is correct, then I believe we can associate instress with epiphany, which is not inscape but its manifestation, its revelation, its experience, coming "in a flash, at a trumpet crash" (p. 66).

In part, Hopkins' notions of perception are Romantic; but he was a Catholic priest, and his concepts are essentially religious, objective rather than subjective : he goes back to the tradition of the Metaphysical poets who had—like the Romantics, it is true—attached the highest significance to the most mundane trivia, but who had not gone on to make the significance mundane too. The

Romantics were generally less eager to speak of the object as revealing itself than of insight on the part of the subject; Hopkins, however, while he feels himself active in perceiving inscape, believes
that it is basically the object that flings out broad its name, as proof
that "Christ plays in ten thousand places" (p. 51). There is no doubt
in his mind that the motive power of instress is divine providence,
"God's better beauty, grace" (p. 58), which provides us with mortal
beauty so that we may give it "back to God, beauty's self and
beauty's giver" (p. 54). God's grace frequently takes the form of
artistic inspiration. In describing the highest kind of poetry to his
friend A. W. M. Baillie years before he was received into the
Catholic church, Hopkins even then found it necessary to use the
word "inspiration," but he did so cautiously, almost apologetically,
with a secular interpretation. Later, his concept of inspiration was
of course a strictly Christian one, and by 1885 he was writing
poems that seemed to come "like inspirations unbidden and against
my will" (*Further Letters*, p. 216; *Letters to Bridges*, p. 221).

Above all, the revelation from God is also of God: "I do not
think," he writes in the *Journals*, "I have ever seen anything more
beautiful than the bluebell I have been looking at. I know the
beauty of our Lord by it" (p. 199). To Hopkins, each moment of
existence can, like the original Epiphany, provide a manifestation
of Christ.

II. THE PRESENT OF THINGS PRESENT

> There has never been a time in which I have been con-
> vinced from within myself that I am alive. You see, I
> have only such a fugitive awareness of things around me
> that I always feel they were once real and are now
> fleeting away. I have a constant longing, my dear sir, to
> catch a glimpse of things as they may have been before
> they show themselves me. I feel that then they were calm
> and beautiful. It must be so, for I often hear people talk-
> ing about them as though they were.

Franz Kafka, "Conversation with the Supplicant," *The Penal Colony*, p. 14.

Our age, in the novel, has been the Age of (Fleeting) Enlightenment. Certainly writers, especially poets, have always recognized
the literary value of recording momentary sensations of seeing into

the truth of things; nevertheless, the way this technique has permeated modern fiction is unprecedented. Many things contribute to its new frequency, some of them grounded in the past, others more or less unique to the present. The same trends I have discussed in the first section of this chapter, for example, have persevered into our own time. With a few notable exceptions, the disillusion with religion has continued the shift—already evident by the end of the nineteenth century—from divine revelations, purely religious experiences, to epiphanies, for the most part regarded as secular. Nowadays men modestly interpret their sensations any number of ways—emotionally, psychologically, physiologically—before they ever think, and then usually with reluctance, of looking upon them as holy and consecrated. Not so modestly, they have insisted upon seeking their salvation and enlightenment here, not in the next world, now, not on the millennium. But, just as they have despaired of salvation through God, so have they rejected the coldness of pure, scientific rationalism, having become no less disenchanted with it than with worship.

In literature, these trends have been supplemented and furthered by the persistent influence of the Romantic view of art and life, despite the reaction against it so often expressed by modern poets, critics, and, more rarely, novelists. Even in poetry, the new movements owe much to the Romantic tradition running through the literature of the nineties and into the twentieth century. Frequently poets who begin by attacking it end with embracing it; this is the case with Wallace Stevens, in whose poetry what he, like Conrad, calls "moments of awakening" are very important. At first Stevens says that "we must somehow cleanse the imagination of the romantic," but finally he comes to the conviction that "the whole effort of the imagination is toward the production of the romantic."[21] But the influence of Romanticism can also be found in poets who have never recanted their dislike of it, and so we see it even in those involved in the Imagist movement and its outgrowth, Vorticism.

Other traits, more specifically connected with our own times, also help account for the new prominence of epiphany, and in the rest of this chapter I shall point out a number of them that I think

[21] "Notes toward a Supreme Fiction," in *Collected Poems*, p. 386; *The Necessary Angel*, p. 138; *Opus Posthumous*, p. 215.

particularly noteworthy and occasionally discuss some figures on whom they have had an appreciable effect.

The increasing interest in psychology and psychological processes, in the "spontaneous" actions of the mind, which has so pervaded modern life and letters, has been especially important. As writers lost confidence in their perception and grasp of things outside man's consciousness—feeling that they hardly knew themselves, much less anything outside themselves—they inevitably turned inward to that consciousness for their subject matter. They became determined, with Virginia Woolf, to render it faithfully, to "record the atoms as they fall upon the mind in the order in which they fall," to "trace the pattern, however disconnected and incoherent in appearance, which each sight or incident scores upon the consciousness."[22] Often, this determination led novelists—especially, as we shall see, some of those whose works stress epiphany—to create highly subjective, introspective, even autobiographical art. Another manifestation of this inward bent, which in turn enhances it all the more, is the contemporary preoccupation with the sense of isolation, the despair of ever having true contact with another human being, the fear of always remaining an outcast and stranger among the rest of mankind. No one theme is more important than this in the epiphanies experienced by such outsiders as Marcel, Stephen Dedalus, Joe Christmas, Eugene Gant, and Septimus Warren Smith (or the six characters in search of an end to loneliness in *The Waves*).

Another trend is the widely noted one of modern fiction to move closer and closer toward the characteristics and techniques of poetry. Certainly connected to a more conscious concern with technique, it has often been particularly associated with the technique of epiphany, whether that word has actually been used or not. Thus, in his study of *The Lyrical Novel*, Ralph Freedman describes the "frontier where novel and poem meet" as the "peculiarly modern" one in which "the engagements of men in the universe of action are reexperienced as instances of awareness" (p. viii). When T. S. Eliot praises Djuna Barnes's *Nightwood* by saying that "it is so good a novel that only sensibilities trained on poetry can wholly appreciate it," Leon Edel interprets these words as referring to the fact that the modern novel is read "not as a time-sequence but as a heterogeneous series of perceptions each catching its moment of intensity

[22] "Modern Fiction," in *The Common Reader: First Series*, p. 190.

without reference to what lies on the succeeding pages."[23] Alun R. Jones claims that the new "type of fiction" that "bears the unmistakable characteristics of poetry" has usually been used "to celebrate those intense, personal moments in which some sudden revelation perceptibly alters the structure of reality. . . ." And Dayton Kohler writes that there has been a "progressive break-down of distinctions formerly existing between poetry and prose, in an effort to give to fiction the sudden flash of recognition or the naked moment of perception which in earlier periods was the function of great poetry alone."[24] Kohler, like Freedman, assumes one of the basic theses of my entire study—that in the past the literary epiphany has had a much greater role in poetry than in fiction. *Ulysses, Remembrance of Things Past, The Waves, Look Homeward, Angel, The Sound and the Fury, The Alexandria Quartet*—if these works constantly aspire toward the condition of poetry, it is not merely because of their "lyricism," but because, as Thomas Wolfe admits of himself, their authors try to see life "as a poet sees it" (*Letters,* p. 500). All these works indicate an attitude toward life that must be called "poetic"—and a concept of art that is made explicit when Faulkner defines poetry as "some moving passionate moment of the human condition distilled to its absolute essence" (*Faulkner at Nagano,* p. 202).

The developments in fiction were not restricted to the novel. The Naturalists, for example, with their passion for the most trivial details, greatly influenced the novel, but they also helped turn the short story into the record of a bare "slice of life"; in its own way, the Symbolist movement had the same passion and as much influence. Some writers were able to blend both strains; Chekhov began to write stories which seemed unlike any that had ever been written before. Clearly related to epiphany, such stories were soon being written, apparently independently, by Joyce in Ireland—and then by others throughout Europe and America. In this form there is frequently no apparent "plot" at all; usually fairly short, the finished work seems more like a "sketch" than an actual "story." It

[23] T. S. Eliot, "Introduction," in Djuna Barnes, *Nightwood,* p. viii; Leon Edel, *The Modern Psychological Novel,* p. 137.
[24] Alun R. Jones, "Life Is the Story," *New York Times Book Review,* 27 May 1962, p. 6; Dayton Kohler, "Time in the Modern Novel," *College English* 10 (October 1948): 24. See, also, the discussion of Virginia Woolf in chapter 4.

often ends abruptly, leaving the reader in the air, strangely un-
satisfied and wanting to know more; but any continuation must be
supplied by the reader himself—for the author has gone on to
record other things, apparently saying, as Wordsworth does of
"Simon Lee": "It is no tale; but, should you think, / Perhaps a
tale you'll make it" (lines 71-72). Besides Chekhov and Joyce, the
most famous writers of such stories are Virginia Woolf, Katherine
Mansfield, and Sherwood Anderson.

Some writers seem equally at home with this form and the more
traditional story. Hemingway is a prime example, with the "interchapters" of *In Our Time*, or even such of its stories as "The Three
Day Blow" or "The Battler," balanced by incident-packed tales like
"The Snows of Kilimanjaro" or "The Short Happy Life of Francis
Macomber." The traditional story may, of course, contain an
epiphany—as, perhaps, both these by Hemingway do. But with the
newer form, centering as it does on the attempt to provide insight
into the world it depicts by recording unexciting events, commonplace scenes, or ordinary dialogue, the relationship to the aims of
epiphany is of a different, even more intimate kind: Conrad's tales
are full of moments of revelation, but their form is remote from
that of *Dubliners*; the same may be said of most of the stories of
James, Lawrence, and Faulkner.

The profound changes in both moral and aesthetic values which
the slice-of-life technique reflects are even more worthy of attention, for my purposes, than its accomplishments in the short story.
In their inability or unwillingness to believe in the broad truths that
most of their predecessors had simply assumed, writers now began
to put existential faith in the *details* of reality—external and subjective—that they could see or sense. For people like Joyce, Wolfe,
Samuel Beckett, and Nathalie Sarraute, "the greatest poverty," as
Wallace Stevens puts it in "Esthétique du Mal," "is not to live /
In a physical world" (*Collected Poems*, p. 325). Modern writers
sought to restrict themselves to things that, unlike vague general-
izations, they could at least try to grasp. Through such things they
might even occasionally hint at or grope for something else. They
became especially interested in the artistic depiction of events which,
if it were not for the artist's revealing hand, would seem completely
insignificant. For that matter, it was only the artist's hand that gave
any event significance anyway. An earlier novelist could usually
have been sure that he, his readers, and his fellow novelists would

be in fair agreement about what the major elements in a story were, or about what kinds of actions and reactions were "the true test of a man's character." Everyone, after all, knew what mattered : now, fewer people lay claim to that knowledge—and if they do their notions of what merits being represented in a novel are likely to be ones that only an eccentric would have held a century or two ago (Sterne comes first to mind).

Although one may wonder whether even Henry James might not have raised an eyebrow (not so much in criticism as in curiosity, perhaps) at the lengths to which later novelists were to go in their stress on so-called trivia, he had fought a battle for them in his dispute with Walter Besant. Handled artistically, he argued in "The Art of Fiction," *any* event may become significant. But years later Virginia Woolf still found it necessary to maintain that "the proper stuff of fiction is a little other than custom would have us believe it." "Let us not take it for granted," she pleaded, "that life exists more fully in what is commonly thought big than in what is commonly thought small" (*First Common Reader*, pp. 189-90). Something that major artists have always realized with greater or lesser consciousness has in this century become a commonplace : that a man's achievements, or the events in his life usually regarded as important, are often less useful as keys to his personality than the slight events no one else even notices but that stick in his mind, or the dream he has on a summer night. Here, too, artists have found support in the trends of modern psychology. Freud, for one, always stressed the concern of psychoanalysis with "trivialities," "the inconsiderable events which have been put aside by the other sciences as being too unimportant—the dregs, one might say, of the world of phenomena" (*Introductory Lectures*, p. 27).

The distrust of absolutes had other results as well. Just as modern artists found value in the trivial, so they became fascinated with the fleeting. Doubtful of immortality, they turned against it and cherished mortality; afraid of death, they worshiped life. Since they could endow nothing else with permanence, they began, paradoxically, to attribute it to whatever is most ephemeral, to value things *because* they are evanescent. Part of the appeal of the epiphany lies in its very transitoriness. If it were to last for a prolonged period, its strength would naturally be lessened : its effect is permanent, or at least long-lasting, partially because the experience itself is immediately lost. In the same vein, Judith Sutpen in

Faulkner's *Absalom, Absalom!* reflects that Charles Bon's last letter will insure his permanence more than a marble tombstone "for the reason that it can die someday, while the block of stone cant be *is* because it never can become *was* because it cant ever die or perish . . ." (pp. 127-28).

Yet even those men most aware that there was no longer any such thing as a truth universally acknowledged, if in fact there ever had been, were reluctant to claim that no truth existed whatsoever. To be sure, they felt, truth may be multiple and complex, it may even be Absurd, and certainly it can never be firmly or conclusively known; but some of them hoped to catch a glimpse of it during those rare, delicate, all too evanescent moments when we have a brief sense of some sort of reality. Ultimate revelations of the universe seem harder to come by these days, and the usually less ambitious epiphany is more congenial to the contemporary artist who believes that whatever truth there is remains elusive, to be partially revealed only at isolated, privileged moments. "In itself," Lionel Trilling has pointed out, "the conception of the epiphany makes a large statement about the nature of human life . . . for something to 'show forth' it must first be hidden. . . ."[25] A fine sensibility is needed if one is to take full advantage of such exceptional moments before they disappear; in order to surprise reality into betraying itself, one must, in Henry James's phrase, "be one of the people on whom nothing is lost" (*House of Fiction*, p. 33). The notion that truth is concealed from us except in extraordinary circumstances is central to James's entire technique, as it is to Joseph Conrad's, and is also closely connected to the general roles played by epiphany in their work.

To James, the claim of a narrator to omniscience seems a presumption, and in his own most characteristic work he limits our knowledge to that of one or more "reflectors": characters through whose eyes we see whatever we are allowed to see. The complete facts are obscured, and the full truth is hidden from the characters and, consequently, from us. But at times these "reverberators" surpass their ordinary limitations and come to that most Jamesian of incidents, the achievement of awareness. When that happens, James never demands that we accept the new knowledge thus gained as authoritative, but it would be a mistake to ignore it, for he places

[25] "Introduction," in Isaac Babel, *The Collected Stories*, p. 16.

great emphasis on the whole "process of vision," as he calls it.[26] Often his characters achieve their awareness suddenly, in an epiphany; but the experience of these "sublime instants" (*The Sense of the Past*, p. 168) is not restricted to his characters: James felt them too, as the inspirations described in his prefaces make clear. To him, such moments are important in all phases of the art of fiction, its creation as well as its final product: he believes that "when the mind is imaginative—much more when it happens to be that of a man of genius—it takes to itself the faintest hints of life, it converts the very pulses of the air into revelations." Although the hint lasts "only a moment" and is immediately gone, for the sensitive artist "that moment" is "experience" (*House of Fiction*, pp. 31-32).

The subtle and intuitive insights achieved by people within James's fiction are innumerable. Usually they are minor, but occasionally they attain great significance; frequently they involve a character's recognition that he has distorted his past life, indeed that his whole life has been futile. The most extreme example is "The Beast in the Jungle," where "a thing of the merest chance" reveals to Marcher all that he has thrown away: "It hadn't come to him, the knowledge, on the wings of experience; it had brushed him, jostled him, upset him, with the disrespect of chance, the insolence of accident. Now that the illumination had begun, however, it blazed to the zenith, and what he presently stood there gazing at was the sounded void of his life" (*Altar of the Dead*, pp. 122, 125). Marcher's self-knowledge comes too late to do him any good. In contrast, a similar realization in *The American* seems to come just in time to produce Christopher Newman's salvation, and, through his conversion from "Wall Street" to "Europe," to permit him to live up to his name and feel within himself "a new man" (pp. 31-32).

Joseph Conrad also stresses the "moment of vision"—his own term—as an essential aspect of his view of both life and art. From a critical position generally similar to James's, he goes on to articulate an affective view of aesthetic experience: art makes the person perceiving it do something. In effect, he says that in the greatest literature the reader experiences epiphanies. In the Preface to *The Nigger of the Narcissus*, he writes that his task is "to make you hear, to make you feel—it is, before all, to make you *see*." But he

[26] "Preface," in *The Ambassadors*, I:vi.

then adds that to depict "a passing phase of life" is not enough; he must hold up "the rescued fragment before all eyes in the light of a sincere mood" and "disclose its inspiring secret : the stress and passion within the core of each convincing moment" :

> To arrest, for the space of a breath, the hands busy about the work of the earth, and compel men entranced by the sight of distant goals to glance for a moment at the surrounding vision of form and colour, of sunshine and shadows; to make them pause for a look, for a sigh, for a smile—such is the aim, difficult and evanescent, and reserved only for a very few to achieve. But sometimes, by the deserving and the fortunate, even that task is accomplished. And when it is accomplished—behold !—all the truth of life is there : a moment of vision, a sigh, a smile—and the return to an eternal rest. [Pp. xiv, xvi]

Moments of vision, however, are not simply the results of art; they are also frequently its origin, and on at least three occasions—reminiscent of the incidents recorded in James's prefaces—a moment of inspiration led Conrad to write a novel, whether because he glimpsed the figure upon whom he based his hero, as he did "Almayer" and "Jim," or because he remembered "a vagrant anecdote completely destitute of valuable details," as in *Nostromo*.[27]

Many such moments of vision also occur for his characters, especially Marlow, and above all in *Lord Jim*, which Robert F. Haugh has accurately called "a story developed by epiphany" (*Joseph Conrad*, p. 40). The most climactic occurs at the very instant of Jim's death, for, as Marlow says, "it may very well be that in the short moment of his last proud and unflinching glance, he had beheld the face of that opportunity which, like an Eastern bride, had come veiled to his side" (*Lord Jim*, p. 416). But they also occur in otherwise minor passages : the "revealing moment" when the figure of the captain of the *Patna* "fixed itself . . . for ever as the incarnation of everything vile and base . . ." (p. 21), or the "moment of vision" produced by a remark of the French officer. Marlow's comment in this passage that "perhaps it's just as well" that we are usually dull to such moments or soon "fall back again into our agreeable somnolence" (p. 143) anticipates a later observation he makes when Jewel tells him about her mother's death : "It had the power to drive me out of my conception of existence, out of that shelter

---

[27] *A Personal Record*, p. 76; *Lord Jim*, p. ix, *Nostromo*, p. vii.

each of us makes for himself to creep under in moments of danger, as a tortoise withdraws within its shell. For a moment I had a view of a world that seemed to wear a vast and dismal aspect of disorder. . . . But still—it was only a moment : I went back into my shell directly. One *must*—don't you know?" (p. 313).

Other men had also come to believe that we all live by illusions, that the real truth remains secret; but the idea that this is fortunate, that somehow the epiphany is undesirable and dangerous, and that we should or even must suppress its revelation, receives an emphasis I find unique in Conrad. Its most powerful statement is Stein's famous plea for us "to follow the dream, and again to follow the dream" (pp. 214-15). And in "Heart of Darkness" Marlow reflects that "the inner truth is hidden—luckily, luckily" (*Youth and Two Other Stories*, p. 93). Why luckily? Perhaps because if we came upon the inner truth it would reveal to us, as it does at last to Kurtz in his "supreme moment of complete knowledge" on his dying bed, "The horror! The horror!" (p. 149). "Human kind," as T. S. Eliot also notes, "cannot bear very much reality" ("Burnt Norton," *Complete Poems*, p. 118).

While the epiphany was becoming increasingly important in the works of a number of novelists, philosophers were devoting more and more attention to problems related to it and providing for the moment of illumination new bases to replace older, theological ones that now seemed to many people insufficient or unacceptable. William James is important here, especially through his studies of religious experience and his willingness to recognize the legitimacy of faculties beyond that of reasoning. But an even more significant figure is Henri Bergson, with whom James agreed on many essential points, and whom he greatly admired. For in addition to stressing intuition, Bergson is the most conspicuous representative of the philosophical concern with time that has had, directly and indirectly, so great an effect on modern literature. More than any previous period, perhaps, the first half of the twentieth century saw philosophical problems largely in terms of time. In his reaction against this emphasis, Wyndham Lewis quite properly concentrates his fire in *Time and Western Man* on Bergson, whose influence he finds both pervasive and horribly "romantic."

One reason for Bergson's great influence is, in fact, that he attempts to provide a scientific and philosophic basis for concepts which had always been relegated to the realms of "romantic" daydreaming, theology, or even superstition. He not only tries to give clinical evidence for metaphysics itself, but insists that such a notion as intuition (to take the most important example of his rejection of strict rationalism) is a perfectly normal faculty which explains many everyday occurrences as well as more exceptional ones, like artistic inspiration and creation. And to him the tale of the drowning man who, in an experience akin to that of William Golding's Pincher Martin, briefly recaptures "all the forgotten events of his life" tells of a valid phenomenon there is no cause to doubt.[28]

Bergson gives his clearest discussion of intuition in *An Introduction to Metaphysics*, where his first sentences distinguish between "two profoundly different ways of knowing a thing. The first implies that we move round the object; the second that we enter into it. . . . The first kind of knowledge may be said to stop at the *relative*; the second, in those cases where it is possible, to attain the *absolute*" (p. 1). The distinction turns out to be between "analysis" and "intuition": "By intuition is meant the kind of *intellectual sympathy* by which one places oneself within an object in order to coincide with what is unique in it and consequently inexpressible. . . . To analyze, therefore, is to express a thing as a function of something other than itself" (p. 7).

Bergson fully realizes the place of his concept of intuition in the history of philosophy, and he sets it off against Immanuel Kant, who chose "to raise an impassable barrier between the world of phenomena, which he hands over root and branch to our understanding, and the world of things in themselves, which he forbids us to enter" (*Time and Free Will*, p. 235). Kant's mistake is in his failure to comprehend the true nature of duration, which leads him to suppose that the obstacle to union between subject and object is space, when it is actually time. To end the dualism between perceiver and perceived that has so plagued philosophy, we must turn to memory, which "is just the intersection of mind and matter"; if we could somehow "eliminate all memory, we should pass thereby from perception to matter, from the subject to the object" (*Matter and Memory*, pp. xii, 77). The role of memory is essential in Bergson's thought and controls his concept of metaphysics; he argues that "memory must be, in principle, a power absolutely independent

---

[28] *Matter and Memory*, p. 200. Conrad especially likes to refer to this legend: see the death of Kurtz, or, more explicitly, *Typhoon*, p. 52, and *The Secret Agent*, pp. 87-88.

of matter," and consequently if "spirit is a reality, it is here, in the phenomenon of memory, that we may come into touch with it experimentally" (p. 81).

Memory is also connected to Bergson's chief contribution to modern thought, his emphasis on duration, on the complete fluidity of time; for time is continuous rather than made up of a sequence of separate moments, while without the "survival of the past" through memory "there would be no duration, but only instantaneity" (*Metaphysics*, p. 45). Carrying some of his statements to their apparent logical conclusions might easily lead one to suppose that another philosophy—emphasizing, in contrast, the discontinuity of time, and therefore stressing the uniqueness of each instant more than Bergson does, although he too is aware of it— would at least superficially seem more amenable than duration to epiphany and its attempt to arrest and preserve a single moment. Yet in addition to the type of epiphany that stresses the significance of the present point of time alone, there is the one that recaptures the past—a type of epiphany greatly encouraged by the Bergsonian view of time as duration, for it is clearly easier to recapture a past forever part of the present than one ineluctably separated from it.

Proust, like the good Bergsonian that he is, implies his recognition of this fact near the end of *The Past Recaptured*, when Marcel realizes the meaning of his ability to hear—rather than simply remember—sounds from his childhood : "for me to have been able to hear the sound again, there must have been no break of continuity, not a moment of rest for me, no cessation of existence, of thought, of consciousness of myself, since this distant moment still clung to me and I could recapture it, go back to it, merely by descending more deeply within myself" (2 : 1123). The *"temps perdu"* is not totally lost after all. In *Cities of the Plain*, too, when Marcel feels that he has "suddenly become once again" the person he had been years before when his grandmother was still alive, it seems to him that he has done so "without loss of continuity, immediately after the first evening at Balbec long ago" (2 : 114). Thus it is, paradoxically, the nature of the very time whose destructive force Proust's work stresses in so many ways that after all enables things to be preserved—indeed, enables us to say that they are as real as ever, that *then* entails no less reality or being than *now*, just as *there* entails no less existence than *here*. Proust's novel never really has deviated from this view of the continuity of time, although there are passages in which his imagery does seem to describe time as fragmentary, "a succession of momentary flashes" (*Sweet Cheat Gone*, 2 :718); he is a good Bergsonian, not a perfect one.

Other writers, equally concerned with artistic effect while less concerned with philosophical consistency, have felt freer to vacillate between the two views, according to whichever happened to suit the works—or epiphanies—at hand. In another context, Walter J. Slatoff discusses this tendency "to emphasize both the pastness of the past and its presentness" in Faulkner, and points out that although "it is true that Faulkner is very much concerned with the idea of the past fusing with the present either in someone's consciousness or in a realm outside time . . . his method is such that the past exists largely as moments or flashes with gaps in between and with gaps between them and the present" (*Quest for Failure*, pp. 93, 92).

This same unwillingness or inability to choose between continuous or discontinuous time makes it possible for writers in whom moments of revelation are important to arrest a moment—the moment itself, not just our perception of it—and insist that time must have a stop, and elsewhere to stress its continued life in the future. Joyce's Stephen Dedalus, who says it is the function of the artist to record the most evanescent of moments, and to whom the "instant" of inspiration seems to have "flashed forth like a point of light," can also believe that "the past is consumed in the present and the present is living only because it brings forth the future" (*Portrait*, pp. 217, 251). Joyce himself had earlier taken a view of time as duration : "the past assuredly implies a fluid succession of presents, the development of an entity of which our actual present is a phase only" (*Workshop*, p. 60). Virginia Woolf, it is true, usually emphasizes the frozen moment—saying, with Mrs. Ramsay, "Life stand still here" (*To the Lighthouse*, p. 249)—but she also implies the utter fluidity of time in novels like *Orlando*, *The Years*, and *Between the Acts*, all of which show how the past flows into the present and never dies. This apparent incongruity perhaps explains why one critic claims that Mrs. Woolf "accepts the flow of linear time," while another says that her moments of vision confirm her belief in "*le principe de la discontinuité temporelle*."[29] Thomas Wolfe discusses much the same problem when he distinguishes

[29] J. W. Graham, "A Negative Note on Bergson and Virginia Woolf," *Essays in Criticism* 6 (January 1956):73; Maxime Chastaing, *La Philosophie de Virginia Woolf*, p. 146.

among the three "time elements" he tried to include in his work : "actual present time"; past time, which insures that men will be affected not only by the present moment, "but by all that they had experienced up to that moment"; and "time immutable." The attempt to reconcile these elements, Wolfe admits, "almost defeated" him (*Story of a Novel*, pp. 51-52).

It is hard to tell how much Bergson directly influenced Joyce, Virginia Woolf, Faulkner, and Wolfe, for they all had strong "Bergsonian" tendencies of their own. Actually, his effect on them was probably not very great, and in any case the question is not especially important as long as we see how he contributed to the general temper of their age.

In regard to Marcel Proust, however, Bergson's influence would seem far more certain. In fact it appears so pervasive that one is at least surprised when Proust asserts in a letter that, though he does sometimes "concur" with Bergson, "there has never been, insofar as I am aware, any direct influence" (*Letters*, p. 405). In an earlier letter, he goes so far as to state, in pointing out that his work is dominated by the distinction between involuntary and voluntary memory, that this is "a distinction which not only doesn't figure in Bergson's philosophy but which is even contradicted by it" (p. 226). Even if one were fully to accept this doubtful claim,[30] the similarities remaining between their works would still be undeniable. Although both believe that time cannot stop, they also feel that during certain experiences it can be transcended—largely through memory, which enables us to live in pure time. And living in this state is, in effect, the same as living outside of time. As early as *Jean Santeuil*, Proust writes that "in the sudden leap which follows on the impact between an identical past and present," the imagination is "freed from time" (p. 410). Later, in his major work, he says that during these moments of timelessness, so to speak, we transcend not only time but mortality; "our true self . . . receives the celestial nourishment brought to it" and "the permanent essence of things . . . is set free":

A single minute released from the chronological order of time

---

[30] See the discussion of this point in Shiv K. Kumar, *Bergson and the Stream of Consciousness Novel*, pp. 26-30.

has re-created in us the human being similarly released, in order
that he may sense that minute. And one comprehends readily
how such a one can be confident in his joy; even though the
mere taste of a *madeleine* does not seem to contain logical
justification for this joy, it is easy to understand that the word
"death" should have no meaning for him; situated outside the
scope of time, what could he fear from the future? [*Past Recaptured*, **2**:996]

Marcel's history, accordingly, is like T. S. Eliot's: "a pattern of
timeless moments" ("Little Gidding," *Complete Poems*, p. 144).

Proust's use of the phrase "celestial nourishment" should no more
be regarded as a sign of belief in grace or even in God than Joyce's
use of the ecclesiastical term "epiphany." Like Pater, Proust almost
makes his belief in his privileged moments his religion. In *Within
a Budding Grove*, Marcel describes how he had to permit a carriage
to drive away from three trees without his having fully explored the
sensation they had given him: "I was as wretched as though I had
just lost a friend, had died myself, had broken faith with the dead
or had denied my God" (1:545). Proust's experiences of timelessness
are not at all like those of the mystics, for they lead him not to self-
denial but to self-expression: seeking a "spiritual equivalent" for
what he has felt, he finds it to be nothing "other than to create a
work of art" (*Past Recaptured*, 2:1001). Like, ultimately, all the
figures I am examining, he puts his faith in art. (For Samuel
Beckett, Proust's privileged moment is "religious experience in the
only intelligible sense of that epithet. . . ." [*Proust*, p. 51]).

When Proust's art is seen against the background of earlier fiction,
nothing is more striking than the way it frustrates the reader's
traditional expectations of what is supposed to be significant in a
hero's life. "Little weight," he says in *Jean Santeuil*, "actually
attaches to things that we are inclined to see as important" (p. 5).
So in *Remembrance of Things Past* only the most casual reference
is made, for example, to the several duels Marcel seems to have
fought, or to his having joined the army; none at all is made to his
first sexual experience, which we would expect to have been a
crucial event for a man like him. Instead, we hear about trivia. But
when Proust—"this delectably myopic genius," as José Ortega y
Gasset calls him[31]—examines trivial events, they seem far from

---

[31] "Time, Distance, and Form in Proust," *Hudson Review* 11 (Winter 1958-
59):507.

trivial, almost through the sheer bulk of his detailed commentary upon them.

Yet the most truly distinctive basis of Proust's fiction is his handling of the relationship between the past and the present. In the choice between them (and Proust does not doubt that a choice is necessary), he decides emphatically in favor of the past, or our present memory of it; for although even the most intense memory must of course take place during a present moment, it must in Proust also battle against it. The present, inevitably, emerges victorious—"but it was ever the vanquished that seemed to me the more beautiful" (*Past Recaptured*, 2 :997). For Proust "the only true paradise is always the paradise we have lost" (2 :994)—as for all true Romantics perhaps. In Joyce's expatriate words, there is "no placelike no timelike absolent" (*Finnegans Wake*, p. 609).

This extreme retrospection turns out to be, in Proust, not the deathly sin of Lot's wife but an invigorating force for the imagination. His outstanding contribution to modern fiction is, indeed, his artistry in depicting "the recapture of the past." I have already had occasion to use this phrase, and both the experience and technique it refers to are important in all the novelists I shall concentrate upon, and many others as well. But they receive their most elaborate treatment in Proust himself, and any commentary on them should pay special attention to his work. First, they must be distinguished from the kind of delayed revelations I call "retrospective epiphanies." When the past is recaptured, the *past* event need not take on the character of a revelatory experience, since it is in fact the past that is *revealed*. The most famous example occurs in *Swann's Way*, when Marcel takes the madeleine dipped in tea and is brought back to the Sunday mornings of his childhood at Combray, when his aunt Léonie used to give him a taste of such a madeleine, dipped in lime-flower tea : "And once I had recognized the taste of the crumb of madeleine soaked in her decoction of lime flowers . . . immediately the old grey house upon the street, where her room was, rose up like the scenery of a theatre . . . and with the house the town, from morning to night and in all weathers, the Square where I was sent before luncheon, the streets along which I used to run errands, the country roads we took when it was fine" (1 :36).

There is no implication that all the various occasions on which his aunt gave him a madeleine are now epiphanies, or even that they have a symbolic or other significance when seen in retrospect. What has happened is that in a present epiphany Marcel has suddenly revived the past of his childhood. In the same way, when he later recaptures in Paris the sensation of the uneven pavement of the Piazza San Marco (*Past Recaptured*, 2 :991-92), it is not on the meaning of the past moment that he centers his attention, but on the significance of his recapture of that moment—not so much on lost time as on the search for it. Upon the foundation provided by such experiences the entire structure of Proust's novel is built. If in a few spots the structure is awkwardly buttressed—the way the entire narrative of Marcel's life at Combray leans precariously on the madeleine experience is, I think, a case in point—there is nevertheless no doubt that the edifice as a whole stands magnificently.

Proust emphasizes that he does not speak merely of the remembrance of things past; they are, rather, relived and recreated, with all their physical and mental associations : the result is "not strictly speaking memory at all, but the transmutation of memory into a reality directly felt" (*Jean Santeuil*, p. 408). In *The Past Recaptured,* a servant of the Princesse de Guermantes gives Marcel a napkin, the texture of which calls up his youth at Balbec so vividly that the moment he is "reliving" is "fused with the real present" : "these resurrections of the past are so complete that they do not merely oblige our eyes to become oblivious to the room before them and contemplate instead the rising tide or the railway track edged with trees; they also force our nostrils to inhale the air of places which are, however, far remote, constrain our will to choose between the various plans they lay before us, compel our entire being to believe itself surrounded by them . . ." (2 : 993, 998).

Other modern novelists also stress the importance of such physical sensations as both a cause and a result of the recapture of the past, tending to agree with Faulkner's Rosa Coldfield that "there is no such thing as memory : the brain recalls just what the muscles grope for : no more, no less . . ." (*Absalom*, p. 143). The same general notion appears in Oscar Wilde's *The Picture of Dorian Gray*, where Lord Henry tells Dorian : "Life is a question of nerves, and fibers, and slowly built-up cells in which thought hides itself and passion has its dreams . . . a chance tone of color in a room or a morning sky, a particular perfume that you had once loved and that brings subtle memories with it . . . —I tell you, Dorian, that it is on things like these that our lives depend. . . . There are moments when the odor of *lilas blanc* passes suddenly across me, and I have to live the strangest month of my life over again" (p. 263). It seems that it is by no means necessary to undergo precisely the same sensations; they are in fact usually only vaguely similar. Marcel need not go to Venice to feel that he recaptures his past; what he must do is experience an impression reminiscent of the one he had undergone while there. An actual return to the scene might never have provided the "Open, Sesame" (*Past Recaptured*, 2:760) needed to unlock the door to the past.

It is, consequently, impossible to know beforehand when one may suddenly stumble into lost time. Throughout his writings, Proust places his greatest emphasis on the sudden, unexpected, "involuntary" nature of the memories involved in recapturing the past. Their spontaneity must, in fact, "surely be the hall mark of their genuineness. I had not set out to seek the two paving stones in the court which I struck my foot against. But it was precisely the fortuitous, unavoidable way in which I had come upon the sensation that guaranteed the truth of a past which that sensation revived . . ." (2:1001). After the sensation has come, one may— and of course Marcel does—painstakingly try to analyze it and discover its source, but the sensation itself always arises spontaneously. Otherwise, what we have is simply "voluntary recollection," which does "not engage more of our faculties than flipping the pages of a picture book" (2:996). At best, voluntary memory forces us to use our mere intellect, but involuntary memory—"true" memory—engages the creative, re-creative imagination.

This experience, as Proust describes it, seems to begin in, but go beyond, the feeling psychologists call *déjà vu*. William James does not use this term, but he speaks in *The Varieties of Religious Experience* of the "pronounced step forward on the mystical ladder" that is to be "found in an extremely frequent phenomenon, that sudden feeling, namely, which sometimes sweeps over us, of having 'been here before,' as if at some indefinite past time, in just this place, with just these people, we were already saying just these things" (p. 383). Many attempts have been made to explain this sensation. For Freud, who rejects the easy answer that it is an illusion, "the feeling of '*déjà vu*' corresponds to the recollection of an unconscious phantasy," but he also wonders in passing if "this phenomenon . . . has ever been seriously offered in proof of an individual's previous psychical existence" (*Psychopathology*, 6:266,

265). Although such an idea runs counter to Proust's whole interpretation of the psychology of memory, other writers, including
Joyce, have played with *déjà vu* as evidence of metempsychosis—or,
perhaps, of some sort of collective unconscious, racial memory; a
character's claim that the "flashes of insight" which *déjà vu* provides
are clues to our "secret history," for example, figures importantly in
William Golding's *Pincher Martin*.[32]

The psychological relativity of time so essential to Proust—and
to the basic concept of *Pincher Martin*, too, for that matter—has
been an extraordinarily pervasive theme in twentieth-century literature. My chapters on Joyce, Virginia Woolf, Wolfe, and Faulkner
will indicate its immense role in their fiction, and these writers are
far from exceptional in this regard. The first thing Thomas Mann's
Hans Castorp learns when he ascends the magic mountain is that
"they make pretty free with a human being's idea of time, up here"
(p. 7). But few writers convey the strange, dreamlike universe of
temporal (and spatial) relativity so hauntingly as Franz Kafka.
Kafka once conjectured in his diary that "something very like a
breakdown" he had suffered was a result of the fact that his "inner"
and "outer" clocks were "not in unison" (*Diaries*, pp. 201-2). In his
fiction, time—both inner and outer—is constantly being shrunk or
stretched out. The country doctor setting out to pay an emergency
call is surprised to find himself in a moment "already there." In *The
Castle*, where all effort to be consistent in regard to the passage of
time seems deliberately abandoned, K. is confused when evening
comes no "more than an hour or two" after morning. Similar scenes
occur in "Jackals and Arabs" and "A Common Confusion," while
in *The Trial* a contrasting experience has Joseph K. open a door in
his bank to be shocked by the sight of the Whipper and two warders
exactly as he had first seen them the previous evening.[33] These
scenes are anything but mere gimmicks, and they say a good deal

[32] P. 156. Other interesting recent examples include the sensations of the
chaplain in Joseph Heller's *Catch-22* (for example, p. 202), and the first
poem in Lawrence Durrell's *Collected Poems*, which speaks of "Mneiae—
remembrance of past lives . . ." (p. 13).
[33] "A Country Doctor" and "Jackals and Arabs," in *The Penal Colony*,
pp. 138, 150; *The Castle*, p. 23; "A Common Confusion," in *The Great
Wall of China*; *The Trial*, p. 111; cf. the deleted passage in the appendix,
describing K.'s dream of Titorelli, p. 309.

about Kafka's attitudes toward man's place in his temporal world. "The history of mankind is the instant between two strides taken by a traveler," he writes in his notebooks (*Dearest Father*, p. 66)— almost as if in direct answer to Bergson's question, "And might not all history be contained in a very short time for a consciousness at a higher degree of tension than ours . . .?"[34]

What Ezra Pound calls "crap like Bergson"[35] has made itself felt in poetry, too. T. E. Hulme, the most important theorist of Imagism, gratefully acknowledged his indebtedness and translated *An Introduction to Metaphysics*. It is the nature of Bergson's influence on him that best shows how related the basic ideas underlying the Imagist movement are to epiphany, as well as to the Romantic tradition. At first, of course, an attempt to trace Hulme's ideas to that tradition seems hopeless, for he expends much of his energy attacking what he regards as its very bases. Yet even a cursory examination of his theories shows that they are not as "classical" as he thinks. Hulme believes that images, rather than being merely decorative, play an essential role in intuition; through them the artist is able "to pierce through here and there, accidentally as it were, the veil placed between us and reality by the limitations of our perception" and "to see things as they are in themselves" (*Speculations*, pp. 147, 154). It is "essential to prove that beauty may be in small dry things" (p. 131), and in his emphasis on things rather than ideas Hulme comes close to aspects of Schopenhauer and Joyce as well as Bergson. Examining the aesthetic relationship between persons and things, he distinguishes between "extensive" and "intensive" manifolds : extensive manifolds are those objects that "can be resolved into separate elements or atoms" (p. 177) and therefore can be analyzed by the intellect; things that cannot be so broken up—intensive manifolds—can be understood only by intuition. Poetry must produce in the reader such an intuition, one related to that experience of "a moment of tension, when a man is moving on the level of the fundamental self" and has "a knowledge of what is happening in him which is of a fundamentally different character to the ordinary kind of knowledge" (p. 187). To accomplish this aim, the artist must write a poem which is concrete—dry and hard.

[34] Quoted in G. Turquet-Milnes, *From Pascal to Proust*, p. 174.
[35] "This Hulme Business," reprinted in Hugh Kenner, *The Poetry of Ezra Pound*, p. 308.

Hulme himself did not succeed in writing such poetry—the few experiments by him that we have are rather mushy, it seems to me. The most famous practitioner of the Imagist notions is Ezra Pound, whose "In a Station of the Metro" is the classic example of the Imagist poem, although one has to interpret some of his own critical statements on Imagism fairly loosely in order to be able to apply them to the *Cantos* as well. Despite his expressed contempt for such "crap," he uses Bergsonian terms to describe "the one-image poem," saying that in it "one is trying to record the precise instant when a thing outward and objective transforms itself, or darts into a thing inward and subjective."[36] Pound's definition of the image itself as "that which presents an intellectual and emotional complex in an instant of time" is even more relevant to epiphany : "It is the presentation of such a 'complex' instantaneously which gives that sense of sudden liberation; that sense of freedom from time limits and space limits; that sense of sudden growth, which we experience in the presence of the greatest works of art."[37] That is, the perception of the single image is instantaneous, intuitive, timeless (as well as free from space), revelatory ("sense of sudden growth"), and produced by art. Very like an epiphany.

I have spoken a good deal of the growing disillusion with orthodox religions. But in some men this disillusion was not kind enough to bring with it indifference as well, and a number of artists, especially, continued to feel a need for spiritual emotions or experiences that would produce some sense of revelation and perhaps even of salvation. Occasionally they felt compelled to evolve highly individual religions, as did two such otherwise different personalities as George Bernard Shaw and D. H. Lawrence. Even Aldous Huxley's mysticism was as much his own formulation as it was the "perennial philosophy" he called it. More recently, we have the ambiguous mysticism apparent in the work of J. D. Salinger, and the interest of others in Zen. William Butler Yeats, much earlier, had turned to occultism, which gave him a chance to regard art as a supernatural force and the symbol or image as deriving from the *Spiritus Mundi*. The concept of the *Spiritus Mundi* is reminiscent of Jung's theory of the Collective Unconscious and its archetypes, but while Jung provided a "scientific" substitute for God's grace, the occult notion of racial

[36] Quoted in Kenner, *The Poetry of Ezra Pound*, p. 73.
[37] "A Few Dont's by an Imagiste," *Poetry* 1 (March 1913): 200-201.

C

experiences also produced such a substitute and at the same time kept for these experiences their full spiritual overtones.

Most men, however, were unable to accept any of these concepts as satisfactory alternatives for either the agnosticism of their contemporaries or the orthodox views of their fathers. A few discovered that they could find solace only in traditional faith—in God, and not a substitute for God. One thinks of W. H. Auden, Evelyn Waugh, Graham Greene. Another is T. S. Eliot, whose religion is intimately connected with his use of something similar though not identical to epiphany. Eliot's treatment of religious experience is no less illuminating in its contrasts to earlier attitudes toward revelation than in its contrasts to the trend toward secularization I have been tracing, for he remained a product of his times even as he resisted their drift.

In such a brief discussion as this, the best way to examine the relation between Eliot's religious beliefs and the moment of revelation is to concentrate on one image that runs throughout his poetry : the rose garden, and the girl or lady associated with it. Leonard Unger, who has written the best discussion of this theme, connects it to Eliot's essay on Dante published in 1929. (Unger has already shown elsewhere that "the ideas of devotion to a woman and the religious experience of approaching union with God are held by Eliot in a single conceptual pattern."[38]) Discussing the importance of the experience of ecstasy that Dante claimed to have had at the age of nine, Eliot says that this "type of sexual experience . . . is by no means impossible or unique." However, he does doubt that it "could have taken place so *late* in life"; "a distinguished psychologist" confirmed him in his impression that "it is more likely to occur at about five or six years of age" (*Selected Essays*, p. 233). In a compromise between Dante and Freudian psychology, Eliot has the waiter in "Dans le Restaurant" describe himself as having been seven years old.

"Dans le Restaurant" contains almost all the elements in Eliot's version of Dante's sexual-religious experience as it will appear in his own later poems. The role played by memory, for example, is essential. Forcing the diner to listen to his tale of an encounter he

---

[38] "T. S. Eliot's Rose Garden" and "Ash Wednesday" (p. 352), in *T. S. Eliot: A Selected Critique*. For an examination of the connection between Eliot's treatment of moments of ecstasy and his concept of the "still point," see Ethel F. Cornwell, *The "Still Point."*

had long ago had with a little girl, the waiter seems completely
futile. Yet the experience he recalls is strikingly reminiscent of the
one Eliot describes in his comments on Dante, though the thought
of Dante tickling Beatrice is, to say the least, ludicrous :

> ". . . J'avais sept ans, elle était plus petite.
> Elle était toute mouillée, je lui ai donné des primevères." . . .
> "Je la chatouillais, pour la faire rire.
> J'éprouvais un instant de puissance et de délire."
>
> [*Complete Poems*, p. 31]

But as the waiter continues his story, we discover that nothing event-
ful really happened. Frightened by a dog, he left the girl alone.
"C'est dommage."

In this account of the moment of intensity or vision, Eliot strikes
a new and unusual note. The experience, to which Eliot gives as
much spiritual significance as Dante does, is one which was forgone
in childhood; as Unger shows, the incident in the rose garden "may
not actually have occurred, may be only imagined; yet it is significantly implied that the experience is a goal to which one might
return, as if it should have happened but did not . . ." ("Rose
Garden," p. 383). Just as Prufrock probably never does force the
moment to its crisis, the adult need never have undergone the experience to feel its effects. Eliot writes in "Burnt Norton" :

> What might have been and what has been
> Point to one end, which is always present.
> Footfalls echo in the memory
> Down the passage which we did not take
> Towards the door we never opened
> Into the rose-garden. [*Complete Poems*, p. 117]

In *The Family Reunion*, Harry is as much a person "to whom
nothing has happened" as the people about whom he uses the expression. He tells Agatha, "I was not there, you were not there, only
our phantasms/And what did not happen is as true as what did
happen . . ." (pp. 234, 277). In effect, an event which never occurred
seems almost epiphanized.

Agatha's reply to Harry points up another unique element in
Eliot's version of the moment of intensity, when she tells Harry that
"We do not pass twice through the same door / Or return to the
door through which we did not pass" (p. 277). It is true that Eliot
seems to believe that in one sense the rose garden experience is very

common—that it or a similar one happens to everyone : "De quel droit," the diner asks the waiter, "payes-tu des expériences comme moi?" (p. 32). But to each person the moment of vision is not merely rare; its occurrence (or the moment when it should have occurred) seems to come only once, at the most twice. The protagonist of *The Waste Land* says that he has "heard the key / Turn in the door once and turn once only" (p. 49). In the scene in which Harry and Agatha both recall the experience they never had, Agatha says :

> There are hours when there seems to be no past or future,
> Only a present moment of pointed light
> When you want to burn. . . .
> . . . They only come once,
> Thank God, that kind. [P. 274]

Yet at least a second chance does seem possible; it can perhaps account for Harry's new and irrational sense of happiness at his "different vision" (p. 275), and, for that matter, for the poet's fulfillment evident in "Ash Wednesday" and "Four Quartets," where for the first time he gives the rose garden theme overt and emphatic religious significance. In "Ash Wednesday," Eliot has arrived at traditional worship, and the rose becomes more than itself : "The single Rose / Is now the Garden . . ." (p. 62). And the end of "Four Quartets"—in which the "moment of the rose and the moment of the yew-tree / Are of equal duration," in which "the fire and the rose are one" (pp. 144-45)—may remind us of the vision at the end of the *Paradiso*. Despite this affirmation, however, one still notices how different Eliot's religious vision has been from, say, that of Hopkins. Certain of his God even in the "terrible" sonnets, Hopkins experiences him in innumerable epiphanies; in Eliot, man must constantly seek to recover the one chance for revelation he may have irrevocably missed.

I would like to mention just one more aspect of modern thought that sheds light on the general context against which epiphany has appeared in fiction before I go on to look at its place in four specific writers : the stress recent philosophers have laid upon the role of the symbol. Symbolism, which has been studied so exhaustively by psychologists and been so important in modern literature, has seemed to put philosophy in a new key. To thinkers like Ernst Cassirer, Ludwig Wittgenstein, and Susanne K. Langer, various though their positions may be, "the study of symbol and meaning" (to use Mrs. Langer's phrase) "is a starting-point of philosophy . . ." (*Philosophy in a New Key*, p. xiv). The modern symbolist viewpoint tries to meet head on the problem of the dualism between subject and object which has so worried past philosophers and aestheticians : "absolute dualism," as Charles Feidelson, Jr., points out, is abandoned, and "subject and object fade before the unitive reality created by the symbolic medium . . ." (*Symbolism and American Literature*, pp. 52-53). In their different ways, the neo-Thomists and the Phenomenologists also stress the attempt to unite the subjective and objective worlds. In the terms of Stephen Dedalus' aesthetics, such a unity is achieved at the moment of epiphany.

It is with an emphasis on this unity that M. A. Natanson, a professor of philosophy, tries to develop a theory of language and rhetoric around the concept of epiphany. Starting with an approach which in a number of ways is close to Susanne Langer's, Natanson attempts to show "the power of language to epiphanize transcendent meanings through its own instrumentality."

> The moment, then, is revealed in language because its very character is constituted of language : the image of the real *is* the real or as much of it as man can grasp, and language draws us into the vortex of full expression. The points in language when such perfection of meaning and image, of word and reality, is achieved are epiphanies; they are, we may say, *privileged moments* of consciousness. And now the full relationship of rhetoric and language may be seen, for rhetoric, as we choose to interpret it in our present framework, is the complete expression which embodies an epiphany, and makes of it a privileged moment.[39]

Natanson goes so far as to say that "the greatness of an artist may be measured by the epiphanies he gives us"—a rather extravagant statement, to say the least, even if we interpret epiphany more loosely than his own definition of it as "a momentous and instantaneous manifestation of reality" (p. 146) will permit.

I am not really concerned here with the truth of these remarks in themselves. They are, however, an indication of the great critical significance now granted to Stephen Dedalus' theory : a significance

[39] "Privileged Moment: A Study in the Rhetoric of Thomas Wolfe," *Quarterly Journal of Speech* 43 (April 1957): 144, 149.

we can see both in comments like these and in the frequency with which one comes across the term "epiphany." By 1944, when *Stephen Hero* was published and "epiphany" began to be a literary catchword, two of the writers besides Joyce to whom I devote separate chapters were dead, and the other had written most of his major work. Although Joyce influenced them all, they did not derive their use of epiphanies from him. Anything they might have needed was to be found in their literary and philosophical tradition. Still, Joyce's word is a helpful and suggestive one; and in any case it is now the definitive name for an experience and technique which —while the shock of recognition has begun to run the whole circle round—has come to be especially important in the work of a number of major novelists.

3

James Joyce: The Bread of Everyday Life

—Don't you think, said he reflectively, choosing his
words without haste, there is a certain resemblance
between the mystery of the Mass and what I am trying
to do? I mean that I am trying in my poems to give
people some kind of intellectual pleasure or spiritual
enjoyment by converting the bread of everyday life into
something that has a permanent artistic life of its own
... for their mental, moral, and spiritual uplift, he con-
cluded glibly.

Stanislaus Joyce, *My Brother's Keeper,* pp. 103-4

The most famous of James Joyce's methods of converting the bread
of everyday life into art of permanent value was to record what he
liked to call "epiphanies." But when we try to determine just what
he meant by that term, our first difficulty is that he did not invent
a new word, he adapted an old one. Stephen Dedalus once told his
dean that "one difficulty . . . in esthetic discussion is to know
whether words are being used according to the literary tradition or
according to the tradition of the marketplace" (*Portrait*, p. 188).
Joyce himself used "epiphany" in neither way, for he took a
theological word and applied it to a literary tradition. By this
clever device he was able to make use of suggestive spiritual meanings and connotations to help get across his own ideas, while at the
same time he avoided the necessity of overthrowing any previous
literary contexts. Instead, the context is theological, and the word
of course refers to the manifestation of Christ on the twelfth day,
January 6, the Feast of the Epiphany. The word would therefore necessarily have been known to the young Joyce, and as
a Catholic he need not have waited, as Oliver St. John Gogarty
has suggested he did, to learn its meaning "as an aside in his Latin
class."[1] Joyce did not know Greek, but he may have known the

[1] *As I Was Going down Sackville Street*, p. 295. In *Finnegans Wake,* Joyce

original meaning of ἐπιφάνεια: "manifestation, striking appearance, *esp.* an appearance of a divinity," according to the *Oxford English Dictionary,* which also relates it to the Greek for *manifest* and *conspicuous,* as well as to the verb *to manifest.* In English, the word has for the most part kept its theological context, although the *OED* does cite figurative adaptations of it. The attempts to determine sources other than the ecclesiastical one for Joyce's application of it have been unconvincing.

Joyce tried to describe what he was driving at in his autobiographical novel, *Stephen Hero,* where Stephen, before he presents his theory, is carefully portrayed as a boy who is "often hypnotised by the most commonplace conversation," who has "his ears and eyes ever prompt to receive impressions"; and just before he begins the exposition of epiphany, Stephen thinks of Emma: "in every stray image of the streets he saw her soul manifest itself . . ." (pp. 26, 30, 210). At last he experiences the eponymous literary epiphany:

He was passing through Eccles' St one evening, one misty evening, with all these thoughts dancing the dance of unrest in his brain when a trivial incident set him composing some ardent verses which he entitled a "Vilanelle of the Temptress." A young lady was standing on the steps of one of those brown brick houses which seem the very incarnation of Irish paralysis. A young gentleman was leaning on the rusty railings of the area. Stephen as he passed on his quest heard the following fragment of colloquy out of which he received an impression keen enough to afflict his sensitiveness very severely.

The Young Lady—(drawling discreetly) . . . O, yes . . . I was . . . at the . . . cha . . . pel . . .

The Young Gentleman—(inaudibly) . . . I . . . (again inaudibly) . . . I . . .

The Young Lady—(softly) . . . O . . . but you're . . . ve . . . ry . . . wick . . . ed . . .

This triviality made him think of collecting many such moments together in a book of epiphanies. By an epiphany he meant a sudden spiritual manifestation, whether in the vulgarity of speech or of gesture or in a memorable phase of the mind itself. He believed that it was for the man of letters to record these epiphanies with extreme care, seeing that they themselves

---

seems to go back to the original meaning, "manifestation," when a character says, upon hearing that HCE's trousers have fallen, "How culious an epiphany" (p. 508).

are the most delicate and evanescent of moments.[2]

The most important fact about the "fragment of colloquy" overheard by Stephen is that it is "trivial," a "triviality," the kind of incident that on the surface seems hardly worth noticing: it was precisely "the significance of trivial things," as he once told Stanislaus, that Joyce wanted to convey to his readers (quoted in Ellmann, *Joyce*, p. 169). Refusing to mourn the death of epic tradition and heroic adventure, he wrote in his early essay "Drama and Life" that "even the most commonplace . . . may play a part in a great drama" (*Critical Writings*, p. 45). This conviction eventually enabled him to devote a very long novel to the events of an apparently quite unsingular Dublin day. For the true artist is a priest who converts the bread of mere everyday life, the "daily bread of experience" in the words of the *Portrait*, "into the radiant body of everliving life" (p. 221).

In the actual definition of epiphany, the first adjective is the word "sudden," and throughout his work many of Joyce's comments stress the instantaneous character of revelation. In a notebook now at Cornell University, he writes under "Esthetic" that "the instant of inspiration is a spark so brief as to be invisible."[3] And in his early essay on "James Clarence Mangan" he declares that poetry "sets store by every time less than the pulsation of an artery, the time in which its intuitions start forth, holding it equal in its period and value to six thousand years" (*Critical Writings*, p. 81). These words are adapted from Blake's *Milton,* though the sentiment is close to that of some passages from Sterne, Shelley, Bergson, and other writers I also quote in my first chapter.

Yet, despite Joyce's use of the word "sudden," it has been fashionable to speak of one or another of his entire works as "an" epiphany. Such statements are extravagant and pointless at best, and at worst misleading and distorting. Works of art, to be sure, often "reveal"

---

[2] Pp. 210-11. Throughout my quotations from *Stephen Hero* I preserve its spellings but omit the editors' graphic devices indicating that the manuscript is underlined in crayon.

In *My Brother's Keeper*, Stanislaus—who does not refer to this passage—relates how the young Joyce was walking one evening with Mary Sheehy, who was at least partly the basis for Emma, when he made an obliquely disrespectful remark about the Church. Not as shocked as she should have been, perhaps, the young lady replied, "I think you are very wicked" (p. 150).

[3] "The Trieste Notebook," in *Workshop*, p. 96. Cf. *Portrait*, p. 217.

things; but they are no more epiphanies by virtue of that fact alone than is the *Encyclopaedia Britannica*. If an epiphany is "sudden," as it is, then works as long as the average short story— and certainly any novel—simply cannot "be" epiphanies, for they cannot be "experienced" or apprehended immediately. Most paintings or sculptures can; certainly they can and should be carefully analyzed and examined, just as a novel is, but the first reading of a novel and the first sight of a painting take enormously different periods of time—though there are exceptions in the spatial arts as well, such as Chinese roll paintings. Even Joseph Frank readily admits, in a final note to the revision of his extraordinary and important essay, "Spatial Form in Modern Literature," that "since reading is a time-act, the achievement of spatial form is really a physical impossibility" (*The Widening Gyre*, p. 60). For while a painted mimetic record of a frozen moment may perhaps be called "an" epiphany, in regard to a novel the most one can say is that at the end a general recollection of all that has been read may lead up to a sudden revelation—but that is a momentary experience not to be confused with all the time one has spent on the book.

By an epiphany, Joyce also meant a sudden "spiritual" manifestation, and he once told Yeats that he wanted this new form to "respond to the motions of the spirit" (Ellmann, *Joyce*, p. 106). Yet Joyce was no exception to the general trend away from the religious interpretation of moments of new awareness; whenever he uses the word "spiritual," he seems to refer to the world of emotions, art, intuition—in terms of his aesthetic theory, all that cannot be analyzed (It is in the context of that theory that Stephen calls literature "the highest and most *spiritual* art" [*Portrait*, p. 214, my italics].) In Joyce's usage the word "spiritual" need not have a religious reference, and the phrase "spiritual manifestation" is more a figure of speech than an actual sign of religious feeling. It is true that Joyce, like Stephen, was never completely able to break away from the Catholicism of his youth; but it is quite another thing to say that he retained his faith.

Nor should we let the use of the ecclesiastical term "epiphany" mislead us, for that would be to mistake the robes for the priest. A consideration of Joyce's use of Saint Thomas Aquinas will show what I mean. In *Stephen Hero*, we are told that Stephen's aesthetic theory "was in the main applied Aquinas," derived "partly from a genuine predisposition in favour of all but the premisses of scholasticism" (p. 77)—that is, all but the belief in God and the Church, without which one can hardly be called, as C. G. Jung has called Joyce, "a pious Catholic."[4] In the *Portrait*, Lynch grasps precisely why Stephen can go only so far with Aquinas and must both trim and expand upon him : "After all Aquinas, in spite of his intellect, was exactly a good round friar" (pp. 209-10). So when years later Joyce speaks in *Finnegans Wake* of the "panepiphanal world" of the "inside true inwardness of reality, the Ding hvad in idself," he stresses that epiphany is non-Catholic as well as nonrational by remarking that no "Rumnant Patholic" could "catch all that preachybook" (p. 611).

Yet in some way the experience is spiritual; it is not merely an intense moment of emotion or a sudden feeling of exhilaration, it is a sudden spiritual "manifestation." Something is revealed, there is a feeling of new knowledge gained instantaneously and apparently irrationally. The realization may be relatively minor, as it seems to be in the colloquy overheard between the young lady and gentleman in *Stephen Hero*, or it may affect one's entire life, as in Stephen's vision of the wading girl in the *Portrait*, or it may even take on both psychological and metaphysical overtones, as in the Nighttown episode of *Ulysses*, or it may become positively cosmic in its reference, as in "the night of the Apophanypes" in *Finnegans Wake* (p. 626). But, whatever its quality, there has to be some such revelation—and it is here that we must beware a common misconception that confuses Joyce's epiphany with the leitmotif, the obsessive image which keeps coming back into the consciousness of a character or into the work as a whole but which at no single time involves any special, sudden illumination. In the same way, and despite obvious associations, we cannot identify epiphany with symbolism either, for epiphany involves not merely representation but revelation as well. The epiphany per se is not a symbol or image, though it may arise from one.

Stephen believes that the manifestation essential to epiphany may result from a variety of causes. The first ones he mentions are "the vulgarity of speech or of gesture or . . . a memorable phase of the mind itself." Vulgarity of speech" figures in the colloquy he has just overhead, while "gesture" is important in many epiphanies throughout Joyce's work (in *Ulysses*, Stephen calls it "a universal

4 " 'Ulysses': A Monologue," *The Spirit in Man, Art, and Literature*, p. 120.

language . . . rendering visible . . . the first entelechy"[5]). In the early
twentieth century, Joyce's unusual fascination with apparently
irrelevant details of speech and gesture was probably matched only
by Sigmund Freud's interest in parapraxes and similar phenomena.

The words "memorable phase of the mind" are more ambiguous,
and it is perhaps impossible to find an epiphany that does not arise
at least in some way from an external stimulus; but the purest
example is probably the "dream-epiphany," for during sleep one is
at least supposedly "senseless" and unaware of the objects around
him. Joyce recorded a number of dreams as "epiphanies," and
several of them have found their way into his published works. He
was always fascinated by the interpretation of dreams, though, as
Richard Ellmann shows, his interest was in "revelation, not scientific
explanation," and probably had its source not in Freud but in the
Dublin poets, such as George Russell and Yeats (*Joyce*, p. 89). However, he did not share their mystical theories. In *My Brother's
Keeper*, Stanislaus Joyce summarizes the significance of this
interest :

> There is no hint . . . that he considered dreams anything but an
> uncontrolled rehash of our waking thoughts, though he may
> have hoped they would reveal things our controlled thoughts
> unconsciously conceal. I preserved them [the dream-epiphanies]
> because I suspected they might be his good-bye to poetry,
> an indication that prose was taking the upper hand. And I could
> see what he was driving at : the significance of unreflecting ad-
> missions and unregarded trifles, delicately weighed, in assaying
> states of mind for what is basic in them. The noise and pomp of
> big events and our own imagination are so apt to mislead us.
> [P. 127]

The dream-epiphanies play a major role in the *Portrait* and are the
basis for three of the entries in Stephen's diary at the end (March
25, April 10, and April 16).[6]

A more imperfect, elusive, and also more significant revelation
through "a memorable phase of the mind" is the one that arises
from memory. There are in Joyce several hints of recaptures of the

---

[5] P. 432/425. In references to *Ulysses,* the page number before the slash
refers to the corrected Random House edition, which is the one quoted; the
subsequent number refers to the page in Random House editions prior to
1961.
[6] See "The Epiphanies," in *Workshop,* pp. 39, 37, 40.

past, as when the playful stroke of Heron's cane suddenly carries Stephen back "as if by magic" to an earlier time when Heron and some other boys had bullied him (*Portrait*, p. 78). Yet I am never absolutely certain whether Stephen actually recaptures the past, or whether he simply recalls it, even during his visions in the Nighttown episode of *Ulysses*. In any case, far more important in Joyce's fiction—as we shall see—are what I call retrospective epiphanies, those occasions when an event seems trivial while it occurs and assumes importance only long after it has passed. Originally, it provides no illumination at all, but for some reason it lingers in the mind, perhaps consciously forgotten, until one day, even if many years later, it is remembered and produces a revelation—but only in retrospect.

An epiphany may also arise, Stephen goes on to tell Cranly, from the apprehension of a concrete object, such as the clock of the Ballast Office—which they happen to be passing at that moment :

> —Yes, said Stephen. I will pass it time after time, allude to it, refer to it, catch a glimpse of it. It is only an item in the catalogue of Dublin's street furniture. Then all at once I see it and I know at once what it is : epiphany.
> —What?
> —Imagine my glimpses at that clock as the gropings of a spiritual eye which seeks to adjust its vision to an exact focus. The moment the focus is reached the object is epiphanised. [*Stephen Hero*, p. 211]

Although such an epiphany would arise from the perception of something external, Joyce's emphasis is generally on the perceiving consciousness, the subject who actively adjusts his "spiritual" vision to focus on the object, which in turn "is epiphanised." Realizing this point helps us to understand Joyce's attitude toward epiphany, which is related to his whole view of the act of perception and consequently to his aesthetic theory. His stress on the perceiver is in line—as we have seen in chapter 2—with the general development in epistemology from an emphasis on the object that reveals itself, fundamentally through God's grace, to an emphasis on the role of man's mind and imagination : from revelation by the object to insight on the part of the subject. For Joyce to have given the primary role to something outside man's consciousness would have involved him in metaphysical problems which he avoids. Yet his language is occasionally ambiguous, and there are a few expressions in

Stephen's exposition of aesthetics—at one point he mentions that "the object achieves its epiphany" (p. 213)—which in themselves might lead one to suppose that Stephen regards epiphany as a non-subjective phenomenon. Nevertheless, I think Hugh Kenner is basically mistaken when he supports his doubtful claim that Joyce is anti-Romantic by saying that "it is radically impossible to understand what Joyce is talking about from the standpoint of the post-Kantian conviction that the mind imposes intelligibility upon things" (*Dublin's Joyce*, p. 138). According to Kenner, "it is *things* which achieve epiphany under the artist's alchemical power, and not his own soul which he manifests . . ." (p. 141). Because he recognizes that this viewpoint seems to contradict the statements in *Portrait* which "emphasize Stephen's highly subjective bent," Kenner assumes that the treatment of aesthetics in that novel is ironic (p. 137).

The tendency to focus on the object stems partially, I think, from a misleading concentration on some vague implications in Stephen's general aesthetic theory, when it is more worthwhile to look at his actual epiphanies. There is not one in which the "otherness" of the object is as significant as the revelation produced in the perceiver. When, in the *Portrait*, Stephen sees an inscription of the word *Foetus*, he does not learn a thing about the carving, but a good deal about himself and his place in the world. Later in the novel he sees the wading girl, and what he and the reader learn about her does not have nearly the significance of what they learn about Stephen. These examples could be multiplied indefinitely and would only demonstrate Joyce's full awareness of what Proust's Marcel realizes even as he tastes the madeleine dipped in tea : "It is plain that the object of my quest, the truth, lies not in the cup but in myself" (*Swann's Way*, 1 :34).

One could also miss the subjective nature of Joyce's epiphany by failing to recognize his strong tendency toward Romanticism, a trait of which he was fully aware, though he may never have been able to reconcile himself to it. The young artist in *Stephen Hero* insists on "the classical style" (p. 78) and claims that his "entire esteem is for the classical temper in art" (p. 96). But we also learn—significantly, in the same paragraph that introduces the concept of epiphany—that it is "hard for him to compel his head to preserve the strict temperature of classicism" (p. 210). The concept of epiphany itself is of course extremely Romantic, as is Joyce's presentation of it. The phrase about the "spiritual eye" reaching its exact focus recalls comments by a number of Romantic poets on the highly subjective vision we attain through what Wordsworth, in "I Wandered Lonely as a Cloud," calls the "inward eye." When Stephen tells his brother that he has burned all his poems because "they were romantic" (p. 226), we may recall the fate of most of the manuscript of *Stephen Hero* itself.

Thus far I have been examining Stephen's definition—but he goes beyond definition to make it clear that to him epiphany is an essential part of the function of the literary artist, whose duty is "to record these epiphanies with extreme care, seeing that they themselves are the most delicate and evanescent of moments." Stephen shares this view with Joyce himself and, as I indicated in my Introduction, with a number of other major modern novelists as well. Of course, we should not let the fact that the exposition in *Stephen Hero* centers on the moment of inspiration mislead us into forgetting the great consciousness Joyce demanded of the artist. There is nothing inconsistent between inspiration and long, hard effort. "A man might think for seven years at intervals and all at once write a quatrain which would immortalise him seemingly without thought or care—seemingly" (*Stephen Hero*, p. 185). Though "he sought in his verses to fix the most elusive of moods," Stephen "put his lines together not word by word but letter by letter" (p. 32). The inspiration he experiences while passing the young lady and gentleman leads as it should to the composition of a work of art—a poem, the "Vilanelle of the Temptress"—but it has a more sweeping result as well : it makes "him think of collecting many such moments together in a book of epiphanies." In *Ulysses*, Stephen reflects : "Remember your epiphanies on green oval leaves, deeply deep, copies to be sent if you died to all the great libraries of the world, including Alexandria?" (p. 40/41). Richard Ellmann reports that Joyce told his brother that if he died "copies of both his verses and epiphanies should be sent to all the great libraries of the world, the Vatican not excepted" (*Joyce*, p. 113). Presumably, it is not known if they were to be on green oval leaves.

Epiphany is central not only in Joyce's concept of the function of the artist, but in his theories of aesthetics, too. Important as it certainly is, however, the relationship of epiphany to his views on art and beauty has occasionally been overemphasized, and sight has thereby been lost of its far more meaningful and fundamental relationship with all experience, aesthetic and nonaesthetic. Yet the exposition of aesthetics in *Stephen Hero* begins as Stephen tells Cranly that "it is just in this epiphany that I find the third, the supreme quality of beauty" (p. 211). His discussion is duplicated in the *Portrait* with different emphases and no mention at all of epiphany, but in both works it is broadly based on Aquinas, who speaks of "three conditions," or qualities.[7] (Aquinas, as William T. Noon points out, says nothing about these conditions being elements in any sequence [*Joyce and Aquinas*, p. 46], but in Joyce they are "phases of artistic apprehension" as well as "qualities of universal beauty" [*Portrait*, p. 211]. It is difficult to see why Joyce made this change; certainly epiphany, stressing as it does immediate perception, would better be served by a theory in which the phases were in an abstract, logical sequence rather than an actual temporal one.) The first element in the act of perceiving an object is *integritas*: we recognize that a thing has wholeness, "integrity," that it is *one* thing, with a bounding line drawn about it. We have here "the synthesis of immediate perception"; it is followed by "the analysis of apprehension" (p. 212), or *consonantia*. In this analytical phase, we perceive the symmetry of the object; it is a complex structure of parts related to parts and to their sum. We now not only see it as *a* thing; it is a *thing*. It has harmony. Finally, through *claritas*, we recognize the thing in itself—"its soul, its whatness": "This is the moment which I call epiphany" (*Stephen Hero*, p. 213).

But it is a distortion to look at epiphany primarily in the context of Joyce's aesthetic theories rather than primarily in the context of his novels, for epiphany is, as I have said, an element in *all* human experience. When, for example, we look at Joyce's own epiphanies, both in his manuscripts and in his published works, we see that they are experiential rather than aesthetic in emphasis; they are manifestations of psychological truth, of character, of society, not manifestations of beauty. Stephen tells Cranly that the clock of the Ballast Office is "capable of an epiphany," but at the end of his exposition he confesses that "it has not epiphanised yet" (pp. 211, 213). Stephen's epiphanies are in fact usually not like that—nor are

---

[7] *Basic Writings of Saint Thomas Aquinas*, 1 : 378. Aquinas' comments on aesthetics are inseparable from his theology, although Joyce separates them anyway. Here, for example, Aquinas goes on to consider each quality of beauty as "a likeness to the property of the Son."

Joyce's. They are produced much less frequently by concrete objects than by events, people, snatches of talk, gestures, dreams, phases of the mind. Even when an epiphany does center on an "object," it is still not essentially an "aesthetic" experience. When Stephen sees the carving of the word *Foetus*, the interest centers not in beauty, but in meaning.

Clearly, epiphany was important in Joyce's view of his art, just as epiphanies are clearly important in his books, which include many experiences which he certainly felt—and often meant the reader to feel—involved sudden spiritual manifestations. Sometimes these experiences seem purely fictional, with little or no biographical basis. At times—indeed, with astonishing frequency—they are based on the incidents he had preserved as "epiphanies" after they had actually occurred to him. Usually he combined these two methods, changing and modifying until he produced something which, though it may have arisen from the everyday world in which Joyce found himself, exists permanently in the world he created.

Joyce presents a cross section of that world in the Wandering Rocks episode of *Ulysses*, which consists of nineteen separate fragments, fleeting revelatory snatches from the life of Dublin that all occur around the same time. Every major character and most of the minor ones appear and reappear in its various scenes, and, although each fragment is separate, they are all connected through a complex series of references. For example, the episode begins with Father John Conmee, who is out taking a walk. In the second paragraph, he blesses a one-legged sailor; we soon meet this sailor again, but in the meantime we continue to see the activities of Dublin through the eyes of the priest. When we leave him, there is a much briefer scene in which we meet Corny Kelleher, an undertaker whose establishment Father Conmee has passed. Here we are told, in a subordinate clause and with apparent irrelevance, that while Corny is walking, elsewhere, in Eccles Street, an arm is tossing a coin from a window. In the third fragment, we again encounter the one-legged sailor. He turns out to be rather disagreeable : a sour, violent, and grumbling beggar. "Two barefoot urchins" (p. 225/ 222), who are fascinated and apparently frightened by his stump, stare at him. When a hand—and by now we realize it is none other than Mrs. Bloom's—flings a coin from a window, one of the children picks it up and gives it to the sailor. Suddenly we are transported to another scene where we are given a snatch of conversation between Katey and Boody Dedalus, and then to other scenes until the end of the episode.

The bit of trivia about the sailor is reminiscent of a passage in some newly discovered pages of the manuscript of *Stephen Hero*, where "a ragged boy" and "an equally ragged friend" are confronted by another "lame beggar," who accuses them of having called out names after him the day before. He threatens them viciously while young Stephen watches horrified (p. 244). Joyce had himself witnessed such a scene, and he recorded it in one of his "epiphanies":

> [In Mullingar : an evening
> in autumn]

> The Lame Beggar—(*gripping his stick*). . . . It was you called out after me yesterday.
> The Two Children—(*gazing at him*). . . . No, sir.
> The Lame Beggar—O, yes it was, though. . . . (*moving his stick up and down*). . . . But mind what I'm telling you. . . . D'ye see that stick?
> The Two Children—Yes, sir.
> The Lame Beggar—Well, if ye call out after me any more I'll cut ye open with that stick. I'll cut the livers out o' ye. . . . (*explains himself*). . . . D'ye hear me? I'll cut ye open. I'll cut the livers and the lights out o' ye. [*Workshop*, p. 25]

The passage in *Stephen Hero* is very close to this incident, but while the one in *Ulysses*—written many years later—also seems to have been suggested by this scene, it makes many changes as well, and one might easily fail to recognize the connection between the two beggars. Nevertheless, the scenes in *Stephen Hero* and *Ulysses* evidently both have their source in the slight manuscript fragment young James Joyce had composed in accordance with his view of the function of the artist.

Most frequently, of course, a reader has no way of knowing whether an event recorded in a novel originated in what Joyce would have called one of the author's own "epiphanies." In Joyce's case, fortunately—"fortunately" if we assume, as I think we must, that such knowledge has intrinsic value and interest—we have a large number of his original manuscript fragments, and copies of others made by his brother Stanislaus. Twenty-two of them are in the Wickser collection at the State University of New York at Buffalo. A slightly larger collection is at Cornell University, although only one, dealing with Oliver St. John Gogarty, is in Joyce's own hand (unlike those at Buffalo, it seems to be a first draft). Twenty-four others appear in Stanislaus Joyce's "Selections in Prose from Various Authors," a commonplace book dated October 7, 1901, although Stanislaus made entries in it for a few years after that. They are in his hand, although all but four, which have no signature, are signed "Jas. A. Joyce." Seven of these epiphanies also appear in the Wickser collection at Buffalo. In addition, Cornell has two other copies of three of them on the reverse of some of the sheets Stanislaus later used for the journal he kept from September 26, 1903 to April 27, 1905.

All these epiphanies have now been published by Robert Scholes and Richard M. Kain in their *Workshop of Daedalus*. Scholes, who edited them for that volume, points out that "most of them seem to be the work of the years 1900 to 1903" (p. 5). He has sensibly placed them in a rough sequence based both on our knowledge of Joyce's life and on some numbers (perhaps but not certainly in Joyce's hand) discovered by Peter Spielberg on the backs of the sheets of paper at Buffalo. These numbers, ranging from 1 to 71, clearly suggest that the number of epiphanies recorded by Joyce originally ran at least into the seventies. Not nearly that many have survived, however. Although some entries in Joyce's "Trieste Notebook" also seem to me to be like records of epiphanies, there is no objective evidence to indicate that he thought of them as such. Without counting this notebook, then, or any other manuscripts which we cannot be absolutely certain Joyce recorded and preserved as "epiphanies" and not simply as notes for future reference, we are aware of fifty-three manuscript copies of epiphanies—forty, not including duplications. Of these, to my knowledge twenty-five are definite sources for passages in published works (if we include *Stephen Hero*), while several others seem to have provided suggestions. Twelve appear in *Stephen Hero*, three of these later used elsewhere as well (two in the *Portrait* and one in *Ulysses*). Eleven are used in the *Portrait*, four in *Ulysses*, and one in *Finnegans Wake*. Less definite suggestions—like the use of the lame beggar in the Wandering Rocks episode—also appear in all these works and some of Joyce's others. There are, of course, many other epiphanies in Joyce's novels based on his own experience, but which were not first recorded in such manuscripts or for which we do not have copies.[8]

[8] Robert Scholes cites slightly different figures in "Joyce and the Epiphany: The Key to the Labyrinth?" *Sewanee Review* 72 (Winter 1964):73: thirteen for *Stephen Hero*, nine for *Portrait*, five for *Ulysses* (and presumably none for *Finnegans Wake*).

Critics of Joyce have differed—sometimes enormously—in their interpretations of epiphany, but almost all have agreed on its profound importance in Joyce's aesthetics and fiction; in the suggestive argument of this essay, Scholes is an exception, though not quite the only one. Robert M. Adams' "low estimate of the epiphanies" is one of the "conscious heresies" against which he frankly warns the reader of his *James Joyce: Common Sense and Beyond* (p. ix). Actually, Joyce himself has recorded an early instance of what we may call the Nora Barnacle school of epiphany criticism: "when she saw me copy Epiphanies into my novel she asked would all that paper be wasted . . ." (*Letters,* 2:78).

But Scholes's essay remains the only thoroughly developed statement of this view. He seems initially to arrive at it out of a quite legitimate reaction against critics who argue that in *Portrait* Stephen is seen ironically, that he has no theory of epiphany because he is incapable of one: "when devotion to the theory goes so far that its absence from *Portrait* is held against Stephen, it is time to call for a return to sanity." That is a true and valuable observation, but Scholes seems to go on to assume that such absence should somehow be held against the theory. He tries to prove that critics have placed too much emphasis on epiphany by claiming that Joyce himself abandoned it, since it "seems never to have been in his recorded thoughts" after *Stephen Hero*, except for one comment in *Ulysses* (p. 72). For what it is worth, however, that is not true: we have a number of interesting remarks in revealing contexts in *Finnegans Wake*, some of which I have already quoted (see the *Wake*, pp. 508, 611, 626). Moreover, it was at the time Joyce started *Ulysses* that he wrote *Giacomo Joyce*, which was about as close as he ever came to fulfilling his original desire to compose a volume of "epiphanies."

Scholes attacks the manuscript epiphanies that have survived as "trivial and supercilious," although he admits that "their chief significance is in the use Joyce often made of them in his later works" (p. 73). (Elsewhere, in fact, he has himself observed that they became Joyce's "principal building blocks" for *Stephen Hero*, and that by reading them in the right sequence "we can see Joyce's novel taking shape" [*Workshop*, p. 6].) Scholes also implies that since fewer of these early epiphanies reappear in *Ulysses* than in *Portrait*, and fewer there than in *Stephen Hero*, the mature Joyce was placing less importance on his old theory. But surely the significant fact is not that only four or five appear in *Ulysses*, but that after so many years any of the original epiphanies still appear at all.

I hope in any case that my discussion of Joyce's epiphanies in the rest of this chapter is in itself a general refutation of Scholes's contention (which he briefly reiterates in a criticism of Florence L. Walzl's "The Liturgy of the Epiphany Season and the Epiphanies of Joyce," *PMLA* 80 [September 1965]:436-50; see Robert Scholes and Florence L. Walzl, "The Epiphanies

As Joyce's artistry matured, he became increasingly able to adapt the fragments to fit into his longer artistic forms, but at first his treatment was frequently awkward; he seems to have been so conscious of their original fragmentary nature that he was afraid the reader would not grasp their full significance. He therefore tended to "explain" them, to point out exactly what they ought to "manifest" or "reveal." But the strength of the epiphany technique is in its ability to dramatize meaning and do away with the necessity for explanation. Joyce realized this long before he wrote the Wandering Rocks; but when the lame beggar appears in *Stephen Hero*, an entire paragraph is devoted to Stephen's reaction to him : we learn that "he had never before seen such evil expressed in a face," and that it "struck a fine chord of terror" in him (p. 245). In the *Portrait*, only the more climactic epiphanies are made explicit; by *Ulysses*, none are. In one of the manuscripts, Joyce records the dialogue of some young girls as they tease a little boy by asking him who his sweetheart is (*Workshop*, p. 48). An expanded version of this epiphany appears in the Nausicaa episode of *Ulysses* (pp. 347-48/341-42), where Joyce shifts the style to suit the parody of cheap fiction in which the episode is written and makes some changes to show the vindictive attitude of her friends toward Gerty; but although the passage is expanded, it is not in the least made more explicit. Although it is clearer, the clarity arises not from any comment by the author, but from the general context in which the incident appears. When given such a context, of course, an epiphany *needs* less clarification than when it stands alone, and a passage that is merely ambiguous as a separate manuscript may become powerful when put against a narrative background.

However, even where Joyce does explicate his published epiphanies, they may in some ways be great improvements upon the originals. The following passage from *Stephen Hero* is based on one of four manuscripts arising from the death of Joyce's brother Georgie, who becomes Isabel in the novel. Only the dialogue appears in the original version (*Workshop*, p. 32).

---

of Joyce," *PMLA* 82 [March 1967] : 152-54). I first examine the changes Joyce made in the various versions of his manuscripts and how the use of epiphanies in his fiction developed; then I go on to a discussion of especially significant moments of revelation—some based on the manuscript epiphanies and some not—in the context and structure of *Portrait* and *Ulysses*.

McCann was also sympathetic. He came over to Stephen while that young man was looking into a haberdasher's window at some ties and wondering why the Chinese chose yellow as a colour of mourning. He shook hands briskly with Stephen:

—I was sorry to hear of the death of your sister . . . sorry we didn't know in time . . . to have been at the funeral.

Stephen released his hand gradually and said:

—O, she was very young . . . a girl.

McCann released his hand at the same rate of release, and said:

—Still . . . it hurts.

The acme of unconvincingness seemed to Stephen to have been reached at that moment. [*Stephen Hero*, p. 169]

Clearly, a great deal has been gained by the expansion of the incident, as well as by its being placed in context. The additional description of the hands is superb. It tells or seems to tell so much that one wonders how much is really added by the summation of the meaning at the end of this epiphany, which in its place in the novel (though perhaps not in its original form) is one of Joyce's most lucid. Particularly when no such attempt at commentary is made, the values of a context can be immense. For in itself an epiphany is very limited—it is, in the end, a mere fragment. Though it may attain the qualities of that vague genre called the prose poem, those qualities are not after all very major.

The primary interest of the manuscripts thus must lie not in themselves but in relating them to Joyce's finished work. In order to achieve something of permanent artistic value, Joyce had to recognize that his epiphanies were best treated as parts, not as wholes: he had to transform the fragmentary sketch and make it part of a broader canvas, just as a painter takes preliminary pencil sketches of a face, of arms and legs, and transforms them into a single portrait. The work of art then becomes, like the perceived object at the moment of epiphany, "an organised composite structure" in which "the relation of the parts is exquisite" (*Stephen Hero*, p. 213). The inherent dangers and limitations of presenting a collection of epiphanies without benefit of a dramatic context are, I think, displayed in such a work as Nathalie Sarraute's *Tropisms*. They are even suggested in the preciosity of Joyce's own *Giacomo Joyce*—although the composition of that collection of epiphany-like pieces, years after he had given up the idea of a separate volume of epiphanies, shows that despite its risks the idea kept its attraction, and that Joyce felt drawn back to it. But as soon as he realized that his epiphanies could have a place in his longer works—if, indeed, he did not always realize it—he must have become especially conscious of the necessity of making changes in his treatment of the fragments, though at first these tended to be slight.

While Georgie was on his dying bed, an incident occurred which Joyce later recorded :

> [Dublin : in the house in
> Glengariff Parade : evening]

Mrs Joyce—*(crimson, trembling, appears at the parlour door)* . . . Jim !

Joyce—*(at the piano)* . . . Yes?

Mrs Joyce—Do you know anything about the body? . . . What ought I do? . . . There's some matter coming away from the hole in Georgie's stomach. . . . Did you ever hear of that happening?

Joyce—*(surprised)* . . . I don't know. . . .

Mrs Joyce—Ought I send for the doctor, do you think?

Joyce—I don't know. . . . . . What hole?

Mrs Joyce—*(impatient)* . . . The hole we all have . . . . . here *(points)*

Joyce—*(stands up)* [*Workshop*, p. 29]

This seems to me one of the most moving of the manuscripts; yet when it is placed in *Stephen Hero* the gains are enormous. There we not only have the relevant background—Isabel's illness—but the epiphany itself is given a much fuller treatment. Joyce sets the scene and creates the proper mood before we even come to the dialogue; instead of "*at the piano*," there is a brief but evocative introduction. The effect, moreover, is not oversimplified by the words *crimson, trembling, surprised,* and *impatient*.

> One evening he sat at his piano while the dusk enfolded him. The dismal sunset lingered still upon the window-panes in a smoulder of rusty fires. Above him and about him hung the shadow of decay, the decay of leaves and flowers, the decay of hope. He desisted from his chords and waited, bending upon the keyboard in silence : and his soul commingled itself with the assailing, inarticulate dusk. A form which he knew for his mother's appeared far down in the room, standing in the doorway. In the gloom her excited face was crimson. A voice which he remembered as his mother's, a voice of a terrified human

being, called his name. The form at the piano answered :
—Yes?
—Do you know anything about the body? . . .
He heard his mother's voice addressing him excitedly like the
voice of a messenger in a play.
—What ought I do? There's some matter coming away from
the hole in Isabel's . . . stomach . . . Did you ever hear of that
happening?
—I don't know, he answered trying to make sense of her
words, trying to say them again to himself.
—Ought I send for the doctor . . . Did you ever hear of that?
. . . What ought I do?
—I don't know . . . What hole?
—The hole . . . the hole we all have . . . here.

[Stephen Hero, pp. 162-63]

This passage ends chapter 22; the next chapter begins with a description of Isabel's death and Stephen's reaction to it.

Despite all the undeniable benefits of placing an epiphany in a
context, there are nevertheless times when it seems a matter of individual taste as to whether a published version is actually an im-
provement. In fact, in some instances I feel certain that the original
fragment is more effective, or at least would be if it were placed
unchanged in the relevant passage. I have already indicated that
at first Joyce's changes occasionally tended to make the newer
versions embarrassingly explicit, surprising as such a fault may be
in the author of *Ulysses* and *Finnegans Wake*. Less surprising, perhaps, is his tendency to be verbose. In one passage in *Stephen Hero*,
the first of three in rapid succession based on Joyce's own epiphanies dealing with games played at the Daniels' (that is, the
Sheehys'), there are a number of helpful facts not in the original
fragment :

[Dublin : at Sheehy's, Belvedere
Place]

O'Reilly—(*with developing seriousness*) . . . . Now it's my turn,
    I suppose . . . . . (*quite seriously*) . . . . Who is your favourite
    poet?
Hanna Sheehy—. . . . . . . German?
                (*a pause*)
O'Reilly—. . . . . . Yes.
                (*a hush*)
Hanna Sheehy—. . . I think . . . . . Goethe . . . . . [*Workshop*,
p. 22]

In *Stephen Hero*, we learn that the boy and girl are apparently trying to impress Stephen with their ability to be serious, and that they are "doing" the same course together; this information helps, yet instead of the brief "a pause," we are told that "Annie thought for a few moments . . . ," and instead of the perfect "a hush" there is the strained irony of the diluted sentence, "Annie thought for another few moments while the table waited to be edified" (p. 43).

In providing the fuller treatment, necessary as it is, Joyce in this case has not been able to preserve the bare simplicity of his original experience. Later, he is able to do so, managing to be brief and yet provide the proper background, taking as much advantage as he can of the differing qualities of both the fragment and the novel. An illustration of this development is the treatment of a manuscript describing two mourners at a funeral, a woman and a girl with "the face of a fish," who looks up at the woman "to see if it is time to cry" (*Workshop*, p. 31). When it appears in *Stephen Hero*, the incident occurs at Isabel's funeral in an almost identical form, the only important addition being the word "viciously" to describe the way in which the two women push through the crowd (p. 167). The epiphany was abandoned for the *Portrait*, where there is no mention of Isabel or her death, but it must have retained its importance for Joyce, for he revived it and put it in *Ulysses*, where it is drastically cut and the language made to fit perfectly into Mr. Bloom's interior monologue during the funeral of Paddy Dignam: "Mourners came out through the gates: woman and a girl. Lean-jawed harpy, hard woman at a bargain, her bonnet awry. Girl's face stained with dirt and tears, holding the woman's arm looking up at her for a sign to cry. Fish's face, bloodless and livid" (p. 101/100). By now, Joyce presents each epiphany as succinctly as possible and with only the minimum suggestion of the necessary background.[9]

So far I have ignored the *Portrait*, but I would like to conclude this survey of the changes undergone by some of the manuscripts with a look at several that appear in that novel. In *Stephen Hero*, the concept of epiphany comes to Stephen as he sees Emma's soul

---

[9] The general tendency toward conciseness which can be traced between *Stephen Hero* and *Ulysses* was in a number of ways reversed between *Ulysses* and *Finnegans Wake*. Even in some of the very latest revisions of *Ulysses*, A. Walton Litz has shown, Joyce began to make increasing use of the "process of inclusion" rather than of "exclusion." See *The Art of James Joyce*, pp. 35-37.

"manifest itself" in "every stray image of the streets," and he over-
hears the colloquy between the young lady and gentleman while on
some sort of "quest" (pp. 210-11). At one point in the *Portrait*,
Stephen discovers that "Dublin was a new and complex sensation,"
and he wanders through the city "in search of Mercedes . . . as if
he really sought someone that eluded him." Though Stephen does
not here go on to a discussion of epiphanies, he is affected enough
by certain incidents to want to record them with extreme care :
while visiting relatives with his mother, "he chronicled with patience
what he saw"—and then comes a series of three passages, at least
two of them based on Joyce's own epiphanies, and all three beginning with the phrase, "He was sitting. . . ." The first deals with
his aunt's admiration for a picture of "the beautiful Mabel Hunter,"
and I know of no manuscript epiphany from which it derives. Next,
however, comes one in which he is sitting in a room with one old
woman, when another comes in and mistakes him for Josephine,
"laughing feebly" at her mistake (*Portrait*, pp. 66-68). This epiphany
is recorded in Stanislaus' "Selections in Prose" (*Workshop*, p. 15),
and its transformation is one of Joyce's most successful; making it
a definite part of the novel, he at the same time manages to preserve
the individual quality of the experience, the sense of a fragment of
life, a sudden, revealing, frozen moment unlike those preceding or
following it.

The third scene begins with the statement, "He was sitting in the
midst of a children's party at Harold's Cross" (*Portrait*, p. 68).
Perhaps no passage in all of Joyce has had a more interesting
history, and few have been used so many times. It, too, originated
in one of Joyce's own experiences, which he set down in a manuscript epiphany :

> The children who have stayed latest are getting on their things
> to go home for the party is over. This is the last tram. The lank
> brown horses know it and shake their bells to the clear night, in
> admonition. The conductor talks with the driver; both nod often
> in the green light of the lamp. There is nobody near. We seem
> to listen, I on the upper step and she on the lower. She comes
> up to my step many times and goes down again, between our
> phrases, and once or twice remains beside me, forgetting to go
> down, and then goes down. . . . . Let be; let be. . . . And now
> she does not urge her vanities—her fine dress and sash and long
> black stockings—for now (wisdom of children) we seem to know

that this end will please us better than any end we have laboured
for. [*Workshop*, p. 13]

Before it appeared in the *Portrait*, this epiphany had also been used
in *Stephen Hero*, where the experience seems, perhaps, less innocent. Thinking of Emma's "warm ample body," Stephen remembers
how one night on the tram he had caressed her hand, and how she
had seemed to feel "obliged to insist on the forbearance of the male
and to despise him for forbearing" (pp. 67-68): this despite the
fact that the experience had occurred when they were children. He
is now remembering something that had happened years before, as
Joyce obviously is in the manuscript fragment—or as a similar
incident is recalled by the waiter in T. S. Eliot's "Dans le
Restaurant."

The first appearance of the incident in the *Portrait* is in the series
of epiphanies I have been discussing, where it is not a memory but
a present experience, and probably for that reason it is greatly
expanded. But, though longer, it is far from being more explicit and
is in fact much more suggestive. The children seem even less innocent in this version; whereas the girl in the fragment "does not urge
her vanities," in the *Portrait* we are told that Stephen "saw her
urge her vanities, her fine dress and sash and long black stockings,
and knew that he had yielded to them a thousand times" (p. 69).
As far as we can tell, therefore, the manifestation is for Stephen
quite different from what it had been for Joyce himself. There is
no mention of the children's hands, but Stephen does recall an even
earlier experience with another little girl, Eileen, whose hands had
been "like ivory; only soft." Consequently, she had made him think
of the Virgin Mary. One day she had broken away from him and
had run off laughing (pp. 42-43); Stephen remembers that incident
and thinks: "She too wants me to catch hold of her. . . . That's
why she came with me to the tram. I could easily catch hold of her
when she comes up to my step: nobody is looking. I could hold her
and kiss her." But, and again rather like Eliot's waiter, "he did
neither" (p. 70).

It is not until the second use of the incident in the *Portrait* that
we come upon the published version that is closest of all to the
original manuscript. All sexual suggestions are minimized, and no
mention whatsoever is made of the girl's "vanities" (p. 222). Perhaps
time has tended to purify Stephen's impression of what had occurred.

Ten years have passed since the incident itself, and, like both the fragment and the version in *Stephen Hero*, this passage records the memory of a past experience. This incident, therefore, is one of Joyce's most Proustian. Not only is there an original epiphany, but its recollection seems to produce another one many years later.

And like many of Proust's, this epiphany has also turned out to be a moment of artistic inspiration, though the art is of doubtful value. In *Stephen Hero*, the event is retrieved from memory to yield "some pages of sorry verse" (p. 67). After its occurrence in the *Portrait*, Stephen tries to write a poem "To E—— C——"; eventually we learn that he has written a poem about the incident itself (pp. 70, 77). Later, when he recalls the incident, he writes "verses for her again after ten years," referring to her as "the temptress of his villanelle" (pp. 222-23). This is especially interesting because the grandfather of all Stephen's epiphanies, the colloquy between the young lady and gentleman which had given him his awareness of the role of the artist as recorder of evanescent moments, had also "set him composing some ardent verses which he entitled a 'Vilanelle of the Temptress'" (*Stephen Hero*, p. 211). By now, the complexity of the relationships among many epiphanies should be becoming apparent.

And we are not finished yet. In the passage just preceding Stephen's recollection of their leave-taking on the tram, he and Emma are at a party; once again he touches her hand, "a soft merchandise," and they speak. Joyce's own original epiphany reads:

> She is engaged. She dances with them in the round—a white dress lightly lifted as she dances, a white spray in her hair; eyes a little averted, a faint glow on her cheek. Her hand is in mine for a moment, softest of merchandise.
> —You very seldom come here now.—
> —Yes I am becoming something of a recluse.—
> —I saw your brother the other day . . . . . . He is very like you.—
> —Really?—
> She dances with them in the round—evenly, discreetly, giving herself to no one. The white spray is ruffled as she dances, and when she is in shadow the glow is deeper on her cheek.
> [*Workshop*, p. 36]

In *My Brother's Keeper* (p. 257), Stanislaus guesses that the affair was actually the engagement party for one of the Sheehy girls. When Joyce adapted the epiphany for the *Portrait*, however, he left out all reference to any "engagement," and there are a number of other significant features in his treatment of it, most noticeably a lack of any definite indication that the moment is for Stephen an especially revealing one—an epiphany. And instead of merely telling Emma that he is a "recluse," Stephen says that he was "born to be a monk"—but she acutely replies, "I am afraid you are a heretic" (p. 219). The relevance of these remarks to Stephen's biography is of course clear : they even prepare for *Ulysses* and Florry's unconsciously perceptive remark, "I'm sure you are a spoiled priest. Or a monk" (p. 523/512).

I have made all these comparisons between manuscript and novel in order to give an idea of the technical methods Joyce used in adapting his own epiphanies to his finished works. But, after all, these manuscripts and their changes tell only part of the story. I believe that a realization of the significance of the epiphany and its role helps to clarify many of Joyce's chief methods and aims as an artist : his concentration on apparently trivial incidents; his structural reliance on key scenes of revelation; the way these or other scenes or events bring together a number of his most important themes; his emphasis on the recollection of previous scenes or events; the special way he chooses some images as leitmotifs over others, which in turn is related to his own peculiar handling of the stream of consciousness and its apparently incongruous associations; and his radical changes in the traditional short story.

However, we need not examine epiphany solely or even primarily in terms of technique. It can also clarify Joyce's attitudes toward his most pervasive themes; and so it is also from a thematic point of view that I shall examine some of the most important epiphanies —many of which never appear in the manuscripts—in the Dedalus-Bloom novels, and try to show how the main themes of these works are carried forward chiefly through climactic epiphanies.

First I ought to say a few words about the technique of *Dubliners,* for, preliminary though both the volume itself and its use of epiphany may be, both are enormously significant in the history of the modern short story. In a sense, the works in this collection represent a new type of story which seems written almost in order to provide an introduction and background to an epiphany—although this "new" form is so similar to Chekhov's that one might assume an influence if Joyce had not denied that he had read Chekhov before he wrote *Dubliners* (Ellmann, *Joyce*, p. 171). As the form is handled by Joyce, the epiphany almost invariably comes at or toward the end and is fully prepared for by a meticulous writer. In "An Encounter," for example, the narrator realizes his own lack of human sympathy and regrets his previous contempt for Mahony. This occurs after his encounter with the pervert—whose stick and veiled threats to the young boy, incidentally, are vaguely reminiscent of the stick and coarser threats of the lame beggar. (This association is strengthened by Joyce's so-called "Ur-Workbook" for *Finnegans Wake*, published under the title *Scribbledehobble*; in an entry under the pages on "An Encounter," he writes of "self & onanism: . . . Oscar=beggar" [p. 37]—presumably references to Oscar Wilde and the assailant-beggar who confronts HCE in the *Wake*, but probably back to the earlier, lame beggar as well.[10])

Another moment of self-revelation—apparently for the same boy —occurs at the end of "Araby," where his illusions about the fair are not the only ones that are shattered: "Gazing up into the darkness I saw myself as a creature driven and derided by vanity; and my eyes burned with anguish and anger" (*Dubliners*, p. 35). Like many a pilgrim before him, he has discovered that the bazaar is still Vanity Fair. In "A Little Cloud," the wailing of his son interrupts Little Chandler's Wordsworthian attempt to recapture an earlier "poetic" sensation and reveals to him that he is "a prisoner for life" (p. 84). "Ivy Day in the Committee Room," which obeys all the unities of time, place, and action, and is presented almost as a prolonged fragment of conversation, comes as close as a story its length ever could to creating the impression of a single epiphany. But it, too, is climaxed by the rather special manifestation of the "*Pok!*" from the gas in the wine bottle. Two stories closely related to each other, both in theme and in the revelations they lead up to, are "A Painful Case" and "The Dead": in each, a beast comes out

---

[10] For a fuller discussion of these motifs and their significance in Joyce's epiphanies and fiction, in a context in which I am able to include a consideration of *Finnegans Wake*, see my essay, "The Wooden Sword: Threatener and Threatened in the Fiction of James Joyce," *James Joyce Quarterly* 2 (Fall 1964):33-41.

of the jungle of the past to reveal to the protagonist the futility and barrenness of his whole life.

My subject, however, is not the modern short story, but the modern novel, where the role of epiphany has been even more important; in the rest of this chapter I try to show that Joyce's two novels actually develop and proceed by epiphany. (I do not include *Stephen Hero* and *Finnegans Wake*. We cannot examine the structure of the one since, as we have it, it is not a novel but a fragment, while the other is a . . . well, a something else.) By examining a selected number of epiphanies in the *Portrait* and *Ulysses* in more or less chronological order—ignoring a good many, including those I have already discussed—I hope to demonstrate how they serve Joyce both structurally and as his primary means of presenting his major themes.

Ever since Hugh Kenner wrote that "every theme in the entire lifework of James Joyce is stated on the first two pages of the *Portrait*," many critics have seen the truth of this statement, and several have followed it through with interesting analyses, especially of the scene in which Dante and Mrs. Dedalus try to get Stephen to "apologise." Marvin Magalaner has some especially valuable comments on this scene, while Ruth Von Phul has based upon it what amounts to a psychoanalytic examination of Joyce and his guilt feelings, much of what she says being generally deprecatory.[11] Despite these studies, however, a few further comments are necessary in a discussion of epiphany, for besides being so thematically crucial this scene is the first of many in the *Portrait* and *Ulysses* that are based on one of Joyce's own epiphanies. In the original manuscript, he records an early childhood experience:

> [Bray: in the parlour of the house
> in Martello Terrace]
>
> Mr Vance—(*comes in with a stick*) . . . O, you know, he'll have
>   to apologise, Mrs Joyce.
> Mrs Joyce—O yes . . . Do you hear that, Jim?
> Mr Vance—Or else—if he doesn't—the eagles'll come and pull
>   out his eyes.
> Mrs Joyce—O, but I'm sure he will apologise.

[11] Hugh Kenner, "The Portrait in Perspective," p. 142; Marvin Magalaner and Richard M. Kain, *Joyce: The Man, the Work, the Reputation*, pp. 112-14; Marvin Magalaner, *Time of Apprenticeship: The Fiction of Young James Joyce*, pp. 30-31; Ruth Von Phul, "Joyce and the Strabismal Apologia," pp. 119-32.

Joyce—(*under the table, to himself*)
    —Pull out his eyes,
    Apologise,
    Apologise,
    Pull out his eyes.

    Apologise,
    Pull out his eyes,
    Pull out his eyes,
    Apologise. [*Workshop*, p. 11]

On the biographical level, of course, this scene is interesting in regard to the eye trouble of both Stephen and Joyce; but when we first encounter it in the *Portrait* it seems to refer above all to the theme of guilt—it records an attempt to make a child feel guilty. It seems, in fact, to have no other major reference, since Joyce presents it with no explication whatsoever, in contrast to his earlier methods in *Stephen Hero*.

But, in the light of all that happens in the rest of the two novels, this retrospective epiphany takes on a great many other meanings. The threat of the eagles clearly represents an attempt not only to make Stephen "apologise," but to make him submit—recalling, Hugh Kenner has suggested, the birds who gnaw at Prometheus ("The Portrait in Perspective," p. 141). Submit to what? It is in the answer to this question that we see how this epiphany is related to every one of Joyce's major themes, for the refusal to apologize seems to foreshadow all the things against which Stephen later rebels: home, fatherland, and church. Notice that in the version in the *Portrait*, the main oppressive role is taken from Mr. Vance—who carries the stick common to all threatening figures in Joyce, such as the lame beggar who threatens to cut "the lights" out of the two boys—and given to Dante, who has just been associated with Irish nationalism through her two brushes, one for Michael Davitt and one for Parnell. Eventually, however, she becomes antagonistic to this cause in the vehemence of her defense of the church—the central reason for taking the role from Mr. Vance, who is a Protestant. Later, some boys approach Stephen after a class in which Mr. Tate, the English master, has said that "This fellow has heresy in his essay"; prodded on by Heron's cry to "catch hold of this heretic," they strike him with a cane and try to make him . . .

    —Admit that Byron was no good.

—No.
—Admit.
—No.
—Admit.
—No. No. [*Portrait*, pp. 79, 81-82]

Finally, Stephen succeeds in driving his tormentors off, his eyes "half blinded with tears." In an outline for some of the chapters of *Stephen Hero* appear the words "Belvedere. Essays." One of the phrases across from these words is "Fight with Heron," while below them is written "Epiphany of Mr. Tate" (*Workshop*, pp. 70-71).

In the earlier, "apologise" scene, the instrument of the church had been a more powerful one than a group of bullies : his mother had been the one who, with Dante, had urged Stephen to submit—just as later she tries to persuade him to perform his Easter duty. This request comes after Stephen's loss of faith, and he denies it. When Cranly asks him why, he replies, "I will not serve"; as Cranly points out, "that remark was made before" (*Portrait*, p. 239). From having once been terrified by Father Arnall's speculation in the retreat sermon—with what Joyce called its "Epiphany of Hell" (*Workshop*, p. 69)—that Lucifer's sin "was the sin of pride, the sinful thought conceived in an instant : *non serviam: I will not serve*" (*Portrait*, p. 117), Stephen has come round to the imitation of Satan. He nows seems to feel—as, according to Stanislaus' testimony, Joyce felt—that his mother represents "the Irishwoman, the accomplice of the Irish Catholic Church" (*My Brother's Keeper*, p. 238). All this, of course, is only anticipated in the "apologise" epiphany—which, however, also looks forward to the one major theme in the novel that I have not yet mentioned : even at the very beginning Stephen's independence finds expression in art, and the little boy hiding under the table composes a verse about his plight.

With what have since become almost stock situations in fiction, the sensitive young artist continues to be bullied. Because Stephen refuses to trade, for example, Wells pushes him into a slimy ditch, where "a fellow had once seen a big rat jump into the scum" (*Portrait*, p. 10). This experience causes Stephen to go to the infirmary, where he has a curious, half-wakeful dream :

> He saw the sea of waves, long dark waves rising and falling, dark under the moonless night. A tiny light twinkled at the pier-head where the ship was entering : and he saw a multitude of

D

people gathered by the waters' edge to see the ship that was
entering their harbour. A tall man stood on the deck, looking
out towards the flat dark land : and by the light at the pierhead
he saw his face, the sorrowful face of Brother Michael.

He saw him lift his hand towards the people and heard him
say in a loud voice of sorrow over the waters :

—He is dead. We saw him lying upon the catafalque.

A wail of sorrow went up from the people.

—Parnell! Parnell! He is dead! [P. 27]

The first two sentences of this passage are based on one of Joyce's
own dream-epiphanies, which has been drastically changed to fit
into this context; in the original there is no mention of Parnell, and
Joyce probably did not have him in mind when he recorded the
dream.[12] From now on, Stephen will associate rats with the church
—and with death, especially Parnell's and his own : frightened by
Father Arnall's powerful words, he will think with horror of how
he is doomed to the grave, "to be devoured by scuttling plump-
bellied rats" (p. 112). (Later, Mr. Bloom, seeing an "obese grey rat"
in the cemetery, will reflect with his usual, quietly understated over-
statement : "One of those chaps would make short work of a fellow.
Pick the bones clean no matter who it was" [*Ulysses*, p. 114/112-
13].) Much earlier, the ill young Stephen feels the prefect's "cold
damp hand" on his forehead : "That was the way a rat felt, slimy
and damp and cold." The little boy tries to assure himself that rats
are after all just rats by reflecting that "when they were dead they
lay on their sides. . . . They were only dead things" (*Portrait*, p. 22).
And soon, during the Christmas dinner, Mr. Dedalus accuses the
Church and its priests of having turned on Parnell "to betray him
and rend him like rats in a sewer" (p. 34).

Dante, who is now unmistakably associated with the Church, is
certainly right when, in regard to the talk at that dinner, she warns
that Stephen will "remember all this when he grows up . . ." (p. 33).
Like many others, the epiphanies in this scene serve as a means of
dramatizing important conflicts—conflicts sometimes expressed

[12] *Workshop*, p. 38 : "A moonless night under which the waves gleam
feebly. The ship is entering a harbour where there are some lights. The sea
is uneasy, charged with dull anger like the eyes of an animal which is about
to spring, the prey of its own pitiless hunger. The land is flat and thinly
wooded. Many people are gathered on the shore to see what ship it is that
is entering their harbour."

through imagery reminiscent of the "apologise" passage, as when Mr. Casey tells how he had spit into the eye of an old woman who had berated Parnell. She had screamed, "*O Jesus, Mary and Joseph! . . . I'm blinded! I'm blinded and drownded!*" (p. 37). By the time it is over, this family get-together has touched upon just about everything against which Stephen eventually rebels. Furious at what she has heard, Dante cries, "God and religion before everything! . . . God and religion before the world!"; this drives Mr. Casey to be equally vehement: "No God for Ireland! he cried. We have had too much God in Ireland. Away with God!" (p. 39). It can be said that Stephen, who is profoundly affected by this scene, eventually decides that if the Church and Ireland both claim supremacy over everything else, he will refuse to submit to either; rather, he will cry: away with God, away with Ireland—and away with family.

Up to now, the theme of the family has for the most part centered on Stephen's attitude toward his mother, as in fact it does until *Ulysses*. Yet occasionally there are important scenes where it is his father who is revealed to Stephen; such is the epiphany that occurs during the trip to Cork. Mr. Dedalus takes his son for a tour through his old school, where Stephen sees the word *Foetus* cut into the wood of one of the desks. "Startled" by the "sudden legend," he is disturbed by a sense of the presence of the absent students and "a vision of their life." He shrinks from that presence, while "the word and the vision" also reveal to him the full hollowness of his father's sentimentality and what Mr. Dedalus' youth must have really been like—and, as well, the universality of the "monstrous reveries" which until then Stephen had deemed "a brutish and individual malady of his own mind" (pp. 89-90). This intensely negative scene is not recorded in any known manuscript epiphany, though it may be based on an actual incident (see Ellmann, *Joyce*, p. 37).

Stephen does not yet completely reject his family or become a rebel; first he must find a cause. Much later than this scene, in fact, he seriously listens to the director's proposal that he become a Jesuit priest. It is the abrupt necessity for this decision that makes him realize "the frail hold which so many years of order and obedience had of him when once a definite and irrevocable act of his threatened to end for ever, in time and in eternity, his freedom" (*Portrait*, pp. 161-62). This rejection of the Catholic priesthood quickly leads

Stephen to lose his faith; at the same time, it prepares him for the realization of his true calling, art, and to become instead the "priest of eternal imagination" he later calls himself (p. 221). Very soon after his interview with the director, Stephen, walking along the shore, feels that the air is "timeless," and all ages seem "as one to him." Suddenly, he realizes the significance of his name, the name of the fabulous artificer: "a hawklike man flying sunward above the sea, a prophecy of the end he had been born to serve . . . , a symbol of the artist forging anew in his workshop out of the sluggish matter of the earth a new soaring impalpable imperishable being" (pp. 168-69).

This comparison extends the bird imagery first begun as a threat in the "apologise" epiphany and thus prepares Stephen for his vision of the wading girl, where the imagery remains a sign of promise and of freedom, not of punishment. This is the most important epiphany as well as the structural climax of the novel, the moment when he becomes a conscious artist, when the rebel finds his cause. Continuing his walk along the strand, Stephen sees a girl who seems "like one whom magic had changed into the likeness of a strange and beautiful seabird."

> She was alone and still, gazing out to sea. . . . The first faint noise of gently moving water broke the silence, low and faint and whispering, faint as the bells of sleep; hither and thither, hither and thither: and a faint flame trembled on her cheek.
> —Heavenly God! cried Stephen's soul, in an outburst of profane joy.
> He turned away from her suddenly and set off across the strand. . . .
> Her image had passed into his soul for ever and no word had broken the holy silence of his ecstasy. Her eyes had called him and his soul had leaped at the call. To live, to err, to fall, to triumph, to recreate life out of life! A wild angel had appeared to him, the angel of mortal youth and beauty, an envoy from the fair courts of life, to throw open before him in an instant of ecstasy the gates of all the ways of error and glory. [Pp. 171-72]

Coming as it does after a rejection of the priesthood, this epiphany of his calling in art is nevertheless couched in very ecclesiastical terms. The girl herself is strongly reminiscent of Beatrice, and the description of her flesh as "softhued as ivory" makes her, like Eileen and Emma before her, an image of the

Virgin Mary, the Tower of Ivory. Stephen's reaction to her is conveyed in such terms as *worship, Heavenly God!, soul, holy silence
of his ecstasy, a wild angel.* But despite all these phrases his emotion
is far from religious and is in fact, like his joy, "profane." She is not
a vision from another world, but "the angel of mortal youth and
beauty, an envoy from the fair courts of life." She makes him feel
"above him the vast indifferent dome and the calm processes of the
heavenly bodies," while the earth, on the contrary, "had taken him
to her breast" (p. 172).

The importance of this incident in the novel is clear; it was
apparently no less important to Joyce himself, to whom it seems to
have occurred in 1898 (Ellmann, *Joyce*, p. 151). Its personal significance is indicated not only by the role it plays in the *Portrait*, but
by the fact that it is one of the few incidents that also appear in the
early sketch, "A Portrait of the Artist," written on January 7, 1904
—unfortunately missing the Feast of the Epiphany by one day. The
unnamed hero walks in "silent and lonely places," watching the
waders along the shore, until he begins "to be conscious of the
beauty of mortal conditions." In a partially destroyed passage in
the manuscript, there is the ambiguous information that "the lights
in the chambers of the heart were unextinguished, nay, burning as
for espousal."[13] The context seems to be about a girl he had seen on
the beach, and he immediately goes on to call her "Dearest of
mortals!" and "Beneficent one!"; and again she is "an envoy from
the fair courts of life" (pp. 65-66). The repetition of this phrase
begins to make it clear that to Joyce this vision had revealed much
the same thing that he had learned from Georgie's death, or
Stephen from Isabel's—that life is a valuable "gift," and that everything else is "uncertain."[14] The girl may also have appeared in the
lost parts of *Stephen Hero*, for at one point in the surviving fragment Stephen, walking along the River Liffey,[15] reflects dejectedly

[13] *Workshop*, p. 65. The phrase "as for espousal" is used in one of Joyce's
epiphanies (p. 34); in the passage in the *Portrait* based on that epiphany,
the words refer to the soul (p. 152).

[14] *Stephen Hero*, p. 165. The passage is based on Joyce's epiphany in *Workshop*, p. 30, which ends with the sentence, "Everything else is so uncertain."
In *Exiles*, Richard hears Beatrice make the same remark, her reference being
to death: "And does death not move you, Mr. Rowan? It is an end.
Everything else is so uncertain!" (p. 23).

[15] Compare also the stirring of the water by the girl's foot moving "hither
and thither, hither and thither" in the *Portrait* with the "hitherandthithering
waters" of Anna Livia in *Finnegans Wake*, p. 216.

that "he met no other Lucy," and "that if he had made his proposal
to Lucy instead of to Emma he might have met with better luck"
(pp. 230-31).

The vision is also anticipated in the *Portrait* itself. While still a
child, Stephen broods upon his loneliness and returns to his image
of Mercedes, confident that someday he will meet this image "in
the real world" : "and in that moment of supreme tenderness he
would be transfigured. He would fade into something impalpable
under her eyes and then in a moment, he would be transfigured.
Weakness and timidity and inexperience would fall from him in
that magic moment" (p. 65). This is a great deal to ask of a mere
mortal, but much of it is actually accomplished by the girl on the
beach, although the final touches are not complete until Stephen's
brief encounter with, of all people, the rather commonplace yet
Beatrice-like Leopold Bloom. In the meantime, Stephen's ecstasy is
ironically offset by the depressing scene in the Dedalus kitchen
which immediately follows it : "He drained his third cup of watery
tea to the dregs and set to chewing the crusts of fried bread that
were scattered near him, staring into the dark pool of the jar"
(p. 174).

Stephen feels oppressed by this environment and at last decides
that he must leave Ireland, for as yet he fails to realize that he cannot leave for good until he is finally saved by a citizen of the very
city he is trying to escape. While there are a number of epiphanies
toward the end of the novel, the most significant is probably the
very last, in which the power of Stephen's compulsion to go away
is revealed to him in a dream he records in his diary; this entry is
in almost exactly the same words as one of Joyce's own dream-
epiphanies, which reads :

> The spell of arms and voices—the white arms of roads, their
> promise of close embraces and the black arms of tall ships that
> stand against the moon, their tale of distant nations. They are
> held out to say : We are alone,—come. And the voices say with
> them : We are your people. And the air is thick with their com-
> pany as they call to me their kinsman, making ready to go, shak-
> ing the wings of their exultant and terrible youth.[16]

[16] *Workshop*, p. 40. In a letter to Stanislaus written on February 7, 1905,
Joyce says that these words "mark the precise point between boyhood
(pueritia) and adolescence (adulescentia)—17 years" (*Letters*, 2 : 79). See the
first of the "Additional Manuscript Pages" of *Stephen Hero*, p. 237.

The white arms of the roads also cast their spell on Stephen. He, too, feels impelled to leave, and despite the rhetoric about the kinsmen who call to him, or rather because of it, no epiphany since the little boy tried to hide under the table has provided more convincing evidence for Harry Levin's point that "each epiphany . . . leaves him lonelier than the last" (*James Joyce*, p. 54).

But though Stephen's essential isolation remains permanent, this time his exile is only temporary. We discover in *Ulysses* that he is recalled from Paris by the death of his mother.

While he was away, and before her death, Joyce had dreamed of his own mother and then recorded the following dream-epiphany:

> She comes at night when the city is still; invisible, inaudible, all unsummoned. She comes from her ancient seat to visit the least of her children, mother most venerable, as though he had never been alien to her. She knows the inmost heart; therefore she is gentle, nothing exacting; saying, I am susceptible of change, an imaginative influence in the hearts of my children. Who has pity for you when you are sad among the strangers? Years and years I loved you when you lay in my womb. [*Workshop*, p. 44]

This is surely one of Joyce's most moving epiphanies; it is also one of his most revealing, strangely obscure as it is. Coming to him "from her ancient seat" while he is in exile "among the strangers," his mother is the old woman, Ireland. But, as the "mother most venerable" (a phrase from the Catholic litany), she suggests the Virgin Mary and therefore the Church. And indeed "susceptible of change," she is also his muse, "an imaginative influence" on her child.

In *Ulysses*, when this epiphany is echoed in Stephen's vision of his mother during the Nighttown episode, all these themes appear; but throughout that novel the dream is closely related to another one Stephen has after her death—this one, too, apparently based on an actual dream. It is recorded in Joyce's "Trieste Notebook" under "Mother": "She came to me silently in a dream after her death: and her wasted body within its loose brown habit gave out a faint odour of wax and rosewood and her breath a faint odour of wetted ashes."[17] At first, the echoes in *Ulysses* are almost entirely of this dream, and they begin almost immediately. There are two close

---

[17] *Workshop*, p. 103. Instead of "wasted" (my reading of the manuscript at Cornell), the *Workshop* has "washed."

repetitions in the first episode, and others in the second. They prepare Stephen for his mother's later visionary appearance to him:

> In a dream, silently, she had come to him, her wasted body within its loose graveclothes giving off an odour of wax and rosewood, her breath bent over him with mute secret words, a faint odour of wetted ashes.
>
> Her glazing eyes, staring out of death, to shake and bend my soul. . . .
>
> Ghoul! Chewer of corpses!
>
> No mother. Let me be and let me live. [*Ulysses*, p. 10/12; cf. pp. 5, 27, 38/7, 28, 39]

The two dreams are combined when she comes to him in the vision *"breathing upon him softly her breath of wetted ashes."*

THE MOTHER

Who saved you the night you jumped into the train at Dalkey with Paddy Lee? Who had pity for you when you were sad among the strangers? Prayer is all powerful. Prayer for the suffering souls in the Ursuline manual, and forty days' indulgence. Repent, Stephen.

STEPHEN

The ghoul! Hyena!

THE MOTHER

I pray for you in my other world. Get Dilly to make you that boiled rice every night after your brain work. Years and years I loved you, O my son, my firstborn, when you lay in my womb. [P. 581/565-66]

Apparently, Joyce could not get this epiphany out of his system, and he used its language and tone as late as *Finnegans Wake*: "Pariah, cannibal Cain, I who oathily foreswore the womb that bore you and the paps I sometimes sucked . . . it is to you, firstborn and firstfruit of woe, to me, branded sheep, pick of the wasterpaper-baskel . . . dweller in the downandoutermost where voice only of the dead may come, because ye left from me, because ye laughed on me, because, O me lonly son, ye are forgetting me!, that our turf-brown mummy is acoming . . ." (pp. 193-94). Perhaps the strangest and most haunting correspondence is not in another work by James Joyce, but in the monologue at the end of Thomas Wolfe's "The Web of Earth." Of course Wolfe could not have known the manuscript epiphany, but he certainly was familiar with *Ulysses*, and though there is no way of telling if he is actually echoing Joyce or not, the resemblances between the two passages are striking. Mrs. Gant, who in part represents the past and the American earth, laments that her son comes from "a race of wanderers," and she tells Eugene : "My dear child, eat good food and watch and guard your health : it worries me to think of you alone with strangers. . . . It worries me to think of you like this, alone and far away : child, child, come home again !" (*From Death to Morning*, p. 304). Mrs. Dedalus, who in part represents the past and Ireland, tells Stephen to eat boiled rice every night, that she pities him when he is "sad among the strangers," and begs him to "repent"—in Wolfe's terms, to "come home again."

However, Wolfe's hero discovers that you can't go home again, and Stephen refuses to repent; even at his mother's deathbed he had denied her request to kneel and pray for her, just as when a boy he had refused her admonition to "apologise," and just as during the same visionary scene in the Nighttown episode he shouts, "*Non serviam !*" in one of the climaxes of the entire novel. But there are several major epiphanies in this episode, and we had best take them in their proper order.

The conformation of the episode is ideal for epiphanies, since very little attention is paid to the basic demands of space and time. To the characters victimized by the illusions of this Walpurgis Night, inches often seem like miles, and minutes like years. When Bloom makes a lewdly flirtatious comment to Zoe about the dangers of tobacco, she replies "Go on. Make a stump speech out of it" (p. 478/469). Always obliging, he does, and for twenty pages we have his illusions, which, as in the legendary belief about dreams, occur in the fraction of an instant yet are long and extremely elaborate. He begins with a modest speech which is so successful that an elector hails him as the future chief magistrate; within a short time Bloom has become the hero of Ireland and an object of worship. But he is also cursed and damned, like many another Irish hero, and is martyred by being set on fire. As he dies, a choir of six hundred voices sings the Alleluia chorus—and then Zoe breaks the illusion by continuing her remark : "Talk away till you're black in the face" (p. 499/488). In the same way, time has a stop when Bella Cohen enters the scene (p. 527/515). For twenty-five pages we have a vast number of phantasms, including the metamorphoses of Bella into Bello and Bloom into a slavegirl, all of which occur in an instant, or perhaps in a state of timelessness, ending when Bloom sees that *"the figure of Bella Cohen stands before him"* (p. 554/540).

The "free association" of these illusions prepares us for epiphanies which, obliterating all space and time, can bring together all the themes of *Ulysses,* and of the *Portrait* as well. While some of Stephen's epiphanies during this episode force him to relive his past, they somehow at the same moment free him from it. The elements of space and time begin to be especially confused for him when in his drunken state he has difficulty lighting a cigarette : "Must get glasses. Broke them yesterday. Sixteen years ago. Distance. The eye sees all flat. . . . Brain thinks. Near : far. Ineluctable modality of the visible. (*He frowns mysteriously.*)" (p. 560/546).

The "yesterday" had occurred sixteen years before, when, a little boy at Clongowes, he had been excused from schoolwork by Father Arnall because he had broken his glasses. But such an excuse had not suited Father Dolan, the school's roving sadist. Having first pandied Fleming ("An idler of course. I can see it in your eye"), he then confronts Stephen ("I see schemer in your face"). The astonished boy holds out his hand; it is struck by the pandybat, "and at the sound and the pain scalding tears were driven into his eyes." Stephen feels within him "a prayer to be let off," but he does not submit—even "though the tears scalded his eyes" (*Portrait,* pp. 48, 50). As Marvin Magalaner has pointed out in regard to this scene, "Stephen, the embryo artist and rebel, will not 'Apologise' even when the world seeks to 'Pull out his eyes' " (*Joyce,* p. 114). Stephen never forgets this incident. Although in some ways it is a "retrospective" epiphany and some of its revelation does not come until he is in Bella Cohen's brothel, even from the beginning it does reveal to him a new aspect of the Church, which, he realizes for the first time, can be oppressive and unjust : "The prefect of studies was a priest but that was cruel and unfair" (*Portrait,* p. 52). The same event appears to affect the attitude toward priests in *Stephen Hero;* when Stephen sees evil in the lame beggar's face he thinks of "the faces of prefects as they 'pandied' boys with a broad leather bat but those faces had seemed to him less malicious than stupid, dutifully inflamed faces" (p. 245). Although Stephen recalls the priests as a contrast, their very association with the lame beggar inevitably suggests a comparison. Within the *Portrait* itself, further connections are made through Stephen's reactions to Father Arnall's sermons, and his sense of being called to "Confess! Confess!" : he has come to mortal sin, he feels, "by seeing or by thinking of seeing"—and the fault thus lies in his "eyes," which "see the thing, without having wished first to see. Then in an instant it happens" (p. 139).

Ulysses shows Stephen remembering the incident of the pandying early in the day, when the editor tells him he wants him to write "something with a bite in it. You can do it. I see it in your face" (p. 135/133). However, its main occurrence is not until shortly after the passage from the Nighttown episode that I have already quoted. Zoe, reading Stephen's palm, finds in it "courage."

I see it in your face. The eye, like that. (*She frowns with lowered head.*)

LYNCH

(*Laughing, slaps Kitty behind twice.*) Like that. Pandy bat.

(*Twice loudly a pandybat cracks, the coffin of the pianola flies open, the bald little round jack-in-the-box head of Father Dolan springs up.*)

FATHER DOLAN

Any boy want flogging? Broke his glasses? Lazy idle little schemer. See it in your eye.

(*Mild, benign, rectorial, reproving, the head of Don John Conmee rises from the pianola coffin.*)

DON JOHN CONMEE

Now, Father Dolan! Now. I'm sure that Stephen is a very good little boy. [P. 561/547-48]

Stephen does not simply remember these two priests. He actually sees them before him in a scene which seems at once a vision and a recapture of the past. And both the present and past moments are revelatory; the significance of the cruel pandying by a priest for young Stephen's development is clear, but there is also a sudden revelation inherent in his recalling the incident at this time, for he is about to have his vision of his dead mother. The description of Father Dolan as a "jack-in-the-box" echoes an argument Stephen once had with his mother, caused by his resentment of her having spoken about him to her confessor : "Have you not your own nature to guide you, your own sense of what is right, without going to some Father Jack-in-the-Box to ask him to guide you?" (*Stephen Hero*, p. 209). As Leon Edel says, "the synthesis here, if we examine all the elements that have become fused in Stephen's mind, is that of Mother Church and the mother Stephen defied on her death-bed and the guilt he feels and cannot banish" (*Modern Psychological Novel*, p. 83).

Thus, besides bringing in the themes of the Church and Stephen's "eye" trouble, this epiphany unites them again with the themes of mother, guilt, and submission—or rather his persistent refusal to submit. Yet he is still not ready for his final cry of rebellion, for he must reject not only the priests, but his mother and father as well. He will soon do that, but apparently he first has to find a substitute. How this can be done is revealed in the sequel to the memory of the pandying, a sequel that is an epiphany for both Stephen and the reader, a manifestation of the essential unity between Stephen and Bloom. Zoe, undaunted by the reception of her reading of Stephen's hand, reads Bloom's, quickly divining that he is a "hen-pecked husband." Bloom protests :

(*Points to his hand.*) That weal there is an accident. Fell and cut it twenty-two years ago. I was sixteen.

ZOE

I see, says the blind man. Tell us news.

STEPHEN

See? Moves to one great goal. I am twentytwo too. Sixteen years ago I twentytwo tumbled, twentytwo years ago he sixteen fell off his hobbyhorse. (*He winces.*) Hurt my hand somewhere. Must see a dentist. [P. 563/549]

Right after Stephen has remembered the pandying, Bloom recalls that he too had hurt his hand years before. Then Stephen, using rather weird arithmetic in order to relate the two experiences, winces and says he hurt his hand somewhere. Bloom, meanwhile,

has been called "the blind man," again relating him to Stephen in
a connection which might easily be missed; for the eyes, the broken
glasses, and blindness are all brought in by Stephen's apparently
irrelevant comment that he must see a dentist. He remembers this
because his memory of the pandying had made him think of his
eyes, and for both him and Joyce eye trouble seems to have been
connected with tooth trouble. Furthermore, Stephen's phrase,
"moves to one great goal," recalls the earlier scene with Mr. Deasy,
who had said that "all history moves towards one great goal, the
manifestation of God," directly after having commented of Jews
that "you can see the darkness in their eyes."[18]

Stephen suddenly realizes that Bloom is the protective figure who
had appeared to him the night before in a prophetic dream which
he had earlier recalled : "Street of harlots. . . . I am almosting it.
That man led me, spoke. I was not afraid. The melon he had he
held against my face. . . . Red carpet spread. You will see who"
(p. 47/47-48). Now he has an experience of *déjà vu*; he finally does
"see who," and this knowledge somehow enables him at last to free
himself from his physical father. Raising his forefinger in a Zen-like
gesture, he says, "Mark me. I dreamt of a watermelon."

(*Extending his arms.*) It was here. Street of harlots. . . . Where's
the red carpet spread?

BLOOM

(*Approaching Stephen.*) Look . . .

STEPHEN

No, I flew. My foes beneath me. And ever shall be. World without end. (*He cries.*) *Pater* ! Free !

BLOOM

I say, look . . .

---

[18] P. 34/35. Stephen's answer to Mr. Deasy's remark about history is that
God is "a shout in the street." If this is so, then Stephen later has an
orthodox "Epiphany"—a manifestation of God—only to react to it by
saying, "Damn that fellow's noise in the street" (p. 505/494).

STEPHEN

Break my spirit, will he? *O merde alors!* (*He cries, his vulture talons sharpened.*) [Pp. 571-72/556-57]

Stephen's cry of defiance against his father—"Break my spirit, will he?"—is repeated during the vision of his mother, when its reference is expanded to include her and anyone else who would try to make him serve. She begs him to "repent," warning him of the horrors of hell; enraged, he answers her with his Satanic cry of rebellion : "*Non serviam!*"

THE MOTHER

(*Wrings her hands slowly, moaning desperately.*) O Sacred Heart of Jesus, have mercy on him! Save him from hell, O divine Sacred Heart!

STEPHEN

No! No! No! Break my spirit all of you if you can! I'll bring you all to heel!

THE MOTHER

(*In the agony of her deathrattle.*) Have mercy on Stephen, Lord, for my sake! Inexpressible was my anguish when expiring with love, grief and agony on Mount Calvary.

STEPHEN

Nothung!

(*He lifts his ashplant high with both hands and smashes the chandelier. Time's livid final flame leaps and, in the following darkness, ruin of all space, shattered glass and toppling masonry.*) [Pp. 582-83/567-68]

This is only one of many times that Stephen has made the claim that he will not serve, yet we realize that this time it is probably true and that he will never have to repeat it again. He is at last free. Having already released himself from submission to his father, he now especially rejects the influence of his mother, because only by freeing himself from her—and her words here obviously associate her with the Virgin Mary—can he completely repudiate the church and become independent. In order to make sure that we see the full significance of what is going on, Joyce arranges for the ruin of all space and time.

About all that is necessary after the thematic unification achieved by this epiphany is that Bloom recognize his role. He does so in the most effective moment of vision in all of Joyce, as Bloom bends over the prostrate Stephen :

> (*Silent, thoughtful, alert, he stands on guard, his fingers at his lips in the attitude of secret master. Against the dark wall a figure appears slowly, a fairy boy of eleven, a changeling, kidnapped, dressed in an Eton suit with glass shoes and a little bronze helmet, holding a book in his hand. He reads from right to left inaudibly, smiling, kissing the page.*)

BLOOM

(*Wonderstruck, calls inaudibly.*) Rudy!

RUDY

> (*Gazes unseeing into Bloom's eyes and goes on reading, kissing, smiling. He has a delicate mauve face. On his suit he has diamond and ruby buttons. In his free left hand he holds a slim ivory cane with a violet bowknot. A white lambkin peeps out of his waistcoat pocket.*) [P. 609/593]

Stephen has already recognized Bloom as his father; this climactic epiphany therefore completes the central theme of the entire novel by revealing to Bloom his son in a sudden spiritual manifestation.

4

Virginia Woolf: Matches Struck in the Dark

> The great revelation had never come. The great revelation perhaps never did come. Instead there were little daily miracles, illuminations, matches struck unexpectedly in the dark. . . .
>
> *To the Lighthouse*, p. 249

Reading the published version of Virginia Woolf's diary, one is especially impressed by the many moments of vision she recorded throughout the volume. Sometimes these experiences seem to have had an unusually, even an abnormally powerful effect—at times they even seem to have had an almost mystical quality, as if there were some great revelation hovering nearby, ready to be grasped. Apparently, however, the great revelation never actually came, and in any case most of Mrs. Woolf's moments of vision were, instead, little daily miracles, illuminations. But for all their trivial and everyday character, they are essential to a full understanding of her work; for like Joyce she used her records of evanescent moments as the bases for works of art.

At one point in her diary Mrs. Woolf reflects on the possibility of writing "a book of characters; the whole string being pulled out from some simple sentence, like Clara Pater's 'Don't you find that Barker's pins have no points to them?'" (*Writer's Diary*, p. 99). This particular "simple sentence" was actually transformed into the subtitle and first words of one of Mrs. Woolf's most interesting stories, "Moments of Being: 'Slater's Pins Have No Points.'" Julia Craye, an elderly, genteel music teacher, opens the story by observing, when a pin drops to the floor, "Slater's pins have no points—don't you always find that?" (*A Haunted House and Other Stories*, p. 101). Her pupil, Fanny Wilmot, is startled by the incongruity of this remark, so domestic as it is, coming from Miss Craye. During the few brief moments she spends searching for the pin, Fanny muses upon this comment, and the story consists of her reflections, which take the form of an imaginative recreation of Miss Craye's past life. Fanny even dreams up a courtship, and how the young couple had gone out in a small boat, both of them aware that he was determined to propose. Nervous and reluctant, Miss Craye had rebuked him for careless rowing, and her words had produced "a moment of horror, of disillusionment, of revelation, for both of them" (p. 105). He had gone away angry and without proposing, and she had remained free. Fanny's reverie is suddenly interrupted when she finds the pin : and now her feelings become really complicated, for when she looks up she sees not a lonely old woman, but one who is experiencing "a moment of ecstasy." This ecstasy in turn produces for Fanny another revelation : "All seemed transparent, for a moment, to the gaze of Fanny Wilmot, as if looking through Miss Craye, she saw the very fountain of her being spurting its pure silver drops." The story ends as Miss Craye, laughing this time, repeats her remark that "Slater's pins have no points" (pp. 107-8).

Elsewhere in her diary, Mrs. Woolf exclaims : "How many little stories come into my head! For instance : Ethel Sands not looking at her letters. What this implies. One might write a book of short significant separate scenes. She did not open her letters" (*Diary*, p. 114). The "book of short significant separate scenes" may remind one of a novel Mrs. Woolf had already written, *Jacob's Room*, or perhaps even of Stephen Dedalus' plan for a collection of epiphanies. The incident she remembers here, at any rate, apparently suggested the short story, "The Lady in the Looking-Glass : A Reflection." Like "Moments of Being," this story consists of an imaginative association of ideas, in this case those of the narrator herself, whose thoughts, which dwell on the probable character and background of a woman named Isabella, are provoked by the objects reflected in a mirror in Isabella's home. We get a highly sentimental and romanticized picture of Isabella's profundity, and of the interesting and friendly letters she must receive—until her own reflection finally appears :

At once the looking-glass began to pour over her a light that seemed to fix her; that seemed like some acid to bite off the unessential and superficial and to leave only the truth. It was an enthralling spectacle. . . . And there was nothing. Isabella was perfectly empty. She had no thoughts. She had no friends. She cared for nobody. As for her letters, they were all bills. Look, as she stood there, old and angular, veined and lined, with her high nose and her wrinkled neck, she did not even trouble to open them. [*Haunted House*, pp. 91-92]

I have compared these passages from Virginia Woolf's diary and fiction in order to give an indication of how, in her art, she made use of those actual experiences from her own life that she called moments of vision; she also gave similar experiences to many of the characters in her novels and stories who, as far as we can tell, had no biographical basis. In fact, despite her many experiments with widely differing fictional forms, the technical device of the moment of vision appears in all her work, from first to last. Although she did not evolve anything remotely like a theory to explain such moments, she mentioned and discussed them more frequently than Joyce and even Proust. Moreover, to a large extent they determined the character and especially the structure of her novels, as one can see from even a cursory reading of such books as *Jacob's Room*, *Mrs. Dalloway*, and *To the Lighthouse*. The attitude toward experience which underlies these and her other works is made explicit in *The Waves*—which she once thought of calling *Moments of Being*[1]—by the novelist Bernard, who distrusts "neat designs of life that are drawn upon half-sheets of note-paper. . . . I begin to seek some design more in accordance with those moments of humiliation and triumph that come now and then undeniably" (*The Waves*, p. 169). It would seem that what Bernard and his creator sought was a design based upon something very like epiphany.

Although Mrs. Woolf developed no broad concepts in regard to them, one can discover a good deal about these moments—to which she variously attaches such words as *vision, being,* or *revelation*—by examining her comments on them. Above all, her statements show that to her the moments themselves are far more important than the meanings they involve. As Katharine says in *Night and Day*, quoting Dostoyevsky, it is "the process of discovering" that matters, "not the discovery itself at all."[2] That is, it is the experience

[1] Unpublished manuscript of *The Waves* in the Berg Collection, New York Public Library, title page.
[2] P. 138. See *The Idiot*, p. 375 (III, 5).

of revelation that matters, not what is revealed—which, as often as not, is vague and mysterious. In this and in other respects, Mrs. Woolf is closer to Walter Pater than to Joyce, for like Pater she believes that not the fruit of experience, but experience itself, is the end. She, too, stresses, in both her own impressionistic criticism and her fiction, the importance of the sensibility; she herself had what she called "a terrific capacity . . . for feeling with intensity" (*Diary*, p. 180). In her case, this capacity may have been related to her mental problems, which caused four breakdowns during her life. In fact the symptoms of her "neurasthenia," Leonard Woolf tells us, never completely left her; "at any moment" she "might suddenly 'leave the ground' and give some fantastic, entrancing, amusing, dreamlike, almost lyrical description of an event, a place, or a person." Such moments, Mr. Woolf points out, show how "terrifyingly thin" is the separation between "the inspiration of genius and madness" (*Beginning Again*, pp. 75, 30-31).

There are many similarities between Joyce's epiphanies and the experiences Mrs. Woolf describes, which do of course involve some sort of revelation, despite the fact that it may at times seem incidental and is very often obscure. One of her favorite words for what is revealed is "it," though she realizes that the reference of this pronoun is all too unclear. "Why," she asks, "is there not a discovery in life? Something one can lay hands on and say 'This is it'?"—though as a matter of fact she feels that she does "fairly frequently come upon this 'it'" (*Diary*, p. 86). In "The New Dress," those occasions when one exclaims "This is it!" are regarded by Mabel Waring as "divine moments" (*Haunted House*, p. 56). Another of Mrs. Woolf's favorite words to describe what she discovers is "reality." Frequently she asks the question, "What is meant by 'reality'?" But—and one can hardly blame her—she never gets around to answering it. The most she can do is describe what "reality" does, what its effects are : "It lights up a group in a room and stamps some casual saying. It overwhelms one walking home beneath the stars and makes the silent world more real than the world of speech—and then there it is again in an omnibus in the uproar of Piccadilly . . . whatever it touches, it fixes and makes permanent."[3]

[3] *A Room of One's Own*, pp. 165-66. Cf. *A Writer's Diary*, p. 132: "That is one of the experiences I have had here in some Augusts; and got then to a consciousness of what I call 'reality': a thing I see before me: something

As in epiphany, also, the experience is irrational and intuitive : "the origin of these moments of vision lies too deep for analysis. A red poppy, a mother's reproof, a Quaker upbringing, sorrows, loves, humiliations—they too have their part in moments of vision" (*Roger Fry*, p. 161). The revelations seem to arise "for no reason at all" (*To the Lighthouse*, p. 114); the moments in which "things come together" have an "inexplicable significance" : "Such moments of vision are of an unaccountable nature; leave them alone and they persist for years; try to explain them and they disappear; write them down and they die beneath the pen."[4] They are also, in other words, the most delicate and evanescent of moments. Again like the moments described by Joyce, they have a unifying role in her novels, a role Mrs. Woolf implies in the remark about moments in which "things come together"; this phrase is repeated in *Mrs. Dalloway*, where Peter also reflects on moments "in which things came together."[5] And, as several of the passages I have already quoted indicate, the moments of vision almost invariably arise from a trivial, apparently irrelevant event that takes on surprising importance.

I would not want my comparison of epiphany and Virginia Woolf's moment of being to be understood to imply that she derived her notions from Joyce, the immensity of whose influence on her has been more often assumed than demonstrated. The effect he had on her work—and as far as it went it was significant—did not arise because she found in him something new which she thereupon adapted for her own use. On the contrary, she found techniques and emphases which she herself had already gone a long way toward developing, though it does seem he hurried her a bit. As she wrote her first full-fledged "epiphanic" novel, *Jacob's Room*, she wondered if what she was doing was "being better done by Mr. Joyce." In time, however, she became repelled by his work and found *Ulysses* "an illiterate, underbred book . . . the book of a self taught working man" (*Diary*, pp. 28, 47). But she realized that no one interested in the trend of modern fiction could afford to ignore Joyce's novels; indeed, her comments on them for publication are much less critical than her diary would lead one to expect. And

---

abstract; but residing in the downs or sky; beside which nothing matters; in which I shall rest and continue to exist. Reality I call it. And I fancy sometimes this is the most necessary thing to me: that which I seek."
[4] "Moments of Vision," *TLS*, no. 853 (23 May 1918), p. 243.
[5] P. 167. Cf. *To the Lighthouse*, p. 100.

when she seeks to define what distinguishes Joyce from the novelists who have preceded him, the things she chooses to praise are precisely the aspects of his art that are most relevant to her own use of epiphany :

> In contrast with those whom we have called materialists, Mr. Joyce is spiritual; he is concerned at all costs to reveal the flickerings of that innermost flame which flashes its messages through the brain. . . . The scene in the cemetery, for instance, with its brilliancy, its sordidity, its incoherence, its sudden lightning flashes of significance, does undoubtedly come so close to the quick of the mind that, on a first reading at any rate, it is difficult not to acclaim a masterpiece. If we want life itself, here surely we have it. Indeed, we find ourselves fumbling rather awkwardly if we try to say what else we wish, and for what reason a work of such originality yet fails to compare, for we must take high examples, with *Youth* or *The Mayor of Casterbridge*. [*First Common Reader*, pp. 190-91]

It is no accident that when, despite the "sudden lightning flashes of significance" in his work, she sets Joyce off against "high examples," she chooses Joseph Conrad and Thomas Hardy; if she had been strongly influenced by any novelists in her own first gropings toward epiphany early in her career, it was not by her contemporaries, such as Joyce—or Proust, of whom I shall have more to say—but by Conrad and Hardy. In both of these novelists she found not only the technique, but even the right phrase : "moments of vision."

In the case of Hardy, Mrs. Woolf seems to exaggerate the importance of his use of the technique, and what she finds is perhaps less an essential element in Hardy's fiction than the result of her own subjective reading, the kind of reading that makes her one of the most interesting "impressionistic" critics of the twentieth century : "His own word, 'moments of vision', exactly describes those passages of astonishing beauty and force which are to be found in every book that he wrote. With a sudden quickening of power which we cannot foretell, nor he, it seems, control, a single scene breaks off from the rest. . . . Vivid to the eye, but not to the eye alone, for every sense participates, such scenes dawn upon us and their splendour remains."[6] It is true that moments of revelation do

---

[6] *Second Common Reader*, pp. 247-48. Cf. *A Writer's Diary*, p. 98, and *The Captain's Death Bed and Other Essays*, p. 63.

play a role in Hardy, especially in his later work. In his last novel, *Jude the Obscure*, a number of characters seem to experience them: there is the "momentary flash of intelligence" when Jude and Arabella meet, a perverse example of that ancient type of epiphany, love at first sight; and later, as he gazes at the buildings of Christminster, "for a moment" Jude has "a true illumination" of the equal dignity of his work in the stone yard with that of scholarly study. Such illuminations, however, are perhaps more prominent in Hardy's later poetry than in his fiction : the title poem of his 1917 volume is "Moments of Vision."[7]

Although Mrs. Woolf's view of Conrad is no less impressionistic, her comments on him have a less dubious or subjective basis. I have already discussed in my second chapter the importance of epiphany in Conrad, so let me just point out here that almost all her remarks on him center on his "moments of vision," which as early as 1917 she regarded as "the best things in his books."[8]

More important than the examples of other novelists in the development of her own use of epiphany, however, were her general philosophical and aesthetic views. Of course, these views did not resemble anything so formidable as a "philosophy." Virginia Woolf was not a philosopher, but an artist. Nevertheless, she was naturally affected, directly and indirectly, by some of the intellectual currents of her day.

Everyone agrees that time is important in Virginia Woolf's work; but for the most part agreement among critics ends there, and the precise nature of her notions of time is a subject of dispute. The major reason for this fact, it seems to me, is her emphasis on time as an almost purely subjective phenomenon. In itself, this attitude would not necessarily lead to ambiguity; for example, her view of the psychological basis of time frequently makes her seem to echo Laurence Sterne—whom she greatly admired—on the possibility of, say, making a minute seem a year. This notion is implied in the very form of *Orlando*, where it is also made explicit when she writes that "an hour, once it lodges in the queer element of the human spirit, may be stretched to fifty or a hundred times its clock length; on the other hand, an hour may be accurately represented on the

---

[7] *Jude the Obscure*, pp. 43 (I, vi), 100 (II, ii); *Collected Poems of Thomas Hardy*, p. 401.

[8] "Lord Jim," *TLS*, no. 810 (26 July 1917), p. 355. Cf. *First Common Reader*, pp. 286-87, and *Captain's Death Bed*, p. 80.

timepiece of the mind by one second" (p. 98).

In context, these remarks are fanciful, but her basic point is both serious and clear. Her other comments on the subjectivity of time, however, are sometimes so ambivalent that the only thing clear is that she will not, and perhaps believes one cannot, conclusively choose among ideas which at least appear to be contradictory. Her ambivalence therefore seems largely deliberate; thus, while writing *The Years*—one of her books most concerned with the fluid and continuous passage of time, as its final title suggests—she toyed with the idea of calling it *Here and Now* (*Diary*, p. 211), a title that would have stressed, if anything, temporal discontinuity. Side by side with her intense realization that the present moment is fleeting is an even more intense desire to hold it back somehow, to preserve it, to make it permanent.

This desire is frequently shared by the characters in Mrs. Woolf's novels, many of whom, like Eleanor in *The Years*, want "to enclose the present moment; to make it stay"—only to conclude that the attempt is "useless" (p. 428). Sometimes they may feel they succeed, as Mrs. Ramsay does when she says to herself, "Of such moments . . . the thing is made that remains for ever after. This would remain"—but she feels shortly afterward that the same scene is "vanishing" even as she looks, indeed that it is "already the past" (*To the Lighthouse*, pp. 163, 173). Virginia Woolf could not make up her mind : "Now is life very solid or very shifting? I am haunted by the two contradictions. This has gone on for ever; will last for ever; goes down to the bottom of the world—this moment I stand on. Also it is transitory, flying, diaphanous. I shall pass like a cloud on the waves" (*Diary*, p. 141).

In her fiction, she seems at times to have tried to keep some sort of rough balance between these views, and between what, in a discussion of the problems of the autobiographer, she described as "the two levels of existence" which have to be recorded : "the rapid passage of events and actions; the slow opening up of single and solemn moments of concentrated emotion"—two levels which are recorded, respectively, by "smooth narrative" and passages in which "time stands still" (*Second Common Reader*, p. 139). But the balance is only a rough one, and in the end the reader gets a definite impression that Mrs. Woolf generally leans toward the view that life is not completely fleeting, that the present moment can be made permanent. Some of her characters do, in fact, succeed in preserving it. We are told how Mrs. Dalloway, for one, "plunged into the very heart of the moment, transfixed it" (pp. 41-42). The first page of *To the Lighthouse* tells of people who do have "the power to crystallise and transfix the moment" (p. 11). And, if we are to believe Lily Briscoe, Mrs. Ramsay's apparent failure to stop the moment is after all only apparent: "Mrs. Ramsay making of the moment something permanent (as in another sphere Lily herself tried to make of the moment something permanent)—this was of the nature of a revelation" (p. 249). Of course, the sphere in which Lily makes her attempt is the same as Virginia Woolf's own: art.

Still another view of time held by Mrs. Woolf is that it does not exist at all. She once pondered the idea of writing a "very profound life of a woman, which shall all be told on one occasion; and time shall be utterly obliterated; future shall somehow blossom out of the past. One incident—say the fall of a flower—might contain it. My theory being that the actual event practically does not exist—nor time either" (*Diary*, p. 102). This "theory" is frequently manifest in the moments of vision in her novels. During many of these moments her characters feel that they are in some sort of timeless state—that time does not exist, or that it has been suspended, or that they have escaped it and are outside of it. Thus, in *The Years*, during an experience of intense happiness Kitty feels that time has "ceased" (p. 278); thus, also, Mrs. Ramsay at the dinner table in *To the Lighthouse* is "dissociating herself from the moment" when she feels that the present experience partakes "of eternity" (pp. 162-63). The sense of timelessness would in fact be very much like that of living in eternity, or in a world in which all time is contemporaneous. So Mrs. Swithin, who does not "believe in history," explicitly says that for the people watching the pageant in *Between the Acts*, time does not exist (pp. 203, 100).

Critics have often attributed Mrs. Woolf's interest in time to the influence of Henri Bergson, although, according to her own testimony, she never read him.[9] A superficial comparison of some of her comments on time with some of Bergson's views might tempt one to believe that she must have been exposed to his ideas indirectly, and critics like to point out that her sister-in-law, Karin Stephen, wrote a book on Bergson, or that the daughter of Leslie Stephen

---

[9] Phyllis Bentley, *Some Observations on the Art of Narrative*, p. 34.

must have known of the latest philosophical trends. But more than counterbalancing such vague evidence is the testimony of an authority who should know : Leonard Woolf has stated not only that his wife "did not read a word of Bergson," as well as his doubts "that she ever discussed Bergson with Mrs. Stephen," but also that, in any case, he does not think "that she was influenced in the slightest degree by Bergson's ideas."[10] Even if there was an indirect influence—clearly, there was not a direct one—Mrs. Woolf's views on time, as my discussion of them should have made clear, are by no means systematic enough to be called Bergsonian, and some of them are even "anti-Bergsonian."

At the risk of seeming to substitute one inaccurate term for another, I would suggest that in some ways Mrs. Woolf's treatment of time, especially in so far as it is artistic rather than philosophic, seems less Bergsonian than Proustian. With Proust, incidentally, the possibility of an actual direct influence seems less dubious, for Virginia Woolf began to read his novels in the original French in 1922.[11] By that year, however, only four of Proust's seven volumes had so far appeared, and though she continued to read the volumes as they came out, the one most important in regard to epiphany, *Le Temps retrouvé*, was not published until 1928. But Mrs. Woolf did not need Proust to increase her interest in moments of vision anyway; if anything specific in his work did influence her, it must have been his preoccupation with the relationship between the past and the present. In this respect, her most "Proustian" book is probably *Mrs. Dalloway*, as we shall see. When she finished that novel in 1925, she asked herself : "I wonder if this time I have achieved something? Well, nothing anyhow compared with Proust, in whom I am embedded now" (*Diary*, p. 72). Nevertheless, though the many resemblances in their work and her great familiarity with and admiration for him are all clear, the extent of Proust's actual influence on Virginia Woolf remains in doubt—as uncertain and as difficult to pin down as her views on the subject of time are in general.

Almost as ambiguous as her attitudes toward time are her feelings about the spiritual nature of her sudden revelations, for despite

<hr>

[10] Quoted in James Hafley, *The Glass Roof*, p. 174. Cf. Jean Guiguet, *Virginia Woolf and Her Works*, p. 33.

[11] Floris Delattre, *Le roman psychologique de Virginia Woolf*, p. 146.

some apparently religious traits in her make-up, she had no belief in God. She had been brought up by her father as a nonbeliever, and she remained one, though while a young girl she did write an essay "proving that man has need of a God; but the God was described in process of change . . ." (*Diary*, p. 151). Even then, she apparently made no attempt to prove that there is a God, but merely that man needs one. Later, she would frequently imply that even this was not so, although the need for belief of some sort remains : "I agree, we *do* believe, not in God though : not me anyhow . . . the living belief now is in human beings."[12] In *Mrs. Dalloway*, she seems to agree with Clarissa's view that religion tends to destroy "the privacy of the soul" (p. 140); the representative of religious faith in that novel is the intrusive, "odious," and aptly named Miss Kilman. Mrs. Woolf's distaste for religion is also reflected in a number of the epiphanies in her novels. Mr. Ramsay, stepping onto the rock at the end of *To the Lighthouse*, appears to his son James "as if he were saying, 'There is no God' . . ." (p. 318). At her mother's funeral in *The Years*, young Delia is possessed by a momentary "sense of something everlasting," but the voice of a clergyman interrupts her, this manifestation of orthodox Christianity destroying "her one moment of understanding" (p. 87).

Mrs. Woolf's leading female characters are almost all nonbelievers; spiritual as they are, it can be said of them, as it is of Clarissa, that "not for a moment" do they "believe in God" (*Mrs. Dalloway*, p. 33). Yet there is a vaguely "religious" quality about them all the same. Mrs. Ramsay, in spite of her own lack of faith, shares her children's contempt for "the atheist Tansley" (*To the Lighthouse*, p. 14). This is fitting, for one somehow feels that, regardless of her disbelief in God, the last thing one would ever call Mrs. Ramsay is an "atheist." The same may be said of Virginia Woolf herself, for despite her accord with the modern tendency to secularize revelatory experience, she disliked the cold and frightening logic of pure atheism as much as what she regarded as the straitening effect of Christianity.

The major example in Mrs. Woolf's work of a character who is both religious and sympathetic is Mrs. Swithin in *Between the Acts*, although the contrast between her and her rationalist brother

---

[12] Letter to Victoria Sackville-West, quoted in Aileen Pippett, *The Moth and the Star*, p. 331.

is, significantly, presented not so much in terms of religion and atheism as in those of emotion and logic, vision and reason : "He would carry the torch of reason till it went out in the darkness of the cave. For herself, every morning, kneeling, she protected her vision" (p. 240). This conflict appears throughout Mrs. Woolf's works, and, true to the Romanticism in her nature, she always makes vision more attractive than reason. While she admitted the truth of Lytton Strachey's comment that her limitation was that she was "not a good ratiocinator," she also realized that her instinct probably kept her mind from "analysing" because otherwise she "would impair its creativeness" (*Diary*, p. 246). (She agreed, too, with Strachey's remark that she was "very romantic"[13]—a self-awareness shared by all the writers I focus upon in this study.) Her Septimus Smith goes mad not because he fears that he has lost his reason, but because of his panic that "he could not feel" (*Mrs. Dalloway*, p. 96).

Many of Mrs. Woolf's characters who are "by conviction" skeptics are nevertheless "taken by surprise with moments of extraordinary exaltation" (*Mrs. Dalloway*, p. 63). In effect, some of these moments seem to be what might be called "secular mystical experiences," in which a person feels the sensations but not the convictions of the mystic. He feels himself outside of time, in eternity; he experiences an irrational enlightenment, a new awareness of something that cannot be explained; he feels that he is becoming part of a much broader unity—but, unlike the mystic, he refuses to let his own personality be annihilated, nor does he go on to ignore the surrounding objects of the material world. Virginia Woolf has sometimes been called, in despair of finding a better word, a "mystic"; and she herself occasionally used the word "mystical" to describe her own feelings or her works (for example, in *A Writer's Diary*, pp. 105, 137). But, despite the obvious resemblances between her moment of vision and the mystical experience, the two are not identical and in fact arise from directly opposing traits in personality. Thus in *The Waves* Bernard, while he is having his hair cut, suddenly feels himself being annihilated and becoming part of the "unfeeling universe," but then notices an expression in his hairdresser's face : "It is thus that I am recalled. (For I am no mystic; something always plucks at me—curiosity, envy, admiration, interest in hairdressers and the like bring me to the surface)" (p. 199). What most

---

[13] Virginia Woolf and Lytton Strachey, *Letters*, pp. 103-4.

prevents both him and Mrs. Woolf from experiencing the great revelation is, paradoxically, what most makes them susceptible to little daily miracles and illuminations : their intense sensibility to the material world, their desire to fathom the full meaning of the trivia of experience.

Before I go on to a discussion of Mrs. Woolf's critical views and their relation to epiphany, I ought to discuss one of the most important forces in the development of her aesthetic ideas—her association with the Bloomsbury Group, and especially its interest in the concept of significant form. The mentor of Bloomsbury was G. E. Moore, a professor of philosophy at Cambridge; the aspect of his philosophy that Bloomsbury most emphasized was the concept of "states of mind." As described by one of the members of the group, "These states of mind were not associated with action or achievement or with consequences. They consisted in timeless, passionate states of contemplation and communion, largely unattached to 'before' and 'after.' Their value depended, in accordance with the principle of organic unity, on the state of affairs as a whole which could not be usefully analysed into parts."[14] Such a notion is clearly relevant to Virginia Woolf's moments of vision, and she occasionally implies a reference to it in her fiction. In *Mrs. Dalloway*, for instance, when her "atheist" is "taken by surprise with moments of extraordinary exaltation," he realizes that "nothing exists outside us except a state of mind . . ." (p. 63; cf. *Orlando*, p. 286). Her circle had long included so many young men who had gone to Cambridge and been influenced by Moore that it is natural to conclude that early in her career she was familiar with and affected by his ideas—or, even more important, by those ideas as the young men interpreted and developed them. Among these men were Leonard Woolf, Lytton Strachey, E. M. Forster, and John Maynard Keynes, but the most noteworthy figures in regard to her aesthetic views were Roger Fry and Clive Bell.

After a great deal of thought and discussion, these two critics

---

[14] John Maynard Keynes, *Two Memoirs*, p. 83. Cf. G. E. Moore, *Principia Ethica*, p. 188: "By far the most valuable things, which we know or can imagine, are certain states of consciousness, which may be roughly described as the pleasures of human intercourse and the enjoyment of beautiful objects."

As might be expected, Clive Bell's book, *Proust*, for example, stresses the presentation of "that agonising moment when a state of mind has the force and certainty of a sensation" (p. 37).

arrived at a theory which centered on what they called "significant form." Fry, who was very close to Virginia Woolf (she later wrote his biography), seems to have originated the concept and to have done the most to develop it; Bell, who married Virginia's sister Vanessa, coined the term and first made it familiar. Although they believed that in one sense art is completely divorced from life, the basic assumption of their aesthetics is that art is experience, that both the creative act and the appreciation of its product involve emotion—specifically, the aesthetic emotion. (This assumption is perhaps derived from Moore's belief that the most valuable instances of aesthetic appreciation include "not merely a bare cognition of what is beautiful in the object, but also some kind of feeling or emotion" [*Principia Ethica*, p. 189].)

In a short book, *Art*, Bell writes that all works of art—that is, all "objects that provoke this emotion"—have one thing in common, the "one quality without which a work of art cannot exist": significant form (pp. 6-7). According to Bell, when a man, any man, has "a sudden vision of landscape as pure form," for that moment he sees "with the eye of an artist" (p. 53). Attempting to explain what an artist meant by telling him that the aim of painting is "a passionate apprehension of form," Bell points out that "occasionally when an artist—a real artist—looks at objects (the contents of a room, for instance) he perceives them as pure forms in certain relations to each other, and feels emotion for them as such. These are his moments of inspiration: follows the desire to express what has been felt" (pp. 51-52).

There is a striking similarity between this view of the artist's moment of inspiration and Joyce's representation of the moment of *claritas*, which also involves the "passionate apprehension of form." One is therefore not surprised when a neo-Thomist writer describes Aquinas' *claritas* as "the splendour of form" that irradiates a being "from within, the light of ontological truth."[15] Even such a Thomist phrase as "the light of ontological truth" does not claim more than Bell claims for significant form:

> Shall I be altogether fantastic in suggesting, what some of the profoundest thinkers have believed, that the significance of the thing in itself is the significance of Reality? . . .

[15] Emmanuel Chapman, "The Perennial Theme of Beauty and Art," in *Essays in Thomism*, pp. 339-40.

If this suggestion were accepted it would follow that "significant form" was form behind which we catch a sense of ultimate reality. [*Art*, p. 54]

With the introduction of meaning, of something revealed, into the artistic form, we begin to see a relationship with Virginia Woolf's moment of vision—which, like epiphany, involves a sudden spiritual manifestation. The word "spiritual" is used not only by Joyce, but also by Roger Fry, to whom "the emotions resulting from the contemplation of form were more universal . . . more profound and more significant spiritually than any of the emotions which had to do with life," and who therefore believed "that the contemplation of form is a peculiarly important spiritual exercise."[16]

The presence of meaning—significance—as opposed to an interpretation of form that would regard it as merely visually pleasant also makes it possible for the concept to be applied to the literary arts; and it thereby permits Fry to believe that, as Virginia Woolf puts it, "Cézanne and Flaubert were, in a manner of speaking, after the same thing" (*Roger Fry*, p. 180). The elements placed in spatial relation to each other in the visual arts correspond in literature to what Charles Mauron, in adapting Fry's aesthetics to literary needs, puts under the heading of "spiritual" or "psychological" elements. In an essay published by Leonard and Virginia Woolf at the Hogarth Press, he asks what we shall find in literature analogous to the "volume" of spatial art and then answers that we must transfer the notion of volume "from the domain of space to that of the spirit. . . . The psychological reality, the psychological complex—there is the material which the writer should work upon."

The simplest entities that literary art admits are states of mind, or perhaps one ought to say moments of the spirit. They are what we are at a given moment: the landscape that we contemplate, the sentiment which agitates us, the wonderful rhythm of a respiration, the movement of a palm tree. The external reality blends with the interior, or rather there is only one reality. Those divisions, useful enough for the life of action, into external objects, sensation, and sentiment, are abolished. It is the central principle of all lyric poetry.[17]

---

[16] Letter to Robert Bridges, quoted in Woolf, *Roger Fry*, p. 230.
[17] Charles Mauron, *The Nature of Beauty in Art and Literature*, pp. 66, 74.

By directly linking Fry's "significant form" to Moore's "states of mind"—the synthesis that would naturally occur to the members of Bloomsbury—Mauron arrives at a view of art that is singularly amenable to epiphany.

Virginia Woolf never developed her own theory of aesthetics, but she did have some firm and clear views on the subject of art in general and literature in particular. These views are expressed in her many critical essays, which provide a more revealing—as well as more eloquent—account of her ideas than the records we have for most of our important novelists. Her criticism, though highly personal and impressionistic, includes some of the most influential essays of the century. At least, they are usually regarded as such: the development of her critical ideas has so curiously paralleled the general development of modern literature that it is often difficult to tell when her statements were important rallying cries or when they were belated symptoms of what other novelists were already doing. The reason for this difficulty, of course, is that they were both.

In 1919, a significant date in history and therefore a convenient dividing point in literature, she wrote one of her most famous essays, "Modern Fiction." In it she takes stock of the English fiction of the recent past, which she finds exemplified in the work of three figures who always seem, when she mentions them, rather futile and pathetic—Mr. Wells, Mr. Bennett, and Mr. Galsworthy. Examining the world depicted in their novels, she asks:

Is life like this? Must novels be like this?

Look within and life, it seems, is very far from being "like this." Examine for a moment an ordinary mind on an ordinary day. The mind receives a myriad impressions—trivial, fantastic, evanescent, or engraved with the sharpness of steel. From all sides they come, an incessant shower of innumerable atoms; and as they fall, as they shape themselves into the life of Monday or Tuesday, the accent falls differently from of old; the moment of importance came not here but there; so that, if a writer were a free man and not a slave, if he could write what he chose, not what he must, if he could base his work upon his own feeling and not upon convention, there would be no plot, no comedy, no tragedy, no love interest or catastrophe in the accepted style, and perhaps not a single button sewn on as the Bond Street tailors would have it. Life is not a series of gig lamps symmetri-

cally arranged; life is a luminous halo, a semi-transparent enve-
lope surrounding us from the beginning of consciousness to the
end. . . . We are not pleading merely for courage and sincerity;
we are suggesting that the proper stuff of fiction is a little other
than custom would have us believe it.

. . . Let us record the atoms as they fall upon the mind in the
order in which they fall, let us trace the pattern, however disconnected and incoherent in appearance, which each sight or incident scores upon the consciousness. Let us not take it for
granted that life exists more fully in what is commonly thought
big than in what is commonly thought small. [*First Common
Reader*, pp. 189-90]

Mrs. Woolf's own practice is not wholly consistent with her comment about recording the atoms "as they fall," for she exerted much
more control over her material than these words imply. But there
is no question of inconsistency between her criticism and her novels
when she remarks that "the accent falls differently from of old,"
for the stuff of her fiction is clearly "a little other" than custom
would have had it; firm in her conviction that life does not necessarily exist more fully "in what is commonly thought big than in
what is commonly thought small," she tried to record the *atoms* that
fall upon the mind. The intense concern with what is apparently
insignificant, evident in so many modern novelists, can be found in
all her work; as she says in *Jacob's Room*, "it's not catastrophes,
murders, deaths, diseases, that age and kill us; it's the way people
look and laugh, and run up the steps of omnibuses" (p. 133). It is
therefore appropriate that when Erich Auerbach emphasizes the importance of "minor, unimpressive, random events" in twentieth-
century literature, he takes as his text a scene from *To the Lighthouse* (*Mimesis*, p. 546).

The two novels that Mrs. Woolf had written by 1919—*The
Voyage Out* and *Night and Day*—could by no means be said to
have "no plot, no comedy, no tragedy, no love interest or catastrophe in the accepted style"; far from it. But her next novel, *Jacob's
Room*, published in 1922, showed how far she was willing to follow
the logical conclusions of her statements in "Modern Fiction." "Disconnected and incoherent in appearance," the book seems to have
no links between each of the brief passages, the significance of many
of the individual scenes is questionable, and the story line is almost
nonexistent. She must have decided, as Isa puts it in *Between the*

Acts, that it is best not to "bother about the plot : the plot's noth-ing" (p. 109); in any case, from *Jacob's Room* on her novels do not have strong plots in the traditional sense. Instead, they consist of a series of intense scenes, many of them moments of being, often with little or no attempt to provide logical transitions between them—or any transitions, for that matter. Like Joyce's novels and modern fiction in general, her work became increasingly dramatic and relied less and less upon broad narrative summary, until a novel like *The Waves* seems literally to dispense with such summary altogether.

In 1924 Mrs. Woolf published another essay that contrasted the work of Mr. Wells, Mr. Bennett, and Mr. Galsworthy with what she was trying to achieve. In "Mr. Bennett and Mrs. Brown" she at-tempts to show the limitations of these three Edwardians when con-fronted with a new character or situation, and she uses as an example a woman—she calls her Mrs. Brown—with whom she had traveled for a while in the same railway carriage. She studies the slice of life that was briefly exposed to her in the carriage and, even more, examines the flood of impressions that "shot through" her own mind : "The impression she made was overwhelming. . . . What was it composed of—that overwhelming and peculiar impression? Myriads of irrelevant and incongruous ideas crowd into one's head on such occasions; one sees the person, one sees Mrs. Brown, in the centre of all sorts of different scenes" (*Captain's Death Bed*, pp. 98, 100-1). She engages in complex conjectures about Mrs. Brown's character and background, much as Fanny does about Miss Craye in "Moments of Being," or the narrator about Isabella in "The Lady in the Looking-Glass"—or, indeed, as a number of people do in similar passages in Virginia Woolf's work that also take place in railway carriages.

Two stories in *A Haunted House* rely on this situation. One be-gins with the sentence, "Such an expression of unhappiness was enough by itself to make one's eyes slide above the paper's edge to the poor woman's face—insignificant without that look, almost a symbol of human destiny with it" (p. 14); this statement and the title of the story, "An Unwritten Novel," would be just as applicable to the description of Mrs. Brown—only here she calls the woman "Minnie Marsh." In "The Shooting Party," the other story that begins with reflections resulting from a vision of a woman in a railway carriage, the woman's initials are again "M. M." In *The Waves*, Bernard describes one of the number of traits he shares with

Virginia Woolf: "I am abnormally aware of circumstances. I can never read a book in a railway carriage without asking, Is he a builder? Is she unhappy?"[18]

A twist is put on the situation in *Jacob's Room* when we get the point of view of the woman—whom we never see again—while she is riding with Jacob. The incident bears little direct relationship to what precedes or follows it in that fragmentary novel, and in fact the short stories built upon this situation are also fragments; like the incident centering on Mrs. Brown herself, they are "without any point" (*Captain's Death Bed*, p. 101). With only the one brief impression, Mrs. Woolf is no more able than Mr. Wells, Mr. Bennett, or Mr. Galsworthy to write a complete work of art about the stranger on the train, and in the end, as she fully realizes, she does not really capture Mrs. Brown and make her live.

Some of the reasons for this failure lie in the intrinsic limitations of the epiphany technique, of which no one was more conscious than Virginia Woolf. People who are seen in a flash can perhaps be *revealed* instantaneously, but they cannot be explained—as Mrs. Woolf cannot help trying to explain Mrs. Brown—without great danger of oversimplification: "Such moments of vision are of an unaccountable nature . . . try to explain them and they disappear; write them down and they die beneath the pen" ("Moments of Vision," p. 243). Mrs. Woolf also comments upon this danger when she discusses the revelations now and then produced by certain passages in George Meredith. Although we may see his people "very brilliantly, in a moment of illumination, they do not change or grow; the light sinks and leaves us in darkness. We have no such intuitive knowledge of Meredith's characters as we have of Stendhal's, Tchehov's, Jane Austen's . . . with Meredith there are no touches; there are hammer-strokes only, so that our knowledge of his characters is partial, spasmodic, and intermittent" (*Second Common Reader*, p. 232). She even found this tendency toward oversimplification in the moments of vision in Conrad, whose characters have a "static quality": "They change and develop very slightly;

---

18 P. 55. As an example of how Mrs. Woolf affected "other people's perceptions through her own," Clive Bell once quoted from a letter written by one of her friends, who described an "odd lady" in a train and the general impression she had given: "This was *literally* her conversation," the friend urged; "could Virginia have invented better?" ("Virginia Woolf," *Dial* 73 [December 1924]: 464).

they are for the most part people whose characters are made up of one or two very large and simple qualities, which are revealed to us in flashes" ("Lord Jim," p. 355). Nevertheless, the power that the moments of vision do provide makes them "the best things in his books"—and the same can be said of her novels too.

For one thing, the epiphanies are a major agent in creating the poetic quality which, difficult as it is to define, is unmistakable in all of Mrs. Woolf's major work. Continuing her rebellion against the conventions followed by the novels of Mr. Wells, Mr. Bennett, and Mr. Galsworthy, she reacted against what she felt were stifling restrictions on prose itself, against the past assumption that, unlike the poet, the novelist must "keep his eyes on the ground, not on the sky : suggest by description, not reveal by illumination" (*First Common Reader*, p. 79). So she strove in her own novels to achieve, as much as possible, the quality of poetry; indeed, we can be even more emphatic and say, with E. M. Forster, that "she is a poet, who wants to write something as near to a novel as possible" (*Virginia Woolf*, p. 23).

However one expresses it, and indefinite and blurred as it may seem, the idea that she wrote "poetic" novels is one of the most constantly heard refrains in all Virginia Woolf criticism. From my point of view, the interesting thing is that the aspect of her art most often chosen as demonstrating its poetry is the moment of vision. For Ralph Freedman, "the *moment* emerges as Virginia Woolf's key . . . to her concepts of poetry and the novel." David Daiches writes of *Mrs. Dalloway* that it is "the sensitive organization of tenuous insights" that "reminds one more of a lyric poem than anything else," while Ethel F. Cornwell connects her feeling that *The Waves* "contains Mrs. Woolf's most poetic prose" with the concentration on "moments of reality" in that book. Similarly, Mitchell A. Leaska associates his observation that *To the Lighthouse* "operates on the plane of poetry" with that novel's "sequence of selected moments of consciousness." Jean Guiguet remarks that Mrs. Woolf is "peculiarly responsive to the moments of intensity which, in prose works, attain the level of poetry." And Alun R. Jones cites Mrs. Woolf's novels as the "most extended" example of the tendency for the new poetic fiction to stress moments of "sudden revelation." Once again we can see that a trait in Mrs. Woolf's work is symptomatic of the whole movement of twentieth-century fiction : according to Bernard Blackstone, "it is in order to convey these fleeting moments of perception that writers like Proust and Virginia Woolf have patiently perfected a new technique of the novel. It is part of the task of the modern writer to show us how these moments can be caught amid the increasing hubbub, the diminishing solitude, of modern life. Formerly it was the poets who did it."[19]

As Virginia Woolf investigated the art of fiction in her criticism, she began, inevitably, to make changes in her own practice of it. Although moments of vision had already appeared in her work, they had not at first been essential elements in her novels. Of Virginia Woolf, perhaps more than of any other novelists, it can be said that as her art improved and her work became more characteristically her own, her use of epiphany also became increasingly significant, until with *Mrs. Dalloway* and her later works it dominates her novels. There are several moments of illumination in *The Voyage Out*, but they are not so pronounced as in her later books and often, for various reasons, do not really seem to be "epiphanies." The same may be said of *Night and Day*, though in that novel such moments, in addition to simple moments of intensity, are much more common and also more significant.

It would seem only natural that writers, before using the epiphany technique in novels, should experiment with it in shorter forms—witness Proust's "Les Regrets, rêveries couleur du temps," Faulkner's New Orleans "Sketches," the "interchapters" or "miniatures" in Hemingway's *In Our Time*, Nathalie Sarraute's "tropismes," or in fact Joyce's manuscript "epiphanies." Mrs. Woolf did so in several of the sketches she put together in 1921, in a volume called *Monday or Tuesday*. A number of them were not so much stories as prose poems, and they therefore enabled her to develop two of her main talents : her lyrical gift, and her ability to "make up situations" or "instantly make up a scene"—which she contrasted with what she felt was her inability to construct plots (*Diary*, p. 116). Epiphanies continue to appear in her later stories too, where they frequently

---

[19] Ralph Freedman, *Lyrical Novel*, p. 192; David Daiches, *Virginia Woolf*, pp. 75-76; Ethel F. Cornwell, *Still Point*, p. 196; Mitchell A. Leaska, *Virginia Woolf's Lighthouse*, p. 116; Jean Guiguet, *Virginia Woolf and Her Works*, p. 164; Alun R. Jones, "Life Is the Story," p. 6; Bernard Blackstone, *Virginia Woolf* (Writers and Their Work), p. 23.

involve the revelation to a character of his own loneliness, or to the reader of the essential isolation in which we all live. Besides some of the stories I have already discussed, such as "The Lady in the Looking-Glass" and "An Unwritten Novel," this type of moment of vision is important in stories like "Together and Apart" and "A Summing Up."

But her main interest was not diverted to the short story, and in *Jacob's Room* she produced her first novel to make genuinely major use of epiphanies, which may even be said to be the basis for its structure. Like Dorothy Richardson's *Pilgrimage*, volumes of which had been appearing for several years, *Jacob's Room* consists of many brief sections by means of which we go from one moment to another, one fragment of outwardly commonplace experience to the next. Each section describes a single scene or conversation, a slice of Jacob's life, a corner of his room, usually as seen by someone other than Jacob himself; then Mrs. Woolf immediately goes on to another fragment, another moment of vision, and in this way Jacob, through a vast series of such moments, is continually revealed to the other characters and to the reader. Obviously, it would have taken a miracle to prevent such an experiment from being choppy and almost incoherent; no miracle occurred. The sketches in *Monday or Tuesday* were not integrated at all, for each had been meant to stand by itself; again in *Jacob's Room*, unfortunately, the scenes are not sufficiently integrated as part of the whole work or related to one another, though now there is at least a unified subject and a unified (though not yet unifying) technique. *Jacob's Room* therefore stands in an intermediate position between her earlier sketches and the later, successful novels. Of these I shall examine two, *Mrs. Dalloway* and *To the Lighthouse*, more closely than the rest.

The number of moments of vision in *Mrs. Dalloway*, Virginia Woolf's first truly major achievement, is amazing; almost every section (there are no chapters) has at least one, usually more. Everyone, like Peter Walsh, is "a prey to revelations" (p. 69), and like him all the characters are fully conscious of this susceptibility and reflect upon it with an uncanny "power of taking hold of experience, of turning it round, slowly, in the light" (p. 88). Septimus Warren Smith notes his "revelations on the backs of envelopes" (p. 28), and his "sudden thunder-claps of fear" (p. 96) that he has lost the power to feel are what have driven him mad. Less an actual "prey" to

them than Septimus, Elizabeth Dalloway calmly muses upon those
moments when the most surprising and trivial objects have the
power "to stimulate what lay slumbrous, clumsy, and shy on the
mind's sandy floor, to break surface, as a child suddenly stretches
its arms; it was just that, perhaps, a sigh, a stretch of the arms, an
impulse, a revelation, which has its effects for ever, and then down
again it went to the sandy floor." Elizabeth's thoughts are interrupted by her desire to know, "what was the time?—where was a
clock?" (p. 151). In the same way Septimus' revelation that beauty
and truth are the same and are "made out of ordinary things" is
interrupted by Rezia's remark, for they have an appointment, that
"it is time." In quiet desperation, Septimus persists :

> The millions lamented; for ages they had sorrowed. He would
> turn round, he would tell them in a few moments, only a few
> moments more, of this relief, of this joy, of this astonishing
> revelation—
> "The time, Septimus," Rezia repeated. "What is the time?"
> [Pp.77-78]

Septimus is forced to keep the revelation to himself, though eventually his vision seems to be shared with Mrs. Dalloway, and to that
extent his essential isolation overcome.

Clarissa Dalloway is the person most sensitive to what she calls
her "secret deposit of exquisite moments." In the principal account
of moments of vision in this novel, her hidden revelatory experience
is cryptically yet unmistakably described as sexual; feeling "like
a nun who has left the world," she thinks of how she has never been
able to dispel from her personality "a virginity preserved through
childbirth which clung to her like a sheet" and because of which
she has sometimes failed her husband :

> . . . yet she could not resist sometimes yielding to the charm of
> a woman, not a girl, of a woman confessing, as to her they often
> did, some scrape, some folly. And whether it was pity, or their
> beauty, or that she was older, or some accident—like a faint
> scent, or a violin next door (so strange is the power of sounds at
> certain moments), she did undoubtedly then feel what men felt.
> Only for a moment; but it was enough. It was a sudden reve-
> lation, a tinge like a blush which one tried to check and then,
> as it spread, one yielded to its expansion, and rushed to the
> farthest verge and there quivered and felt the world come closer,

swollen with some astonishing significance, some pressure of rapture, which split its thin skin and gushed and poured with an extraordinary alleviation over the cracks and sores. Then, for that moment, she had seen an illumination; a match burning in a crocus; an inner meaning almost expressed. But the close withdrew; the hard softened. It was over—the moment. [Pp. 33, 36]

In one sense, Clarissa's revelations of "what men felt" correspond to an experience Virginia Woolf had herself undergone, and which she recorded in *A Room of One's Own*. She had seen a man and a woman get into a taxi and depart together, and the sight, "ordinary enough" in itself, had an extraordinary effect on her imagination (so extraordinary, in fact, that she later used a very similar scene as the climax of *The Years*). As a result of this vision, Mrs. Woolf sketched a view of the soul as a fusion between male and female elements in which one or the other sex predominates. When there is a complete balance, we have the utmost power, and this, she believed, may be what Coleridge meant by saying that the great mind is "androgynous" (pp. 145-48).

In *Mrs. Dalloway*, however, there is a quality to Clarissa's experience that is not simply androgynous, but displays an actual if latent homosexuality. This fact becomes more evident when Clarissa goes on to recall the feeling she used to have many years ago for Sally Seton: "Had not that, after all, been love?" (p. 37). At first Clarissa is unable to recapture her old emotion, but as she removes her hairpins she recalls how once, while doing her hair, she had felt a moment of ecstasy upon realizing that she and Sally were under the same roof. She then remembers another moment, "the most exquisite moment of her whole life," when "Sally stopped; picked a flower; kissed her on the lips. The whole world might have turned upside down! . . . the radiance burnt through, the revelation, the religious feeling!" This incident was innocently cut short by Peter, who was in love with Clarissa; but, fiercely indignant at his interruption, she imagined she could feel "his hostility; his jealousy; his determination to break into their companionship. All this she saw as one sees a landscape in a flash of lightning . . ." (pp. 40-41). In the end, however, it was not her love for Sally that separated Clarissa and Peter, but rather her new and greater love for Richard Dalloway (who, Clarissa tells Rachel in *The Voyage*

Out, "gave me all I wanted. He's man and woman as well").[20] For the rest of the novel, the subject of Clarissa's latent homosexuality is dropped, and the main interest of this very significant passage finally lies in the Proustian way in which the past experience is revived.

Virginia Woolf realized how, in the "perfect rag-bag of odds and ends" of which our memory is the seamstress, "the most ordinary movement in the world . . . may agitate a thousand odd, disconnected fragments" (*Orlando*, p. 78). Thus Clarissa, by performing such a commonplace act as doing her hair, experiences sensations similar to the ones she had felt many years before, and these sensations lead to a complete recapture of the past—significantly, a past which itself had contained a moment of revelation. It is not only the manner of recapture that is Proustian; so is the use to which the recapture is put, for it starts a flashback that provides us with some very important facts about Clarissa's life.

Flashbacks occur more frequently in *Mrs. Dalloway* than in any of Virginia Woolf's other novels—as might be expected, since one of its major themes is the complexity of the relationship between the present and the past. Indeed, recollections of the past are so frequent that the action of the novel may be regarded as taking place on two different time levels: the present day in London, and the summer at Bourton thirty years before. At the beginning of the novel Clarissa realizes that what she loves is "life; London; this moment of June" (p. 6). However, she does not live entirely in the present moment, much as she may love it. Throughout the book we are shown her many memories, and in fact only a few pages later she thinks with pleasure of those moments when friends, from whom one may have been parted for years, "came back in the middle of St. James's Park on a fine morning" (p. 9). She does shortly say to herself that anyone can remember, and that "what she loved was this, here, now, in front of her" (p. 11); but not everyone can remember as vividly as Clarissa Dalloway can. Nevertheless, her feelings about the value of the present moment are sincere; she has an unusual ability to live in both the memory of the past and the here and now.

This characteristic is shared by Peter, who after a number of passages during which he recaptures scenes from the past—"it was

---

[20] P. 65. Peter too, however, is attractive to women who like the sense that he is "not altogether manly" (*Mrs. Dalloway*, p. 172).

extraordinary how vividly it all came back to him"—can still say
that life "here, this instant, now . . . was enough" (pp. 84, 88).
Clarissa and Peter would both prefer to stress the present, but they
are in middle age and worried about growing old, so their minds
almost involuntarily turn to their youth. "If you are young," Mrs.
Woolf writes elsewhere, "the future lies upon the present, like a
piece of glass, making it tremble and quiver. If you are old, the
past lies upon the present, like a thick glass, making it waver, distorting it."[21] In *Mrs. Dalloway*, this remark is verified by the fact
that most, though not all, of Clarissa's and Peter's moments of
vision now recall the past, while the ones they had experienced
when young—such as his "sudden revelation" that she would someday marry the stranger, Dalloway (p. 68)—had anticipated the
future, just as Elizabeth's do now. An exception is young Septimus,
whose disturbed mind cannot forget the war.

Clarissa's fears of old age and her "horror of death" cause her to
develop a transcendental theory which allows her to believe that,
once having had contact with people or things, we may survive
after death in the memories of this or that person, or even haunt
certain places—a notion which anticipates *To the Lighthouse* and
Mrs. Ramsay's continuing presence after her death. Peter's skeptical
refinements on this theory produce fanciful thoughts on immortality
that seem based on "retrospective" epiphanies:

> Looking back over that long friendship of almost thirty years
> her theory worked to this extent. Brief, broken, often painful as
> their actual meetings had been, what with his absences and inter-
> ruptions . . . the effect of them on his life was immeasurable.
> There was a mystery about it. You were given a sharp, acute,
> uncomfortable grain—the actual meeting; horribly painful as
> often as not; yet in absence, in the most unlikely places, it would
> flower out, open, shed its scent, let you touch, taste, look about
> you, get the whole feel of it and understanding, after years of
> lying lost. Thus she had come to him; on board ship; in the
> Himalayas; suggested by the oddest things (so Sally Seton,
> generous, enthusiastic goose! thought of *him* when she saw blue
> hydrangeas). [Pp. 168-69]

Such grasping at straws for some sort of survival results from
Clarissa's and Peter's intense love of life, a love that is even shared

---

[21] "The Moment: Summer's Night," in *The Moment and Other Essays*,
p. 9.

by the suicide, Septimus, who immediately before he kills himself decides to "wait till the very last moment. He did not want to die. Life was good" (p. 164).

And perhaps we are meant to feel that Septimus does achieve a strange, vicarious immortality through a union with other people. After his death, the ambulance rushing to the scene is heard by Peter, who experiences a moment "in which things came together; this ambulance; and life and death" (p. 167). That evening, at one of her frequent parties—parties which she gives because "what she liked was simply life" (p. 134)—Clarissa leaves her guests for a few minutes and goes into a little side room; looking out of the window, she is surprised to see the old woman she had seen climbing upstairs earlier in the day now going to bed and staring "straight at her" (p. 204). The scene resembles a previous one : at the window just before Septimus had jumped, "coming down the staircase opposite an old man stopped and stared at him" (p. 164). Clarissa cannot know of this similarity, but as she reflects that death is "an attempt to communicate," that there is "an embrace in death" (p. 202), she sees the old woman and remembers that someone has mentioned that a young man has committed suicide :

> There ! the old lady had put out her light ! the whole house was dark now with this going on, she repeated, and the words came to her, Fear no more the heat of the sun. She must go back to them. But what an extraordinary night ! She felt somehow very like him—the young man who had killed himself. She felt glad that he had done it; thrown it away while they went on living. The clock was striking. The leaden circles dissolved in the air. But she must go back. She must assemble. She must find Sally and Peter. And she came in from the little room. [Pp. 204-5]

Although Septimus is dead, the revelation to Clarissa of her identity with him paradoxically emphasizes life and stills her fears of death. As so often in Mrs. Woolf's novels, the climax of the book is an integrating epiphany that brings together many of the important themes and characters; and here it serves the specific purpose of revealing the triumph of life and the value of love, of what Sally despairingly calls "human relationships" (p. 211). As Clarissa deserts the vacant little room and comes into the party among her friends, her symbolic force does not go unnoticed :

". . . What does the brain matter," said Lady Rosseter, getting
up, "compared with the heart?"

"I will come," said Peter, but he sat on for a moment. What
is this terror? what is this ecstasy? he thought to himself. What
is it that fills me with extraordinary excitement?

It is Clarissa, he said.

For there she was. [P. 213]

The idea that the brain matters hardly at all compared with the
heart, illustrated here by the figure of Mrs. Dalloway, appears again
in Virginia Woolf's next novel, *To the Lighthouse,* where it is
illustrated by the figure of Mrs. Ramsay. Mrs. Ramsay is an instinctive woman who knows things "without having learnt. Her
simplicity fathomed what clever people falsified" (p. 49). Her husband, however, is one of the "clever people," a distinguished
philosopher with an acute intellect that was "incapable of untruth;
never tampered with a fact . . ." (p. 13). Consequently, in a novel
in which, once more, everyone is "a prey to revelations," Mr.
Ramsay is the major exception. His books are on "subject and
object and the nature of reality," but the irony of the novel is that
he has attained less true understanding of his own field than his
wife, for he has not yet realized that the brain does not matter compared with the heart.

Although I have no desire to turn *To the Lighthouse* into a
treatise on epistemology, it seems to me that here, as in all her
work, the strong implications of Mrs. Woolf's presentation of the
problem of "subject and object and the nature of reality" are that
one can solve the problem only if one grasps two fundamental
truths : that when the true nature of reality is perceived, an intuitive union takes place between the subject and the object, that
is, the person knowing and the thing being known; and that, because the nature of reality is largely a matter of subjective interpretation, objects are very complex, and nothing can be said to be
simply one thing. Despite his intellect, or because of it, Mr. Ramsay
does not realize these two principles as fully as a number of the
other characters in the novel, who are therefore temperamentally
more capable than he of experiencing moments of being.

The notion of an intuitive union between subject and object
certainly sounds reminiscent of Bergson, but if Mrs. Woolf derived
it from anyone it was probably from the philosophy of G. E. Moore
or from his students. I have already quoted Charles Mauron's ob-

servation that the states of mind "are what we are at a given moment: the landscape that we contemplate . . . the movement of a palm tree. The external reality blends with the interior, or rather there is only one reality" (*Beauty in Art and Literature*, p. 74). Such moments are frequently experienced by Mrs. Ramsay, who is, spiritually, the wisest character in *To the Lighthouse*: "Often she found herself sitting and looking, sitting and looking, with her work in her hands until she became the thing she looked at—that light for example." "That light"—the beam from the Lighthouse—exerts an unusual fascination upon her, and she feels strangely united to it. "It was odd, she thought, how if one was alone, one leant to things, inanimate things; trees, streams, flowers; felt they expressed one; felt they became one; felt they knew one, in a sense were one; felt an irrational tenderness thus (she looked at that long steady light) as for oneself" (pp. 100-1).

The second major concept one must grasp in order to understand the nature of reality—that objects are complex and are actually many things—is also important in *Orlando*, where there are so many metamorphoses it is hard to keep track of them; Orlando herself realizes that "nothing is any longer one thing" (p. 305). As Mrs. Woolf explains, "when one has been in a state of mind (as nurses call it)"—Orlando is pregnant—"the thing one is looking at becomes, not itself, but another thing, which is bigger and much more important and yet remains the same thing. If one looks at the Serpentine in this state of mind, the waves soon become just as big as the waves on the Atlantic; the toy boats become indistinguishable from ocean liners." In fact, one realizes that "that's what it is —a toy boat on the Serpentine, it's ecstasy—ecstasy" (pp. 286-88). In *To the Lighthouse*, this principle, like the first one, can be demonstrated in a passage centering on Mrs. Ramsay; to her, the calm rhythm of the waves breaking upon the beach is usually a soothing, comforting sound, a "cradle song, murmured by nature" —yet at times this same sound produces a horrible fear of destruction and makes her "look up with an impulse of terror" (p. 30).

However, the most important realization in the novel of this aspect of the apprehension of reality is not Mrs. Ramsay's, but the one achieved by her son, who comes to it only after many years. James Ramsay, when we first meet him, is only just out of infancy and is looking forward with childish eagerness to the excitement of the next day's journey to the Lighthouse; but the weather is threatening, and the conflict between what Mr. and Mrs. Ramsay each represent is shown mainly through their different attitudes toward the chances of their being able to make the trip. Always rational and factual, Mr. Ramsay thinks it best that the boy should be discouraged from believing that the weather will be good enough for the boat to go out : James hates him for this logic. Mrs. Ramsay, trying to guard the boy from too much pain, can neither give up her own hopes nor completely dash her son's. In the end, Mr. Ramsay of course turns out to be correct; yet we are clearly meant to feel that in some more basic way than that of fact it is he who is wrong and his wife right. Even he seems to sense this, so he apologetically approaches the seated Mrs. Ramsay and, trying at the same time to humor James by tickling and prodding his bare legs, offers to check with the Coastguards for the weather prediction, so they can be sure. But, realizing her husband's discomfort and loving him even more than their son, she yields and admits that of course he is right.

That evening, Mrs. Ramsay looks sadly at James as he goes off to bed : "she was certain that he was thinking, we are not going to the Lighthouse tomorrow; and she thought, he will remember that all his life" (p. 99). And he does, though for a long time it is forgotten and is only remembered ten years later when his father— whom he still resents—has to press him into making the long postponed trip to the Lighthouse. In the boat, James recalls—very vaguely at first—what had happened on that day years before : "He began to search among the infinite series of impressions which time had laid down, leaf upon leaf, fold upon fold softly, incessantly upon his brain; among scents, sounds; voices, harsh, hollow, sweet; and lights passing, and brooms tapping; and the wash and hush of the sea, how a man had marched up and down and stopped dead, upright, over them" (pp. 260-61). At last, as they approach the Lighthouse, James recaptures the past and then also realizes that nothing is simple, that the world and reality are much more complex than he has hitherto realized :

Something, he remembered, stayed and darkened over him; would not move. . . .

"It will rain," he remembered his father saying. "You won't be able to go to the Lighthouse."

The Lighthouse was then a silvery, misty-looking tower with

a yellow eye that opened suddenly and softly in the evening. Now—

James looked at the Lighthouse. He could see the white-washed rocks; the tower, stark and straight; he could see that it was barred with black and white; he could see windows in it; he could even see washing spread on the rocks to dry. So that was the Lighthouse, was it?

No, the other was also the Lighthouse. For nothing was simply one thing. The other was the Lighthouse too. [Pp. 285-86]

James is now ready for the revelation that his father must not be interpreted too simply either, that he is not "simply one thing," a stern unfeeling tyrant. But that revelation will take another epiphany.

In addition to Mrs. Ramsay and James, Lily Briscoe also comes to understand the complex relationship between subject and object and the nature of reality: "One wanted, she thought, dipping her brush deliberately, to be on a level with ordinary experience, to feel simply that's a chair, that's a table, and yet at the same time, It's a miracle, it's an ecstasy" (pp. 309-10). Of the four major characters, consequently, that leaves only Mr. Ramsay in the dark. Yet he is not a stupid man, nor is he completely unemotional—he certainly loves his wife very much. Why, then, has he failed to learn? And why has he had no sudden spiritual revelations?

The answers to these questions can, I think, be expressed in terms of James Joyce's very useful theory of aesthetics. In Mr. Ramsay's own terms, he has managed to reach Q, but not R; in Joyce's, he has reached the apprehension of *integritas* and *consonantia*, but he has yet to perceive *claritas*. He has reached the level of "ordinary experience," as Lily calls it: he feels "simply that's a chair, that's a table"; having realized that an object "is one integral thing, that it is *a* thing," he has achieved the phase of perception called *integritas*. He has also gone on to the next step, *consonantia*, which Joyce appropriately associates with the "analysis" of apprehension: "The mind recognises that the object is in the strict sense of the word, a *thing*, a definitely constituted entity" (*Stephen Hero*, p. 212). So far so good; but Mr. Ramsay's overrational mind prevents him from going beyond analysis. At one point in the novel, his wife perceives his limitation: "His understanding often astonished her. But did he notice the flowers? No. Did he notice the view? No. . . . He never looked at things" (pp. 111-12). What she means is that he does not look at things the way she does, the way Lily speaks of when she says that one wishes "to feel simply that's a chair, that's a table, and yet at the same time, It's a miracle, it's an ecstasy." That is, he cannot enter into the object and experience its radiance, its *quidditas*, its whatness. *Claritas*, the phase of apprehension Joyce associates with intuition and epiphany, is out of Mr. Ramsay's reach. The reason for this incapacity seems clear : he is too dependent upon his intellect. It is only at the end of the novel, when the rationalist insists upon performing his quite "irrational" act of atonement, by going to the Lighthouse at last, that he apparently experiences the nature of reality.

The epiphany in which he does so is not his alone; it is shared by James, Cam, Lily, and even Mr. Carmichael. In this way, all the characters attain what Lily had wished for ten years before, when she leaned on Mrs. Ramsay's knee and thought that "it was not knowledge but unity that she desired, not inscriptions on tablets, nothing that could be written in any language known to men, but intimacy itself, which is knowledge . . ." (p. 83). We need "only connect," another member of Bloomsbury has told us, and we shall be saved. And in *To the Lighthouse*, as in *Mrs. Dalloway* but on a broader scale, Virginia Woolf's characters achieve a measure of union—and salvation—through a climactic moment of being: James and Cam connect with their father, while he unites with them but also with his dead wife, in whose memory he has come to the Lighthouse, and with Lily, who on shore not only connects with him but also with Mr. Carmichael, the poet, and above all with Mrs. Ramsay. As the little boat reaches the island, Mr. Ramsay unexpectedly praises James's steering, and instantly the boy and his sister drop all their antagonism :

> They both wanted to say, Ask us anything and we will give it you. But he did not ask them anything. He sat and looked at the island and he might be thinking, We perished, each alone, or he might be thinking, I have reached it. I have found it, but he said nothing.
> Then he put on his hat.
> . . . He rose and stood in the bow of the boat, very straight and tall, for all the world, James thought, as if he were saying, "There is no God," and Cam thought, as if he were leaping into space, and they both rose to follow him as he sprang, lightly like a young man, holding his parcel, on to the rock.

14

"He must have reached it," said Lily Briscoe aloud, feeling suddenly completely tired out. . . . Ah, but she was relieved. Whatever she had wanted to give him, when he left her that morning, she had given him at last.

"He has landed," she said aloud. "It is finished." Then, surging up, puffing slightly, old Mr. Carmichael stood beside her, looking like an old pagan God, shaggy, with weeds in his hair and the trident (it was only a French novel) in his hand. He stood by her on the edge of the lawn, swaying a little in his bulk, and said, shading his eyes with his hand: "They will have landed," and she felt that she had been right. [Pp. 318-19]

But, though this is the climactic epiphany, it is not the final one—the last is reserved for Lily alone. Mrs. Woolf had been troubled about how to end the novel, and she indicated her problem in the *Diary*: ". . . I had meant to end with R. climbing on to the rock. If so, what becomes of Lily and her picture? Should there be a final page about her and Carmichael looking at the picture and summing up R.'s character? In that case I lose the intensity of the moment" (p. 99). She solved her problem through the unifying epiphany that lets Lily and Carmichael share in "the intensity of the moment"; but she also increased that intensity by giving Lily her own separate vision as well.

Although she is not the main character, Lily Briscoe has more moments of vision than any other figure in *To the Lighthouse*, even Mrs. Ramsay, for as an artist she is peculiarly sensitive to sudden spiritual manifestations. And, like Virginia Woolf, she is acutely aware of their limitations and of the frustration of trying to translate them into worthwhile art. Her attempt to capture in her painting "the thing itself before it has been made anything" is inevitably thwarted by the artist's ancient complaint of the great disparity between inspiration and expression—a disparity which led Shelley to compare the dying vision to a "fading coal" and which now almost brings Lily to despair, in the realization that "one could not say what one meant" (pp. 297, 35). Lily is a painter, but her comments on the impossibility of recording the most evanescent of moments are sometimes expressed in terms that seem more appropriate to the man of letters.

Thus, sensing on the morning of the trip to the Lighthouse that all words seem to become symbols that day, she feels that "if only she could put them together . . . write them out in some sentence, then she would have got at the truth of things"; but one cannot write the words out : "The urgency of the moment always missed its mark. Words fluttered sideways and struck the object inches too low" (pp. 228, 274). Lily's art actually uses not words but visual forms and colors; that the difficulties remain, however, is shown by the fact that it takes four separate moments of inspiration over a period of many years for her to finish her picture. The first had occurred before the action of the novel starts and is remembered as "that vision which she had seen clearly once and must now grope for among hedges and houses and mothers and children—her picture" (p. 86). While visiting the Ramsays during the first part of the book she is working on a view of their house, and at dinner in the evening she has her second inspiration : "In a flash she saw her picture, and thought, Yes, I shall put the tree further in the middle; then I shall avoid that awkward space" (p. 132). The full significance of this moment is not revealed until later, when we also learn that "it had flashed upon her that she would move the tree to the middle, and need never marry anybody . . ." (p. 271). But before she can carry out her intention everyone leaves the Ramsays' summer home, Mrs. Ramsay dies, Lily loses track of her picture, and ten years pass.

Then Mr. Ramsay unexpectedly reopens the house and invites the guests of that summer to visit there again. Confronted with the same scene she had been painting, Lily has her third moment of inspiration when she recalls her previous one. "Suddenly she remembered. When she had sat there last ten years ago there had been a little sprig or leaf pattern on the table-cloth, which she had looked at in a moment of revelation. . . . She would paint that picture now" (p. 228). After some initial difficulty, she works steadily all that morning, and by the moment Mr. Ramsay lands at the Lighthouse her new painting is all but complete. She has paused while she seems to share with Mr. Carmichael the same thoughts about Mr. Ramsay and what he has done, when "quickly, as if she were recalled by something over there," she turns to her canvas and takes up her brush. She then looks at the steps of the house, where she had earlier felt she could see an image of Mrs. Ramsay, but : "they were empty; she looked at her canvas; it was blurred. With a sudden intensity, as if she saw it clear for a second, she drew a line there, in the centre. It was done; it was finished. Yes, she thought, laying down her brush in extreme fatigue, I have had my vision" (pp. 319-20). With these words, which end the novel, it appears that Lily's hopes of capturing her fleeting inspiration and making of the moment something permanent are at last realized.

I have paid special attention to *Mrs. Dalloway* and *To the Lighthouse* primarily because I believe they are Virginia Woolf's greatest novels, but they are also representative of her use of moments of vision in almost all her works after *Jacob's Room*, and there is little reason for me to examine the rest of her books in detail here. Although in many ways each of her later novels experiments with a new departure in fiction, each follows basically the same pattern she first used in *Mrs. Dalloway*: we encounter many epiphanies of varying importance throughout the novel, and then at the end we have a climactic moment of vision which unifies and summarizes a number of the major themes and brings together the separate threads of the story.

For example, the last words of *Orlando*, a novel largely concerned with the passage of time, tell of the heroine's ecstatic realization, for the second time that day, that it is the present moment, "Thursday, the eleventh of October, Nineteen Hundred and Twenty-eight"—which also happens to have been the date on which the first edition of the book was published. As Mrs. Woolf remarks, it is no wonder that Orlando had turned pale upon making the same discovery earlier in the day, "for what more terrifying revelation can there be than that it is the present moment?" (pp. 329, 298). More serious in tone, *The Waves* has an especially large number of moments of vision throughout the novel, many of them almost semi-mystical in character. In the final one, Bernard senses in the world about him an "eternal renewal," as of waves rising and falling, and then comes to a new awareness that "death is the enemy," that it is against death that he must fling himself, "unvanquished and unyielding" (p. 211). In contrast, *The Years* ends with a vision of tranquillity. During a party, Eleanor Pargiter looks out of a window and sees a young man and a girl get out of a taxi, and Eleanor is inexplicably moved when she sees them enter a home together; as she, like Mrs. Dalloway, returns to the party, the sky above wears "an air of extraordinary beauty, simplicity and peace" (p. 435).

Mrs. Woolf's last novel is an exception to this pattern, for *Be-*

tween the Acts does not finish with a major, unifying revelation, although toward the end one does climax the outdoor production staged by Miss La Trobe. After having gone through the entire pageant of English history, the actors stop time at "the present moment" and hold mirrors up to the people in the audience, who are thereby revealed to each other and to themselves; as the audience soon realizes, "that was her little game! To show us up, as we are, here and now" (p. 217). Extended quotations from this pageant form the center of interest in the novel, and, just as the portrayal of Lily Briscoe had demonstrated Mrs. Woolf's views about the origins of art, so the portrayal of Miss La Trobe indicates her views about its aims and functions. While the pageant is still in progress, Miss La Trobe tries to estimate how much effect it has so far produced: "Hadn't she, for twenty-five minutes, made them see? A vision imparted was relief from agony . . . for one moment . . . one moment" (p. 117). Like most true artists, perhaps, she finally decides that she has failed; but she is at least partially wrong, as we can see from the discomfort of the spectators when confronted with their image in the mirrors, and from the powerful and personal effect the pageant has upon Mrs. Swithin.

Whatever degree of success Miss La Trobe may have, however, her aim is clear: she wants, if only for a moment, to impart a vision to her audience. That this is also Mrs. Woolf's aim is shown by the impressionism of her own literary and critical ideas. To her, the function of a novel has been performed if, when one has read it, "one sees more intensely afterwards; the world seeems bared of its covering and given an intenser life" (*Room of One's Own*, p. 166). In every great novel there are certain passages which startle you "into a flash of understanding"; together these passages make up the "book itself," which is actually the "emotion which you feel" (*The Moment*, pp. 129-30). We have already seen this affective view of artistic experience in the concept of significant form, and in Joseph Conrad, who tries to reveal to his readers "all the truth of life" in "a moment of vision" (*The Nigger of the Narcissus*, p. xvi).

Virginia Woolf, too, believes that her task is to make us hear, to make us feel—that it is, before all, to make us *see*.

5

Thomas Wolfe: The Escapes of Time and Memory

> . . . I know there is nothing so commonplace, so dull,
> that is not touched with nobility and dignity. And I
> intend to wreak out my soul on paper and express it all.
> This is what my life means to me: I am at the mercy
> of this thing and I will do it or die. I never forget; I
> have never forgotten.
>
> Thomas Wolfe, *Letters to His Mother*, pp. 51-52

I

Moments of revelation are probably more frequent in the works of Thomas Wolfe than in those of almost any other novelist. Saying that, as we shall see, is by no means the same as saying that in him they are more essential, or more functional, but it does indicate the important role epiphany plays in his novels. Many of the moments of intensity or illumination that Wolfe included in his books were ones he himself had experienced—and which he never forgot, had never forgotten : that, it turned out, was his trouble. His passion for epiphany was akin to that of the other novelists I discuss, but he had much more difficulty than they in controlling that passion and in curbing his urge to record in his art all his own sudden spiritual manifestations. The problem became so acute that he ultimately wrote of his determination to abandon them altogether. And so Wolfe is of special interest particularly because, among modern novelists who make extensive use of epiphany, he was unique in eventually reacting against it. Or, rather, against one type of epiphany, the autobiographical one that involves what he came to consider were escapes from reality—the imprisoning escapes of time and memory.

Wolfe's work is also notable for the fact that in few other writers can the epiphanies be so appropriately divided into two basic groups : either they stress an event in the past (an event which may now be recaptured, or one which may now be given a significance and meaning that went unperceived when the incident originally occurred), or they involve only the present. As in Proust, but in contrast to most novelists, present revelations are less frequent and less prominent in Wolfe than those that in one way or another center on the past; but in many instances they are his most effective epiphanies and are important enough to merit a separate discussion before I go on to consider the general development of his attitude toward the past and one's memories of it.

Though less central in Wolfe's work than those involving memory, epiphanies of the present are plentiful in their own right, and they produce such widely differing phenomena as the embarrassingly infantile awkwardness of George Webber's "squeal," which we are clearly but vainly meant to admire, and the childish beauty of Esther Jack's description to her father and his friend of her ability "to see a forest in a leaf, the whole earth in a single face"; but the most interesting examples are those arising from the experience of riding on a train, an experience Wolfe regarded as "one of the most wonderful things in the world."[1]

Indeed, not a single image in all of Wolfe's novels has more meaning for him than that of the railroad. It pervades all his books, which describe train rides over the mountains of Old Catawba, under the streets of New York City, along the river in New York State, through the countryside in France, across the border from Germany. But by far the most important journey is the one between the southern and northern United States : ". . . so relative are the qualities of space and time, and so complex and multiple their shifting images, that in the brief passage of this journey one may live a life, share instantly in 10,000,000 other ones, and see pass before his eyes the infinite panorama of shifting images that make a nation's history" (*Of Time and the River*, p. 25). This trip, for obvious biographical reasons, was immensely significant to Wolfe, and the excitement of it often produces for his heroes moments of vision greatly resembling those in Virginia Woolf that arise from brief contacts with other passengers in the same railway car. For

[1] *The Web and the Rock*, p. 421; *You Can't Go Home Again*, p. 55.

example, when Eugene Gant goes "out into the world for the first time," riding the train from Altamont to Harvard, he experiences a "glorious moment" of "incredible knowledge" and "illimitable power" as he stares at the prosperous older men who, like him, are heading north (pp. 35-36).

Even more frequent are the mysterious and fascinating visions seen by Wolfe's characters out of the windows of the train. Such scenes, which recur till the very end of Wolfe's last novel, begin as early as Eugene's eleventh year, when he is traveling to and from Florida with his mother: "The picture of flashing field, of wood, and hill, stayed in his heart forever: lost in the dark land, he lay the night-long through within his berth, watching the shadowy and phantom South flash by . . . seeing, in pale dawn, the phantom woods, a rutted lane, a cow, a boy, a drab, dull-eyed against a cottage door, glimpsed, at this moment of rushing time, for which all life had been aplot . . . flash upon the window and be gone" (*Look Homeward, Angel*, p. 171). And later, as he looks back upon his still young life, Eugene wonders at the fact that "so many of the sensations that returned to open haunting vistas of fantasy and imagining had been caught from a whirling landscape through the windows of the train" (p. 202).

We have already noticed passages in Virginia Woolf that parallel Wolfe's interest in trains and their ability to provide revelations; similar passages also figure importantly in Proust, Faulkner, William Styron, Michel Butor, and others. For as an interlude between two points of space and time, a journey structurally lends itself to being treated in fiction as a detached fragment of life, while the experience can, as well, be readily interpreted in terms of pervasive themes in twentieth-century literature—such as the modern urge for movement and speed, the relations of space and time, or each man's essential isolation.

The kind of epiphany that confines itself to what can be seen within a railway car itself is of course peculiar to trains or other vehicles that bring together people who have never seen each other before, and who will leave each other's lives within a very short time. The excitement connected with traveling and the stimulation of the sense of swift movement heighten one's sensibility, especially to the new faces about him; as Wolfe puts it in *You Can't Go Home Again*, "one observes all the other passengers with lively interest, and feels that he has known them forever . . . all are caught upon the wing and held for a moment in the peculiar intimacy of this pullman car which has become their common home for a night" (pp. 55-56). There are also significant reasons for the frequency of the epiphany involving something glimpsed from the window of a moving vehicle. To begin with, the experience is necessarily both sudden and brief. If a train stops at a station or a siding, it will usually do so only for a short time; and when the train leaves, any envisioned scene will be lost not only in time, but also in space, as it is taken miles away from the spectator by his own rapid movement as a passenger in the train. A still more fleeting vision occurs when one train passes a second one, and the riders in each gaze at each other, the relative movement of the two moving trains making the experience strangely impressive and a favorite one with Wolfe. Even briefer is the experience in which a passenger catches a glimpse of a stationary object as he dashes by it.

But a more fundamental basis for the persistence of both kinds of train epiphanies in Wolfe's fiction—as, in fact, in the fiction of the other novelists I have mentioned—lies in the general impression they give of separation, even of isolation, in the ease with which they can be regarded as manifestations of the inherent loneliness of all men. This is especially true of the train window type, in which the passenger is unavoidably separated from whatever he perceives and is being carried farther away from it every second. If he sees a person, he may, and in fact usually does, feel a momentary sense of union with him, but in Wolfe this feeling is almost always one-sided, with the person outside the train rarely so much as aware that he is being watched. Even when the sensation is shared by both figures, its fleeting quality only makes it serve the more to reveal their inevitable solitude.

On one of his trips in *Of Time and the River*, Eugene Gant's express catches up to a local and begins to pass it, while the passengers in each train smile at each other in friendly competition, and it seems to Eugene that he must have always known these people, that they will stay with him forever. But then, despite their smiles, he senses that they too feel sorrow and regret: "For, having lived together as strangers in the immense and swarming city, they now had met upon the everlasting earth, hurled past each other for a moment between two points in time upon the shining rails, never to meet, to speak, to know each other any more, and the briefness of their days, the destiny of man, was in that instant greeting and farewell" (pp. 410-11). The idea that man is doomed to perpetual isolation is one of the central themes in Wolfe's work. From our mother's womb, he tells us in the epigraph to his first novel, we come naked and alone into exile. "Which of us," he asks, "is not forever a stranger and alone?" The theme is not at all limited to the image of the railroad (the crowded city, especially, seems to Wolfe a vast image of loneliness) : manifestations of separateness dominated his books and, despite his occasional Whitmaniacal cries that he contained multitudes, gave his epiphanies an in-rooted and self-absorbed quality they did not begin to shed till his outlook underwent a number of significant changes late in his career.

The train epiphanies play varying roles in each of Wolfe's novels. In *Look Homeward, Angel*, they are especially associated with Eugene's growth and his increasing awareness of the changes brought about by time, as well as with all the other aspects of time in which Wolfe is so interested : the relations among time past, time present, and time immutable; the swiftness of its passage or the sensation that it has stopped; and the confusion between time and space ("time and movement")—all of which are manifested in "the weird combination of fixity and change, the terrible moment of immobility stamped with eternity in which, passing life at great speed, both the observer and the observed seem frozen in time" (p. 202).

But it is in *Of Time and the River*, more than any of Wolfe's other novels, that the train really comes into its own, and in fact a more appropriate title for the book might well have been *Of Time and the Railroad*, for the image of the river does not even approach in importance that of the train. I am not merely referring to the frequency with which railroad journeys appear in this novel, and I am thinking less of the large number of revelations involving trains than of the uses to which those revelations are put; for they lend to the book much of whatever unity it has, connecting all the sections of the novel, early, middle, or late, whether the action takes place in the South or in the North, in America or in Europe. Wolfe himself, when he tried to describe the "design" of the novel, did not refer to the continuous flow of a river, but was forced instead into the realization that he could "liken these chapters only to a row of lights which one sometimes sees at night from the windows of a speeding train" (*Story of a Novel*, p. 54).

Train epiphanies also help integrate *Of Time and the River* as a whole into the sequence of volumes that tell the life story of the Wolfe hero; but in none of the other novels do they play so large a role in providing a degree of internal coherence, limited as it may finally seem even here. Early in the novel, for example, the train taking Eugene toward Harvard stops at Maysville, the last town in Old Catawba; it is night, and as Eugene looks out from his berth onto the depressingly pretentious and artificial gaiety of a small southern town square, "in the wink of an eye, a moment's vision," he is filled with a "feeling of loneliness, instant familiarity, and departure." Under the pressure of the multitude of Eugene's impressions to which we are exposed, we might easily regard this incident as simply one of the many isolated passages that Wolfe so often seems to include in his novels for no other reason than that they interested him, and with no reference beyond themselves. But in this case we would be mistaken. The "familiarity" Eugene finds in the scene arises not only from its being typical of many that can be observed throughout the South, but also because it is an "image of ten thousand lonely little towns like this across the continent" (pp. 31-32).

As a matter of fact, one night several years and hundreds of pages later, we do come across such a town in upstate New York. Eugene's train stops at one end of the station of a small factory town. Once more he looks out of his window, and this time he is able to see into a shabby bar, ornately decorated and containing a number of laughing men, a coarse but friendly-looking prostitute, and a portrait of Warren G. Harding. The train moves on to the other end of the station: "And again, from his dark berth, he could see without moving this whole immense and immediate theatre of human event, and again it gripped and held him with its dream-like magic, its unbelievable familiarity" (p. 473). The word "familiarity" reappears because in essence this northern town is Maysville, Altamont, and all the little towns he has ever known. So when he sees a boy on the street trying to get up the courage to approach a prostitute who is obviously waiting for him, we do not need to be told (though we are) that Eugene is witnessing an image of what he himself has been, of his own desire, indeed "of the desire of every youth that ever lived" (p. 475).

Trains are less important in *The Web and the Rock* than in most of Wolfe's work, though here their symbolic force is recognized by both Esther Jack and George Webber. As a child trying to explain to grown-ups what sort of things can teach you to see "a forest in a leaf, the whole earth in a single face," Esther cites as an example "the people in a train that passes the one you're in : you see all the people, you are close to them, but you cannot touch them, you say good-bye to them and it makes you feel sad." Later, we discover that one of the images that inexplicably persist in George's memory is "the face of a woman passing in another train, an atom hurled through time," just as Eugene, when it was his train that passed another, was especially struck by "a lovely girl, blonde-haired, with a red silk dress"—or just as Thomas Wolfe himself could never forget "a girl who looked and smiled from the window of the other train."[2]

In *Of Time and the River*, some fifty-odd pages near the beginning of the novel were devoted to the train ride that took Eugene from Altamont to the North; in *You Can't Go Home Again*, some fifty-odd pages near the beginning of the novel are devoted to the train ride that takes George back south to Libya Hill. He is traveling on K 19 (the same pullman car that made the run between the North and Wolfe's own Asheville) : "The moment he entered the pullman he was transported instantly from the vast allness of general humanity in the station into the familiar geography of his home town . . . it all came back again, his feet touched earth, and he was home" (p. 52). He is deceived, of course. You can't go home again. But George will not fully realize this until, years later, he experiences the train window epiphany that forms the climax of the novel—when he and his fellow passengers gaze at their former companion, the desperate little man whom the Nazis have caught trying to escape Germany. This passage is one of the most important in all Wolfe's fiction, and I shall later discuss some of its far-reaching implications.

In addition to revelations that concentrate upon present experiences, of which I have taken some involving trains as the chief examples in Wolfe, there are those that center on the past and one's present memories of it. And they, as I have already indicated, are far more important to one who, fascinated as he may be by what

[2] *The Web and the Rock*, pp. 421-22, 455; *Of Time and the River*, p. 410; *The Story of a Novel*, p. 44.

he sees around him here and now, is utterly obsessed with what has passed, with what is perhaps lost forever. Of course, it is not possible to distinguish completely between these two kinds of revelation, and neither one of them can be discussed without sooner or later bringing in the other, but the distinction is nevertheless generally useful, especially in regard to Wolfe. Much the same may be said of the division of the epiphany of memory itself into two further types, the "retrospective" epiphany and that of the past recaptured.

When one recaptures the past, if we are to believe modern novelists, he does not merely recall an event but actually lives through it again in all its original reality. During his privileged moments, consequently, it seems to Proust's Marcel that the past he relives fuses with the present and becomes contemporary with it, while Wolfe writes that once, when George noticed the first signs of spring, the color green so worked upon his memory that "the past became as real as the present, and he lived in the events of twenty years ago with as much intensity and as great a sense of actuality as if they had just occurred. He felt that there was no temporal past or present, no *now* more living than any reality of *then* . . ." (*The Web and the Rock*, p. 541). Eugene has the same experiences, and they always occur in an epiphany, suddenly : "always when that lost world would come back, it came at once, like a sword thrust through the entrails, in all its panoply of past time, living, whole, and magic as it had always been" (*Of Time and the River*, p. 200). Not everyone, however, is capable of recapturing the past; it would seem that one must have a virtually abnormal awareness of the sensations of the present in order to feel them again when they have gone, or at least when most people would say they have "gone." One needs the almost neurotic ultra-sensibility of a Marcel—a quality already part of Eugene's make-up when he is "not quite six" : "his sensory equipment was so complete that at the moment of perception of a single thing, the whole background of color, warmth, odor, sound, taste established itself, so that later, the breath of hot dandelion brought back the grass-warm banks of Spring, a day, a place, the rustling of young leaves, or the page of a book, the thin exotic smell of tangerine, the wintry bite of great apples . . ." (*Look Homeward, Angel*, p. 84).

Thomas Wolfe believed that he himself possessed such a sensibility and that his memory was characterized "in a more than ordinary degree by the intensity of its sense impressions." As an illustration, he describes in *The Story of a Novel* how one day he was sitting in a Paris café, when suddenly and for no apparent reason he remembered the iron railing on the boardwalk at Atlantic City : "I could see it instantly just the way it was, the heavy iron pipe; its raw, galvanized look; the way the joints were fitted together. It was all so vivid and concrete that I could feel my hand upon it and know the exact dimensions, its size and weight and shape" (pp. 31-32).

Wolfe asserts that this experience—and others like it, all of which also took place, paradoxically, in Europe—enabled him to discover his America, which he had begun to feel was lost to him. Both his fictional counterparts also undergo the same discovery while in France : the incident that causes Eugene to look homeward occurs toward the end of *Of Time and the River*, when a church bell in Dijon brings him back to the bell in college at Pulpit Hill, and then even further back to his childhood and "the lost America" (p. 898); the incident that takes George home again occurs in Boulogne, as he enters a hotel room for the first time yet "feels that he has been here before." All the objects seem "like old, immensely familiar, and essential things, although an hour before he did not know of their existence." He is experiencing something very similar to what happens at the beginning of Proust's privileged moments, though no special sensibility is needed to go this far, and most people have had this feeling a number of times. While psychologists speak of it as *déjà vu*, it is known in the terminology of popular song as the It-seems-we've-sat-and-talked-like-this-before-but-who-knows-where-or-when phenomenon. George, however, hears a different song, as he listens to the voices of a man and woman passing under his window :

> Suddenly, just as they pass, a low, rich burst of laughter, tender and voluptuous, wells up out of the woman's throat, and at that moment, by the magic of time, a light burns on a moment of his weaving, a shutter is lifted in the dark, a lost moment lives again with all its magic and terrible intensity, and the traveler is a child again, and he hears at night, beneath the leafy rustle of mid-Summer trees, the feet of the lovers passing by along the street of a little town in America when he was nine years old, and the song that they sang was "Love Me and the World is Mine."
> Where?

In the town of Libya Hill in Old Catawba twenty years ago . . . . [*The Web and the Rock*, pp. 631-32]

Such a passage can leave no doubt that Wolfe's treatment of the past is very similar to Proust's, but it would be quite another thing to say that Proust influenced him. It does seem fairly certain that Wolfe was familiar with Proust's work and greatly admired it, but his own tendency to emphasize the recapture of the past was so strong as to make any actual influence by Proust probably superfluous.[3]

Those epiphanies involving events that produce revelations only long after the events themselves have occurred are so numerous in the novels of Thomas Wolfe that it would be pointless to quote many examples here; they form the bulk of the long catalogues of Eugene's and George's memories that fill so many pages in Wolfe's books, and of which Wolfe wrote in terms that make it clear he regarded these memories as what I call retrospective epiphanies. *The Story of a Novel* describes how, when he began to work on the first book of an intended series, he compiled vast lists of almost every conceivable sort; some of them were put among sections of his manuscripts headed by the words "Where now?" and one of the incidents he uses as an example is the same one we have just seen recaptured by George Webber:

Under such a heading as this, there would be brief notations of those thousands of things which all of us have seen for just a flash, a moment in our lives, which seem to be of no consequence whatever at the moment that we see them, and which live in our minds and hearts forever, which are somehow pregnant with all the joy and sorrow of the human destiny, and which we know, somehow, are therefore more important than many things of more apparent consequence. "Where now?" Some quiet steps that came and passed along a leafy night-time street in summer in a little town down South long years ago; a woman's voice, her sudden burst of low and tender laughter; then the voices and the footsteps going, silence, the leafy rustle of the trees. "Where now?" [Pp. 43-44]

Like his desire and apparent ability to recapture lost time, then,

---

[3] On Wolfe's admiration for Proust, see *Letters*, p. 194, and Daniel L. Delakas, *Thomas Wolfe, la France et les romanciers français*, p. 120.

these manuscripts were the product of the general infatuation with the past that Wolfe brought to his art when he first began to write novels.

For a brief period before then, however, and despite the inclinations of his character, he did try to tone down his preoccupation with his own personal memories. In his writing, this attempt took the form of a number of plays that were not especially autobiographical. His major effort in a purely fictitious plot was *Mannerhouse*, a drama set during and after the Civil War. In the original version, according to a letter young Wolfe wrote to his mother in 1920 or 1921, at the end of the play the hero Eugene and his sweetheart Christine, "glorious forerunners of the New South," were to leave his family's mansion; because of the ruin brought upon Tradition by the War and the years that have followed it, the house is no longer his. "Take one last look at this room, 'Gene," Christine tells him, "and realize that this is past, that this was a fine life but a useless one. We are not living in the Memory of past greatness, but Now and Here. Are you ready to meet it?" As they are leaving, the house is being torn down to satisfy Crass Material Interests and "the inexorable call of Tomorrow. From the distance comes the deadly whirring buzz of the New and the Curtain Falls!" "Well," Wolfe concludes, "I have the stuff for a fine play here" (*Letters to His Mother*, p. 19).

Be that as it may, within a few years he decided to change the ending, adapting it more suitably to the view of the past he then actually held, perhaps in spite of himself. He accomplished this by grafting onto the echoes of Chekhov's *The Cherry Orchard* the image of Samson destroying the Philistines. In the final version, which was not published until 1948, the Young Aristocrat rejects the present and the future, and embraces his past by pulling down a pillar—an act that brings down the house, crushing himself, the Southern Belle, the Poor White Trash who has come up in the world and bought the estate, and the Faithful Old Negro Tod. Clearly, the two endings reflect different attitudes toward the role of the historical past, as well as one's own. Around the same time, Wolfe changed his very art form to one that conformed to his views about the role of one's personal past in art—he began writing autobiographical novels. From then on, his work showed a great emphasis on his memories of his own life, a conscious and deliberate intention to utilize them in his work. He had the major requisite for doing so—

a powerful memory that seemed capable of total recall—and he announced his full determination to rely upon it even before he actually gave up the dramatic form. In 1923, he wrote to his mother :

> . . . I am at the mercy of this thing and I will do it or die. I never forget; I have never forgotten. I have tried to make myself conscious of the whole of my life since first the baby in the basket became conscious of the warm sunlight on the porch, and saw his sister go up the hill to the girl's school on the corner (the first thing I remember). Slowly out of the world of infant darkness things take shape, the big terrifying faces become familiar— I recognize my father by his bristly moustache. . . .
>
> This is why I think I'm going to be an artist. The things that really mattered sunk in and left their mark. Sometimes only a word—sometimes a peculiar smile—sometimes death—sometimes the smell of dandelions in Spring—once Love. [*Letters to His Mother*, pp. 52-53]

It was against the background of this obsession with time and memory that Wolfe wrote his first novel.

II

It would be pointless for me to trace the pattern of epiphanies in *Look Homeward, Angel*, or in any of Wolfe's novels, as I have in Joyce's and Virginia Woolf's, for the simple reason that there really is no pattern. Yet a chronological examination of his work does have value in suggesting how thoroughly moments of passionate illumination pervade it, how related they are to his basic notions of art and the artist, and especially in showing how his views toward the use of the epiphanies of his own past developed and changed.

Early in *Look Homeward, Angel*—as in *A Portrait of the Artist*, with its opening scene of Stephen creating a rhyme out of the demand that he "apologise"—we are given an epiphany that strongly hints at the hero's vocation as an artist. The incident occurs at school, where all the children have been able to learn how to write except Eugene, who draws only jagged lines and is unable even to see any difference. One day his friend Max looks at Eugene's sheet and, commenting that "That ain't writin'," scrawls a correct copy of the exercise on the paper; somehow this act suddenly causes

Eugene to write out the words too—"in letters fairer and finer than his friend's"—and to go on hurriedly to copy the subsequent pages, as the two boys react "with that clear wonder by which children accept miracles."

> "That's writin' now," said Max. But they kept the mystery caged between them.
> Eugene thought of this event later; always he could feel the opening gates in him, the plunge of the tide, the escape; but it happened like this one day at once. Still midget-near the live pelt of the earth, he saw many things that he kept in fearful secret, knowing that revelation would be punished with ridicule. [Pp. 90-91]

Though this episode, like the one in the *Portrait*, may be regarded as revelatory primarily for the author and the reader, it does provide a mysterious new awareness for the two boys as well; and it is immediately followed by another revelation which they—"midget-near the live pelt of the earth," or trailing clouds of glory as it were—cannot communicate and so keep secret : but this time it is a vision of the hidden presence of evil in the world. Watching some workers repair a broken water main in one of the town streets, Eugene and Max are standing next to a fissure in the earth, a window that opens "on some dark subterranean passage," when they suddenly see gliding past them "an enormous serpent" which vanishes into the earth behind the working men, seen only by the terrified children and never revealed by them (p. 91).

Such scenes appear throughout the novel, and many of them seem based on Wolfe's own memories; but art reflects the mind and world of its creator in more ways than one, so in *Look Homeward, Angel* a large number of the purely imaginary incidents, too, involve the recollection or recapture of lost time by various characters themselves. Oliver Gant goes through such a moment when, to his dismay, the local madam buys his statue of an angel for a prostitute's grave. The importance to Gant of this angel has been prepared for by the first epiphany in the novel—one that also dealt with the discovery of artistic longings. Gant, fifteen years old, was walking along a street in Philadelphia when he saw a statue of an angel outside a stone cutter's shop, and it instilled a lifelong desire "to wreak something dark and unspeakable in him into cold stone," to "carve an angel's head," to "seek the great forgotten language, the lost

lane-end into heaven" (p. 3). The angel purchased by the madam
has been imported from Italy, but it is as close as Gant has ever
come to carving his own angel and to finding the forgotten language. As he and the madam conclude their transaction, their
thoughts turning to the years that have gone by since their youth,
they look out upon the town square, where everything seems suddenly "frozen in a picture" :

> And in that second the slow pulse of the fountain was suspended,
> life was held, like an arrested gesture, in photographic abeyance,
> and Gant felt himself alone move deathward in a world of seem-
> ings as, in 1910, a man might find himself again in a picture
> taken on the grounds of the Chicago Fair, when he was thirty
> and his mustache black, and, noting the bustled ladies and the
> derbied men fixed in the second's pullulation, remember the dead
> instant, seek beyond the borders for what was there. . . .

"Where now?" Wolfe asks, "Where after? Where then?" (p. 285).

At the end of the novel, Gant's son Eugene sees in the same
square a vision of his whole past life; in general radiance and
significance, that final vision and the others I have cited are exceptions to most of the epiphanies in the book, which are plentiful and
often individually very effective, but which too frequently have no
real function in relation to the rest of the novel. They reveal a good
deal about specific people, but little in regard to comprehensive
themes, and sometimes they even seem like merely irrelevant in-
trusions. Occasionally, however, a moment of revelation will not
only give us insight into Wolfe's characters, but also serve broader
purposes of form by bringing together various themes or threads
in the story—as with Eugene's climactic experience at the very end,
the evening before he is to leave Altamont.

The vision of Ben concludes the novel with a forecast of the
future, but it serves primarily as a summary of the past. The nature
of that summary seems meant to illustrate Wolfe's assertion in his
note to the reader that "we are the sum of all the moments of our
lives" (p. xvii); gazing upon the town square, Eugene feels that he
sees all his younger selves evoked before him :

> And for a moment all the silver space was printed with the
> thousand forms of himself and Ben. There, by the corner in from
> Academy Street, Eugene watched his own approach; there, by
> the City Hall, he strode with lifted knees; there, by the curb

F

upon the step, he stood, peopling the night with the great lost legion of himself—the thousand forms that came, that passed, that wove and shifted in unending change, and that remained unchanging Him.

And through the Square, unwoven from lost time, the fierce bright horde of Ben spun in and out its deathless loom. Ben, in a thousand moments, walked the Square : Ben of the lost years, the forgotten days, the unremembered hours. . . .

And now the Square was thronging with their lost bright shapes, and all the minutes of lost time collected and stood still. Then, shot from them with projectile speed, the Square shrank down the rails of destiny, and was vanished with all things done, with all forgotten shapes of himself and Ben. [Pp. 658-59]

When the images of the past have disappeared, Eugene experiences another "moment of terrible vision," this time of "his foiled quest of himself," of the same hunger that has "darkened his father's eyes to impalpable desire for wrought stone and the head of an angel"; we are thus brought back to the first epiphany in the novel. Ben reveals in an "apexical summation" that what Eugene seeks must be found within himself ("*You* are your world"), and that the object of his quest—"the forgotten language, the lost world" (pp. 660-62) —involves the past as much as the future. But it is forward that Eugene tries to look as he expresses in his final words his confidence that he will someday find what he desires, just as at the end of *The Story of a Novel* Wolfe himself is confident that we shall all "find the tongue, the language, and the conscience that as men and artists we have got to have" (p. 93). The last chapter of the novel has generally suggested the visions in Joyce's Nighttown episode in *Ulysses*; but it is Stephen's affirmation on the last page of the *Portrait*—that, as artificer, he will forge the uncreated conscience of his race—that is called to mind by the last page of *Look Homeward, Angel*, with the young artist's determination to attain what his father has sought but never found in the carved angel : "the forgotten language, the lost world."

We trace Eugene's progress toward the achievement of his goal in Wolfe's next novel, *Of Time and the River*. Through its portrait of the young artist and his attitude toward his work, we get a good picture of Wolfe's own views on art, and of his own goal. A central description of these views takes its departure from Eugene's feelings as he reads his play—which happens to be called *Mannerhouse*—

to his friends Joel and Rosalind Pierce. Wolfe first deals with artistic genesis, citing Eugene's play as an illustration of the fact that the source of art lies in one's personal experiences—especially in one's moments of inspiration : "the flashes of blind but powerful intuition, which mark the artist's early life here in America" (p. 549). At any rate, they certainly seem to have marked Wolfe's life; if we can trust *The Story of a Novel*, indeed, one such sudden artistic inspiration, which took place in Paris, very much resembles the new self-awareness he attributes to Eugene at the end of *Look Homeward, Angel*: "I saw," he writes, "that I must find for myself the tongue to utter what I knew but could not say. And from the moment of that discovery, the line and purpose of my life was shaped" (p. 35). The words he uses in *Of Time and the River*— "flashes of blind but powerful intuition"—provide one example (we shall see others) of Wolfe's ability to point out both the strengths and weaknesses of his own work, and to do so with something rare in his writing, a concise phrase.

Having commented on the origin of art, Wolfe goes on to describe its aims, which also turn out to involve moments of vision. First, he shares with other writers the belief that the artist's drive to create comes from the hope of recording epiphanies—what Joyce calls the attempt "to fix the most elusive of his moods" (*Stephen Hero*, p. 32). Wolfe, of course, greatly admired Joyce's work, but the important thing to notice here is that he did so largely because he felt that Joyce was able to do successfully what he himself longed to do— to record his evanescent moments with extreme care. Wolfe felt that in *Ulysses* "the effort to apprehend and to make live again a moment in lost time is so tremendous that . . . Joyce really did succeed, at least in places, in penetrating reality . . ." (*Letters*, p. 322). In the passage in *Of Time and the River*, Wolfe refers to this compulsion as "the intolerable desire to fix eternally in the patterns of an indestructible form a single moment of man's living, a single moment of life's beauty, passion, and unutterable eloquence, that passes, flames and goes" (p. 551).

The artist need not be the only one to feel the flash of intuition, however; another of his aims is to impart it to his audience. As Eugene reads his play aloud to his friends and realizes that they are powerfully affected by it, he feels a tremendous sense of elation and learns "in one blaze of light, an image of unutterable conviction, the reason why the artist works and lives and has his being." It is, as we have seen it in other writers, to make his reader experience a revelation, "to snare the spirits of mankind in nets of magic . . . to wreak the vision of his life, the rude and painful substance of his own experience, into the congruence of blazing and enchanted images that are themselves the core of life, the essential pattern whence all other things proceed, the kernel of eternity" (p. 550). The same purpose makes an artist out of Eugene's alter ego George, who, as a boy, laments the inability of people like his Aunt Meg to understand "the life of life, the joy of joy, the grief of grief unutterable, the eternity of living in a moment" and therefore longs for the power to "enlighten their enkitchened lives with a revealing utterance" (*The Web and the Rock*, pp. 24-25).

His belief that the artist is characterized by an extreme propensity for such experiences and an overwhelming need to depict and impart them to others leads Wolfe to call him "life's hungry man, the glutton of eternity, beauty's miser" (*Of Time and the River*, p. 551). This description may not fit most artists, but it does fit Wolfe himself, and it shows how his interpretation of the role of the artist as the recorder of epiphanies is very much related to his artistic tendencies—including his faults. Wolfe sees the artist as the man who is hungry for all experience, who has an insatiable craving to do all things and, unfortunately, to express them all. In Wolfe's own work, this aesthetic gluttony leads to his most basic defects, a failure to control his material and a consequent weakness in structure.

In regard to the structural use of epiphanies, the weaknesses of *Look Homeward, Angel* are in one way alleviated in *Of Time and the River*, where a measure of unity is provided by the many train epiphanies. But the coherence thus achieved, though significant, is perhaps more than offset by the very size of the book and the countless revelations of all types that run through it, with little attempt at relating most of them to one another. Wolfe's problems are further compounded by the novel's climax. *Look Homeward, Angel* had at least ended with a powerful and unifying vision; *Of Time and the River* ends with what is probably the chief example in Wolfe of a nonfunctional and even harmful epiphany, one that seems completely out of place in the novel it is meant to conclude.

In the final scene, Eugene is leaving Europe and returning to America; he is in a small boat with a number of other people, waiting to board the ship that is to take them home. All the travelers feel the strange power of the huge liner as it towers over them, but Wolfe gives special attention to the effect of this "magic moment" on a woman named Esther, whom we have never encountered before. We are then shown her own effect on Eugene, as he turns toward her; from the moment he sees her, his spirit is "impaled upon the knife of love." As if that were not bad enough, "at that instant" he also loses the "wild integrity" and the "proud inviolability of youth" (pp. 910-11). Whereupon the novel ends. As the conclusion to an already ill-structured book, this revelation, which should form the forceful climax to the entire novel, succeeds only in leaving the reader hanging in the air. Eugene's loss of his youth can hardly be regarded as a dramatic or convincing corollary of what amounts to an epiphany of love at first sight. Besides, Wolfe's hero instantaneously loses his youth forever very often, and in this case the supposed loss is so unpersuasive as to be embarrassing. One would like to be able to find some alternative thematic function served by this incident : to regard it, say, as a culmination of the search for a mother—which, despite Wolfe's claim that the controlling idea in *Of Time and the River* is "man's search to find a father" (*Story of a Novel*, p. 39), often seems more central in his work than the father theme. But the scene does not really fit this interpretation either, and, though eventually Esther does in some degree become a mother figure, that role is of course not evident until the George Webber novels. Indeed, no matter how one looks at it, this scene is so unrelated to the context of the rest of the novel that it can only be regarded as a passage that starts threads that are entirely new. Strictly speaking, moreover, those threads were never taken up and no sequel to the book was ever written, for Wolfe never published another novel about Eugene Gant—though in the end, to be sure, we must ignore Wolfe's switch from Eugene to George Webber.

One of the most frequently cited causes of the structural defects of *Of Time and the River*, and of Wolfe's other novels as well, has been his inability or unwillingness to control the flow of memories he so freely permitted himself to record in his fiction—so freely that the flow became a deluge. Of course, Wolfe was correct in believing that there is much to be said for what he called, in a famous letter to F. Scott Fitzgerald, the "putter-inner" (as opposed to the "leaver-outer") approach to fiction (*Letters*, p. 643). But this approach also entails great dangers, and too often Wolfe's own work does not overcome his obsession to be a putter-inner of everything. Yet it is an oversimplification to say that Wolfe's "chief fault," in his own words, was merely that he "wrote too much" (*Story of a Novel*, p. 83); a lack of critical judgment was also involved. He devoted so much space to autobiographical details which the reader can only regard as at best unessential that his novels frequently give the impression—valid or not—that he failed to understand that not every moment personally important to him need also be artistically significant. To Wolfe, all the myriad experiences he gives his hero are important, even essential; all of them at least potentially involve revelations. And the ones explicitly described as revelations are so numerous as to appear in almost every scene. By itself, each might be fully credible—but not as simply one out of a massive crowd; under such conditions, they take on something of the character of a mere artistic "convention." Moreover, Wolfe aggravates his difficulties by treating every one of the illuminations as if it were of cosmic proportions. Instead of subordinating some of them in comparison with others, he uses the same superlative adjectives to describe what would seem to be relatively unimportant moments of insight as he uses in the accounts of those he obviously regards as vital or climactic, such as the ones that end all his novels. We are so frequently told that this or that moment will never be forgotten and produces a revelation completely changing the course of Eugene's life that each such passage loses much of its intended force, and after a while we begin to treat these statements with skepticism—worse, we may even cease to notice some of them.

After finishing *Of Time and the River*—or, rather, after Maxwell Perkins took it away from him when it looked as if he might never stop putting things in—Wolfe published in *The Story of a Novel* an account of how it had been written. No one who reads this account can help being struck by its almost masochistic eagerness to tell the truth, and by its perceptive recognition of the defects as well as the benefits of the methods Wolfe had thus far used in his fiction. Almost everything a reader of the novel is bound to suspect is shown here to have been true. Wolfe admits, for instance, that he "cannot really say the book was written"; rather, it "took hold" of him and "possessed" him, it came "pouring from its depth a torrential and ungovernable flood" (p. 37). When the resulting manuscript was finally deemed almost ready, it was Wolfe's task, with the help of his editor, to work on its mighty maze till it yielded a plan. Inevitably, considering how much easier Wolfe found it to add than to cut, their success was only partial.[4]

The story of the composition of *Of Time and the River* also provides a review of the role that had thus far been played in Wolfe's novels by the memory of the past. He was, of course, much concerned with the whole problem of the representation of time in fiction. But systematic reasoning was not one of his strengths, and his discussion of the three elements of time that he discovered in his material—"actual present time," "past time," and "time immutable, the time of rivers, mountains, oceans, and the earth" (*Story of a Novel*, pp. 51-52)—is after all neither profound, interesting, nor very enlightening in terms of his own work. The one time element that really monopolized his attention, as we have seen, was the past, together with one's memories of its individual moments. Although his preoccupation with it was closely related to a number of the other important themes he discusses here—notably the search for a father and the relationship between Europe and America—it towered above them all in significance. As Wolfe describes how he set about preparing to write his novel, and then how he actually wrote it, it is his "powers of memory"—which at that time "reached the greatest degree of sharpness that they had ever known" (p. 58)— that constantly take the forefront. We have already seen how they formed the impetus that made him compile the "Where now?" manuscripts which were in turn one of the bases for the finished book. In huge ledgers Wolfe listed retrospective epiphanies, writing down "not only the concrete, material record of man's ordered memory, but all the things he scarcely dares to think he has remembered; all the flicks and darts and haunting lights that flash across the mind of man that will return unbidden at an unexpected moment" (p. 46). Like so many modern writers, Wolfe strove to find in "material" details and fleeting trivia the sense of value and permanence for which he longed.

Where now? The phrase figures not only in the manuscripts described in *The Story of a Novel*, but in epiphanies recorded in the

---

[4] Perkins' patient love for Wolfe's work is in part illuminated by the fact that his "passion," according to a colleague, "was for the rare real thing, the flash of poetic insight that lights up a character or a situation and reveals talent at work" (quoted in Andrew Turnbull, *Scott Fitzgerald*, p. 118).

published versions of his novels as well.[5] Yet, after his description of these manuscripts, Wolfe suddenly rejects both them and the uncontrolled use of memory they seem to imply. In an unexpected and disconcertingly brief passage, he writes :

> It may be objected, it has been objected already by certain critics, that in such research as I have here attempted to describe there is a quality of intemperate excess, an almost insane hunger to devour the entire body of human experience, to attempt to include more, experience more, than the measure of one life can hold, or than the limits of a single work of art can well define. I readily admit the validity of this criticism. I think I realize as well as any one the fatal dangers that are consequent to such a ravenous desire, the damage it may wreak upon one's life and on one's work. . . .
>
> . . . And now I really believe that so far as the artist is concerned, the unlimited extent of human experience is not so important for him as the depth and intensity with which he experiences things. [*Story of a Novel*, pp. 46-47]

As here presented, Wolfe's new attitude is as yet vague and undefined, but it does suggest a stronger realization that his work has suffered from his lack of selectivity. It is of course inconceivable that Thomas Wolfe could ever really have become a leaver-outer. But though the "Where now?" method was inevitable and even justifiable for the early stages of his particular career, he now sees that it must be modified to take into consideration the quality of remembered experience as much as, or even more than, its quantity; not every event that had occurred to him is worthy of being recorded in art as a retrospective epiphany. This new point of view indicates a degree of reaction against the almost completely free play he had thus far given his memory in the fictional chronicle of his life; and therefore, as far as it goes, it is a sign of Wolfe's transition from the attitude we have seen in his youthful letter to his mother—"I intend to wreak out my soul on paper and express it all. . . . I never forget; I have never forgotten"—to his eventual conviction that you can't go home again. I say "as far as it goes" because in itself this passage is anything but a clear and emphatic statement, and its context contains further qualifications. Nevertheless, it is one of the first signs of a significant shift in his thinking.

---

[5] See, for example, *Look Homeward, Angel*, pp. 203, 285; *The Web and the Rock*, p. 276.

There are a few less questionable signs in his next published volume, though again only a few. *The Web and the Rock*, like *You Can't Go Home Again* (Wolfe, of course, meant them to form a single novel), was never corrected or even finished by Wolfe himself, and it had to be posthumously edited by Edward C. Aswell. Much of it, moreover, was written as early as *Of Time and the River*, and it is therefore doubly difficult to depend on it in order to trace the development of Wolfe's techniques and ideas. We know, however, that except for a few passages, notably the ending, the last half was written before the first, though he did rewrite "small portions of it" before he died.[6] This situation leads to some awkward discrepancies between various viewpoints expressed within the novel itself, as well as with what Wolfe had said elsewhere.

Conflicts are especially apparent in his comments on the role of memory in George Webber's art, and readers who have read *The Story of a Novel* carefully, but who are unaware of the peculiarities in the chronology of composition of *The Web and the Rock*, will be particularly struck by a number of passages in the novel that contradict the position toward which Wolfe had seemed to be groping. Thus, in the second (earlier) half of the book, Wolfe occasionally speaks approvingly of George's great reliance upon his powers of recollection, which make the past "as real as the present" (*The Web and the Rock*, p. 541). "The majestic powers of memory," we are told, "exerted a beneficent and joyful dominion over his life, sharpening and making intensely vivid every experience of each passing day," and enabling him to possess "a thousand fleeting and indefinable things which he had seen for the flick of an eye in some lost and dateless moment of the swarming past" (pp. 455-56). Yet such remarks, though published after Wolfe's death, are not indications of a late reversion to the attitude that had produced the "Where now?" catalogues, but are rather another early product of that attitude. The newly written sections of the book, in contrast, reflect Wolfe's more recent concern about the pernicious effect on his work of his emphasis on memory.

When George begins to write his first novel, his memory is said to have grown so "encyclopaedic" and preoccupied with the

---

[6] Edward C. Aswell, "A Note on Thomas Wolfe," in Wolfe, *The Hills Beyond*, p. 374. But for a full discussion of the composition of Wolfe's work, see Richard S. Kennedy, *The Window of Memory: The Literary Career of Thomas Wolfe*.

"minutest details" that it impairs his art and becomes, "instead of a mighty weapon," "a gigantic, fibrous million-rooted plant of time which spread and flowered like a cancerous growth." Eventually, as George begins to realize that he has been trying "to pour the ocean in a sanitary drinking cup," he does atttempt to set down merely "a fractional part of his vision of the earth" (pp. 262-63). However, he is not really prepared to control the crushing power of his past, much less to discard it, and in another year his modest effort has— and Wolfe repeats his previous phrase—"spread and flowered like a cancerous growth" : "From his childhood he could remember all that people said or did, but as he tried to set it down his memory opened up enormous vistas and associations, going from depth to limitless depth, until the simplest incident conjured up a buried continent of experience, and he was overwhelmed by a project of discovery and revelation that would have broken the strength and used up the lives of a regiment of men" (p. 273). We have here a description of essentially the same power as the one that had previously been depicted as exerting over George "a beneficent and joyful dominion," only now there is a marked difference in outlook toward its desirability. The later Wolfe was coming to suspect that —to adapt the terminology of the later Freud—the repetition compulsion is nothing less than deathly. Nevertheless, though this and similar passages are significant, they are as yet isolated, infrequent, and counterbalanced by the passages that sharply contradict them.

A more pronounced symptom of Wolfe's doubts about his reliance on his own past in his fiction was his adoption of a new hero, to whom he gave a childhood quite different from his own. This attempt to abandon strict autobiography was, perhaps inevitably, abortive; but it did bring him face to face with one of his most important failings—the almost complete absence from his work of objectivity. The novelist who works in the autobiographical form should not only be able to select the significant from the inconsequential; he should also be able to look at himself with a certain amount of perspective. And if he records his own epiphanies, as Joyce says it is for the man of letters to do, he will be most successful if he can do so with the impersonal self-analysis of a Proust, a Conrad, or of Joyce himself. Wolfe's treatment of many of his epiphanies, on the other hand, is romanticized and theatrical. It would be absurd to condemn his novels because they are autobiographical. But it would, I am afraid, be correct to accuse them of being *too* autobiographical, in the sense that he seems to have seen his hero first as a reflection of himself, and then as a character in a work of art : he usually—though by no means always—failed to achieve that unique blend of subjective interest and objective insight that Edward Bullough called Psychical Distance.

Extreme subjectivity controls not only Wolfe's own attitude toward his experiences, but also the attitudes of his heroes toward theirs. Far from attaining any true and balanced view of the world around them during their moments of revelation, at such times they frequently have a view that is if anything even more individual and distorted than usual. They can see neither themselves nor others in perspective : they are self-deluded as well as self-absorbed. To some degree, they may be looked upon as simply following in this trait the general emphasis of our time on the subjective quality of experience and revelation : young Eugene Gant realizes in so many words that everything he saw from the train had "no existence save that which I gave to it, became other than itself by being mixed with what I then was" (*Look Homeward, Angel*, p. 203). But the egotism of Wolfe's characters is so excessive, and they are so incapable of looking at the world except through their own highly distorted glasses, that the credibility of their moments of supposed insight into the lives of other people is greatly affected. Thus, despite the many moments in which Eugene or George feels an overpowering communion with other people, one's general impression is that of a bitter man more capable of abhorrence than of sympathy. For every stranger in the streets of Boston or New York to whom he feels his heart go out, there is someone, barely an acquaintance perhaps, whom he knows and—consequently—hates, fears, and despises. As a result, the sudden insights during which he is said to fathom completely some person or object are frequently unconvincing, for we find ourselves wondering if he is really capable of such insights. Generally, his abnormally self-centered relationships with other people, and his resulting inability to understand or communicate with them except on his own very peculiar terms and according to his own unusual needs, lessen the stature of the Wolfe hero as a human being; specifically, they lessen the seriousness with which we can react to some of his most important epiphanies, for we tend to regard his moments of compassion as more rhetorical than real.

The rhetoric of the epiphanies at the end of *The Web and the Rock*, when George confronts not someone else but his own reflection in a mirror, is an especially interesting example of some of Wolfe's major tendencies, including his inclination to view his hero too subjectively, and his technical handling of moments of revelation. George is in a hospital in Munich after having participated in a brawl at the October Fair. His face has been beaten into an awful sight, but as he looks at it in the mirror across from his bed he suddenly grins, and then laughs : "The battered mask laughed with him, and at last his soul was free. He was a man" (p. 690). After that last remark, we too are inclined to grin, and perhaps laugh. This is not the first of the spiritual *bar mitzvahs* Wolfe gives his heroes—nor is it the last, for that matter. But the embarrassingly mawkish today-I-am-a-man quality of this scene is particularly noticeable, largely because his treatment of it is so explicit, a trait we have noticed before in some of Wolfe's epiphanies : too often he spoils an excellent effect by pointing out the very things which, with the consummate art of all his undeniable genius, he has just dramatically shown or suggested.

For the final epiphany, the reflection even becomes vocal, and he and George have a dialogue—their talk, as might be expected, centering on the past : George lovingly describes to his image the memories of childhood, "the good time." "But," the reflection reveals in the last words of the novel, "you can't go home again" (p. 695). As a climactic epiphany, this scene is almost as inadequate as the end of *Of Time and the River*, and for essentially the same reasons. It is unprepared for and in its context even seems irrelevant. The revelation it produces seems artificially imposed and is not in the least convincing as the conclusion of all that has preceded it, much of which it in fact appears to contradict. One is therefore not surprised to learn that this scene was probably written much later than most of the last half of *The Web and the Rock*[7]—which dates from the period of *Of Time and the River*, before Wolfe himself had actually come to believe that you can't go home again. Of course, Wolfe did not intend his manuscript to be split in two here, so he can hardly be blamed for the inappropriateness of this scene

[7] Louis D. Rubin, Jr., says that Edward C. Aswell, the editor of Wolfe's posthumous manuscripts, has written to Rubin of his agreement that this scene must have been composed after the bulk of the last two novels (*Thomas Wolfe: The Weather of His Youth*, pp. 176-77). On Aswell's editorial decisions in respect to the ending of *The Web and the Rock*, see Kennedy, *Window of Memory*, p. 390.

to its final position, though as the novel stands it is nonetheless inappropriate. It is also ineffectual and unsatisfactory in itself, despite the fact that Wolfe regarded the whole episode of the October Fair as one of the most central in all his work. At one time, he even planned to use *The October Fair* as the title of the novel dealing with the period of his life covered by both *Of Time and the River* and *The Web and the Rock*.

It is not until the end of *You Can't Go Home Again* that, for the first time since *Look Homeward, Angel*, we have an effective climactic epiphany in one of Wolfe's novels. George, having returned to his beloved Germany as a famous author, is now on a train leaving it once more. At Aachen, the last stop before the border, he and the other travelers in his compartment are shocked to see that one of their fellow passengers—a nervous little man, whom George has privately called Fuss-and-Fidget—has been seized by the authorities. The rumor circulates that he is a Jew who has been caught trying to escape with all his money. As the terrified little man tries to persuade the officers to let him go, since there must be some misunderstanding, he is led past his former traveling companions, his eyes glancing at them for just a moment. But he does not betray them by showing in any way that he knows them, and they board the train, leaving him behind on the platform.

> And the little man . . . paused once from his feverish effort to explain. As the car in which he had been riding slid by, he lifted his pasty face and terror-stricken eyes, and for a moment his lips were stilled of their anxious pleading. He looked once, directly and steadfastly, at his former companions, and they at him. And in that gaze there was all the unmeasured weight of man's mortal anguish. George and the others felt somehow naked and ashamed, and somehow guilty. They all felt that they were saying farewell, not to a man, but to humanity; not to some pathetic stranger, some chance acquaintance of the voyage, but to mankind; not to some nameless cipher out of life, but to the fading image of a brother's face.
> The train swept out and gathered speed—and so they lost him. [*You Can't Go Home Again*, p. 699]

As so often before, Wolfe has used a scene envisioned from a train window to dramatize a symbolic isolation. But this time the person seen is not a complete stranger; he has had some sort of contact with George and the other passengers. Perhaps that is why their sense of union with him seems more real and of a more lasting nature than the union Wolfe's characters have thus far felt in similar situations. In the end, this isolated, helpless little man becomes an image less of solitude than of the unity of all mankind. He has achieved a bond—even an identity—with all men, but especially with the people in the train. He is not even aware of it, and it would be little comfort to him if he were. But it is apparently of the greatest importance to those who see him; and, paradoxically, he could never have attained this bond were he not isolated and manifestly doomed.

This episode is one of the best things Wolfe ever did. Its power relies not so much on the impassioned rhetoric so frequent in his work—though there is still some rhetoric, of the quieter sort—as on its relative calm, the frighteningly low key of its presentation. Even the discussion of the personal significance of this incident for George is treated concisely and with restraint. And the long letter to Foxhall Edwards that then closes the novel discussing some of the broader ramifications of this experience is also handled relatively well; though it follows the climax, it does not really seem anticlimactic. For we soon understand that this event does more than simply reveal to George the true nature of Nazi Germany or even teach him about humanity, though it does both these things; it goes much further and teaches him about himself, enables him to see himself with an objectivity he has never previously known. It thus prepares him for the evaluation of his entire life and career that he undertakes in the letter to Fox. When we begin to see the full significance of all he has learned, we realize that if this vision of a brother may be compared in effectiveness to Eugene's vision of Ben at the end of *Look Homeward, Angel*, it must be contrasted to it in theme. For instead of involving the recapture of the past, it centers on the future. As George's train takes him out of the Germany he has known and loved so well, he realizes all that he has lost : but "he knew also the priceless measure of his gain. For this was the way that henceforth would be forever closed to him—the way of no return. He was 'out.' And, being 'out,' he began to see another way, the way that lay before him. He saw now that you can't go home again—not ever. There was no road back. . . . And there came to him a vision of man's true home, beyond the ominous and cloud-engulfed horizon of the here and now, in the green and hopeful and still-virgin meadows of the future" (p. 704). The little man's capture has been for George a catalytic agent producing a violent reaction against much that he has taken for granted in the past—and, even more important, against his great emphasis upon that past itself. You can't go home again. This time the phrase is packed with meaning, and the rest of this chapter is devoted to an examination of its significance.

George's new discovery comes to him as a sudden shock despite the fact that he has already supposedly learned in a moment of revelation that "you can't go home again"; for the passage at the end of *The Web and the Rock* is a careless addition, as well as a late one. It is completely inconsistent with subsequent passages in *You Can't Go Home Again*, throughout which it is clear that George has yet to discover the truth of this phrase, though he occasionally comes close. Early in the novel, he is on a train heading toward Libya Hill, when he meets his old friend Nebraska Crane. They indulge in nostalgic reminiscences of their childhood, and George agrees with Nebraska's comment that "it don't seem no time, does it? It all comes back!" (p. 69). Yet shortly afterward, on the very same trip, he gets just the opposite feeling, when he meets Judge Rumford Bland, a figure of evil but also of a kind of dark wisdom. "And do you think," Bland asks him, "you can go home again?" (p. 83). George's hesitant, "almost frightened" affirmative response ("Why—why yes! Why—") makes it clear that he has not yet had the new awareness attributed to him at the end of *The Web and the Rock*, that he still has much to learn, but that he is already beginning to be uncomfortable. He realizes that Bland's question refers not merely to the physical act of returning to the town of Libya Hill, and he is beginning to suspect—and this thought represents no less than a revolution in Wolfe's ideas—that lost time cannot be recaptured and that, contrary to Nebraska's words, perhaps it really doesn't all come back.

Indeed, this discovery is the one that George finally makes at the end of the novel. It is then stated, moreover, not simply as an inevitable fact, but also as a moral principle: you *ought* not to recapture the past, you *must* not go home again. The attempt to do so is not merely futile; it is wrong. George's new belief essentially amounts to a rejection of the most important epiphanies in the novels—those involving Wolfe's personal memories. They are rejected because they place an inordinate emphasis upon the recollection of the past. I do not mean to imply that Wolfe rejects the past itself; that would be absurd and useless. Nor does he repudiate his "home" when he sadly realizes that he cannot go there again. Rather, he rejects the idea that you can or should relive the past, that it can entirely control your life and art. The recognition of necessity is not completely sad, however, and if he has in one sense lost the past he has in another gained the present and the future. Thus, in a letter sent to Margaret Roberts a few months before his death, Wolfe wrote that after some initial terror and despair, his new conviction came to seem "triumphantly *hopeful*" : ". . . it was like death almost, because it meant saying farewell to so many things, to so many ideas and images and hopes and illusions that we think we can't live without. But the point is, I have come through it now, and I am not desolate or lost. On the contrary, I am more full of faith and hope and courage than I have been in years" (*Letters*, p. 730).

With his courage came a realization that until then he had been afraid, so afraid that he had always been running away—away from the present and the future and toward the refuge of some dream world of what used to be. Wolfe had once written to Julian Meade of his emphatic conviction that "in no sense of the word" could writing be considered "an escape from reality"; in fact, it is "an attempt to approach and penetrate reality." As an example of what he meant, he cited *Ulysses*, with its "effort to apprehend and to make live again a moment in lost time" (pp. 321-22). But Joyce had been able to exercise strict control over this effort, while Wolfe, as he himself now saw, had made it almost his sole preoccupation. Consequently, he had so distorted its importance that it had become "an escape from reality" after all. The means of escape were the things that make up the mysterious entity of one's past. Wolfe described the essence of his new knowledge in a letter written a few months before his fatal illness to Edward C. Aswell, who adapted Wolfe's words for the bridge between the German episode of the little man and George's letter to Fox :

> . . . the whole book might almost be called "You Can't Go Home Again"—which means back home to one's family, back home to one's childhood, back home to the father one has lost, back home to romantic love, to a young man's dreams of glory and of fame, back home to exile, to escape to "Europe" and some foreign land,

back home to lyricism, singing just for singing's sake, back home to aestheticism, to one's youthful ideas of the "artist," and the all-sufficiency of "art and beauty and love," back home to the ivory tower, back home to places in the country, the cottage in Bermuda away from all the strife and conflict of the world, back home to the father one is looking for—to someone who can help one, save one, ease the burden for one, back home to the old forms and systems of things that once seemed everlasting, but that are changing all the time—back home to the escapes of Time and Memory. . . . But the conclusion is not sad : this is a hopeful book—the conclusion is that although you can't go home again, the home of every one of us is in the future : there is no other way.[8]

The "escapes of Time and Memory" comprehend all the others, and the radical nature of his departure from them, with all its personal, moral, and artistic implications, was not lost upon Wolfe —nor upon George, who admits to Edwards : "No man that I have known was ever more deeply rooted in the soil of Time and Memory . . . than was I" (*You Can't Go Home Again*, p. 739).

As Wolfe indicates in his letter to Aswell, the escapes of Time and Memory had taken many forms, and his repudiation of them meant repudiating a great many of the things that he had always loved. George begins to realize just how much it entails as soon as the epiphany of the little man has ended, for one of the major lessons of this experience is that he must say good-bye to his beloved Germany. The reason he must leave is not that he has to go home, but rather that he must *not* go "back home to exile, to escape to 'Europe' and some foreign land." Europe and not America, para-doxically, symbolizes to George his own past, for it is more like the world of his childhood than is modern, ever changing America. In this sense, the Wolfe hero has long felt more "at home" in Europe, where there has been less progress, where there is more conscious-ness and preservation of the past, and where that past is more easily recaptured. Thus, in *Of Time and the River*, following his recapture of "the America of twenty years ago" at Dijon, Eugene Gant rea-lizes that in this old French town he is "closer to his childhood and his father's life of power and magnificence than he could ever be again in savage new America" (pp. 898-99). It is interesting that

---

[8] Pp. 711-12. Cf. *You Can't Go Home Again*, p. 706.

Europe should specifically bring back his father; it does so, of course, because both are associated with his past. So when the Wolfe hero rejects his general emphasis on that past, he also gives up his quest for his spiritual father : George announces his new attitude in the very same letter in which he announces his decision to break with Edwards, who has been for him an immensely important father figure.

This abandonment of what Wolfe had once called "the deepest search in life" and the consequent break with Edwards imply that George has achieved a new sense of independence; but this independence does not in itself mean that he becomes even more self-centered than ever. On the contrary, his new attitude to a large degree involves, in the broadest sense of the phrase, social consciousness—that is, a consciousness of others besides and beyond himself. One can easily see how such a vision as that of the little man caught by the Nazis could lead to this result, and while still on the train after that episode, George reflects : "There was no road back. Ended now for him, with the sharp and clean finality of the closing of a door, was the time when his dark roots, like those of a pot-bound plant, could be left to feed upon their own substance and nourish their own little self-absorbed designs. Henceforth they must spread outward—away from the hidden, secret, and unfathomed past that holds man's spirit prisoner—outward, outward toward the rich and life-giving soil of a new freedom in the wide world of all humanity" (*You Can't Go Home Again*, p. 704).

This passage suggests that, had he lived, Wolfe might have tried in his subsequent works to tone down the stress on man's isolation and solitude that had so pervaded his previous novels, especially their epiphanies, and perhaps to increase the sense of the possibility of some sort of meeting with other people. In any case, the analogy between George's roots and those of a pot-bound plant feeding upon itself indicates the violence of his reversal in attitude, for, as we can see if we look once more at his confession to Fox, it seems to him that he had been "more deeply rooted in the soil of Time and Memory, the weather of his individual universe," than any other man he has ever known (p. 739). But despite an increased concern with present as opposed to past evils, Wolfe had no intention of writing reform tracts. Rather, in his art his social awareness took the form of a new determination to avoid concentrating on himself or his own past experiences, simply for their own sake; he had now come to regard this practice as just as dangerous as the art for art's sake aestheticism he had long despised. To him, the notion that you can't go home again is both a moral and an artistic concept.

It applies to art in two principal ways : in its essentially moral statement that you can't use art itself as an escape from reality; and, more important for its complete reversal of Wolfe's former views, in its essentially aesthetic statement that you can't create worthwhile art through the particular escapes of Time and Memory. In the latter respect, the end of *You Can't Go Home Again* effectually amounts to a substantial rejection of his reliance on his own recollected epiphanies, which till then had been one of the bases of his work. Wolfe is therefore unique among the novelists I am examining, in that he is the only one to react against the use of a major type of epiphany—in Wolfe's novels, indeed, the most important and prevalent type. His decision seems to arise from an increased understanding of his own peculiar tendencies and needs. He had already come to the realization that a novelist must be selective in his use of the past; perhaps because he has as yet been unable to put this realization into practice to his own satisfaction, he now suspects that one must not use the past at all, and his statements suggest a belief that the attempt to base one's art upon personal memories is *always* mistaken, even if carried out with the utmost selection and control : "He saw now that you can't go home again—not ever" (p. 704). He thus reacts against his former methods even more forcefully than reason might have dictated, though in his case such a fierce reaction is perhaps necessary. In the letter to Fox, George laughs at all the people who have spread rumors that he would never be able to start another novel. The ironic truth is that he has found it impossible to finish anything; his trouble, far from being an inability to begin, is an inability to stop recording all he remembers. His "huge inheritance" had become a "giant web" in which he had entrapped himself; in admitting this to Fox, George repeats the phrases that had become so familiar in Wolfe's novels : "forgotten memories exhumed . . . until I lived them in my dreams," "nothing that had ever been was lost," "I lived again through all times and weathers I had known," "the forgotten moments and unnumbered hours came back" (p. 740). But though this language has appeared before, and despite George's obvious relish in reverting to it, there is now an unshrinking recognition that his "torrential recollectiveness" has been a burden, has brought about a distorted attitude toward life and art, and has produced a "million-fibered integument" which has bound him to the past and therefore stifled his creativity.

Wolfe's statements are not specific enough for us to be able to tell the extent to which he consciously intended his new position as a criticism of all that he himself had so far written, but it is natural that his readers look at that position in terms of the light it sheds upon Wolfe's accomplishments. One's attitude toward it necessarily involves an evaluation of Wolfe's entire career. In so far as one regards the view taken at the end of *You Can't Go Home Again* as valid, then so much lower must his estimate be of all of Wolfe's novels, for the new view rejects their very basis : the assumption that you can return to the past. But it is not a perfectly simple matter to judge the validity of Wolfe's notion that he had been wrong to try to go home again, for, though his memory produced some of the most glaring of his artistic defects, it often contributed much of the value and uniqueness his novels do have. It was at times his strength and at times his weakness.

One critic who believes that Wolfe would have been correct to discard his own past as a subject for fiction is Louis D. Rubin, Jr. Yet at the same time Rubin is convinced that at its strongest Wolfe's memory did produce his most powerful work, and that, because Wolfe's recollections of his childhood were his clearest and sharpest, and because the lapse of many years yielded a degree of perspective, *Look Homeward, Angel* is his greatest novel; when he begins to record his adult experiences his books "exhibit a sharp decline in the quality of the recall" (*Thomas Wolfe*, p. 53). Rubin's position boils down to a disagreement with Wolfe's phrase, "you can't go home again." Like the early Wolfe he admires most, Rubin seems to believe that you *can* go home again, though only to a limited extent and, perhaps, to certain periods of one's life; and Wolfe, so to speak, used up all his homecomings in *Look Homeward, Angel* and a few other accounts of his childhood. In other words, Rubin seems to say that you can go home only so many times. Wolfe, on the other hand, finally goes so far as to say that once you have left it you can *never* go back : "you can't go home again—not ever." Look to the future; there is no other way.

There is much to be said for Rubin's view as he presents it, but I think that in this instance it was Wolfe himself who recognized his problems most acutely. His main difficulty was not that he was too infrequently able to utilize his past, but that he was too exclusively concerned with it. He had allowed his obsession with his memory and its epiphanies to take over and run free, and they had thus impaired even his best work. Rubin feels that it was the poor quality of the memories in them that ruined the last three novels; but in fact those memories were in quality so intense that they could not be suppressed : the stronger Wolfe's recall, the weaker the art. The superiority of *Look Homeward, Angel* by no means shows that Wolfe was at his best when he gave his memory the freest play; on the contrary, it shows that he was at his best when he exerted the most restraint over it. Of all his novels *Look Homeward, Angel* is the one that least displays the defects of too much use of personal memories; shorter than his later books, it nevertheless covers the longest period of time, deals fully with the largest number of characters, and is thereby most selective in the choice of incidents that were powerful enough to be included.

Actually, it is doubtful whether Wolfe ever would or could have given up recapturing the past in autobiographical fiction; and it is at least questionable whether his future work would have been better if he had. One suspects he would have discovered that, like Orpheus, he had to look back whatever the cost. And if in the end Wolfe had found himself unable to write effectively about anything but the memorable moments out of his own past, regardless of all the dangers they entailed, he surely would have gone back to them with little hesitation—he was never one to be entrapped by a consistency, especially a foolish one. But his growing awareness of the dangers inherent in his use of such moments might have led him at last beyond a mere lip-service recognition of the need to control Time and Memory rather than to continue to let his art be controlled by them. He might have come to treat them as tools, not escapes— to create the great novel he never wrote, but which he had it in him to write.

6

William Faulkner: A Flash, a Glare

> And so maybe if you could go to someone, the stranger
> the better, and give them something—a scrap of paper—
> something, anything, it not to mean anything in itself . . .
> it would be at least a scratch, something, something that
> might make a mark on something that *was* once for the
> reason that it can die someday, while the block of stone
> cant be *is* because it never can become *was* because it
> cant ever die or perish. . . .
>
> *Absalom, Absalom!*, pp. 127-28

Evanescent trivia make their indelible mark on the lives of people in all the novels of William Faulkner, from the earliest to the last. Yet only a few of his books—*The Sound and the Fury, Light in August*, and *Absalom, Absalom!*—rely as heavily on epiphanies as do the works of Joyce, Virginia Woolf, or Thomas Wolfe. That these three are Faulkner's novels which most utilize epiphany is not simply a matter of chance, for they are similar in a number of relevant ways. For one thing, they are probably his greatest achievements, though I would be reluctant to argue that there is a necessary correlation between that fact and their use of epiphany. They do, however, share a number of other significant characteristics, and in his other novels as well there seems to be a general ratio between the presence of one or more of these traits and the importance and frequency of sudden moments of revelation.

Most noticeably, perhaps, the narratives of these three novels use what we might call disrupted chronology. Each begins at a specific present time and then goes back to the events leading up to that present and evokes the past in many ways, but particularly by means of epiphany, which Faulkner repeatedly uses as a structural device to introduce a flashback—either through a present epiphany in which a character recalls or recaptures the past, or by relating a past epiphany which has remained in a character's memory. Thus

—as in so many novels making significant use of sudden moments of illumination—the order in which events are presented to the reader is not a chronological and historical one, but a visionary and psychological one.

Perhaps even more important, however, is the fact that, unlike a number of Faulkner's other principal characters, most of those in *The Sound and the Fury, Light in August,* and *Absalom, Absalom!* are people who for one reason or another are capable of experiencing unique moments of intensity. Naturally, novelists like Dostoyevsky, Joyce, Mrs. Woolf, Proust, and Wolfe also give epiphanies only to those characters whom the reader can credibly accept as sensitive enough—or Romantic or irrational enough—to experience them, but for the most part these are the only people with whom those writers concern themselves. At least in this respect, Faulkner's range of characterization is much wider. Of all the people who appear in *The Hamlet,* for example, perhaps only two or three seem capable of ever experiencing a true sudden spiritual manifestation; anyway, no one ever does. In William Faulkner's world, indeed, more than in that of any other novelist of whom I am aware, a character must meet certain curious qualifications if he is to have true moments of illumination; a degree of sensibility is not the only requisite. In *The Sound and the Fury,* Jason Compson's inability to undergo instantaneous revelations also results from his overly rationalistic view of experience—and, especially, from his peculiarly distorted attitude toward time and space.

For it would seem that in order to experience epiphanies in Faulkner's world one must, above all, have some sort of orientation toward the past; although one may try to escape from it, like Thomas Sutpen, or perhaps even transcend it, like Dilsey, he cannot simply ignore it, like Jason. Usually, a Faulkner character will either live in the past, as Benjy Compson and Gail Hightower do, or in some other way be passionately concerned with it and the passage of time : characters like Bayard Sartoris, Quentin Compson, Joe Christmas, Rosa Coldfield, Harry Wilbourne, and Ike McCaslin live in the element of time rather than—almost as opposed to—that of space. On the other hand, those who seem to live primarily in space cannot experience any epiphanies involving the past, and perhaps none at all : Jason, constantly and frantically in motion; the wasted young wanderers of *Pylon;* all the Bundrens except Darl and Addie; above all Lena Grove, who combines a consciousness almost solely in the realm of space with what seems a complete incapacity for illumination.

In no other Faulkner novel is the relationship of the characters toward time more structurally and thematically evident than in *The Sound and the Fury.* Benjy is completely unaware of the passage of time, and at certain moments the past is just as real to him as the present, or more so. Because Quentin is fully aware, his absorption in the past is much more tormenting than Benjy's, so he vainly tries to freeze it and yet escape from it by fleeing from time itself. In contrast, Jason's distortion of time involves an indifference to the past, of which he is indeed almost oblivious. Dilsey has the most transcendental view, including as it does a vision of "the first and the last."

The very form of the first section of *The Sound and the Fury* depends on the fact that Benjy cannot distinguish between the past and the present—that to him, in effect, all time is contemporaneous. "To that idiot," Faulkner has been quoted as saying, "time was not a continuation, it was an instant, there was no yesterday and no tomorrow, it all is this moment, it all is [now] to him" (*Faulkner at Nagano,* p. 106). I have already discussed, in my second chapter, the importance in modern literature of the Augustinian concept of the psychological coexistence of past, present, and future. In passages like the Nighttown episode of *Ulysses,* or in all of *Finnegans Wake,* this notion becomes especially prominent, for such works stress phases of the mind which are normally unconscious, and in which time therefore ceases to seem relevant : in his study, *The Unconscious,* Freud writes that the processes of the unconscious system "are *timeless*; i.e. they are not ordered temporally, are not altered by the passage of time; they have no reference to time at all" (p. 187).

Benjy lives largely or entirely on the unconscious level of experience, completely incapable of temporal order. But he is capable at any moment of total recall, for memory may operate even in the unconscious—better, it may be, than on the conscious level, where time interferes with it. "Memory believes," Faulkner points out elsewhere, "before knowing remembers" (*Light in August,* p. 111). I use the term "memory" to describe Benjy's faculty because it is the only term we have; but he clearly does far more—or, from the intellectual point of view, far less—than recall things : he revives them. He is an idiot, but his ability to recapture lost events is much profounder than that of any normal or sane person. The effect on him of the resurrection of the past is so strong that he is unable to make the slightest distinction between it and present reality. Indeed, even Proust's Marcel cannot put the past on so absolute a par with the present. The experiences of both men in recreating past time are similar, but Marcel's intelligence keeps him aware of what is happening to him, while it never occurs to poor Benjy that he is not actually living through the events and feelings he recaptures with all of his extremely acute senses.

But although all periods of time are equally "present" to Benjy, they are not all equally important to him. It has become a critical commonplace to say that Benjy's mind switches without control from scene to scene. Nevertheless, this section of the novel is very selective, and it presents only a few scenes—which keep coming back—out of the many that have made up Benjy's thirty-three years. Clearly, therefore, there are some criteria behind the selection of the various stimuli Benjy feels, and thus behind the choice of the events he will recapture. Benjy is selective, so to speak, despite his being incapable of any conscious criteria of selection; the criteria are artistic, and they are not his but Faulkner's. Though told by an idiot, the incidents relived by Benjy must not seem to signify nothing—except to him. Their meanings cannot exist for him, but only for the reader through him. The past may manifest itself and cause Benjy to feel *emotion*, but its *significance* can be demonstrated only to us—and in that significance, however ambiguous it may finally seem, lies the artistic justification for presenting each of the past incidents.

Structurally, Benjy's recaptures of the past convey vital information and impressions in brief but illuminating snatches. Usually these flashbacks arise from an object, sensation, or word suggesting a clearly identifiable association between two scenes. Water, for example, is a very frequent associative image, one especially connected with Caddy. When at one point in present time (April 7, 1928) Benjy is told by Luster to sit in the water, he does so and is instantaneously brought back thirty years to the day of Damuddy's death, when Caddy squatted in the water, got her dress wet, and muddied her drawers—producing an image which runs through this and the next section. Later, for example, Caddy climbs up a tree to look into the house and see what the family is doing, as the children below watch "the muddy bottom of her drawers" (*The Sound and the Fury and I As Lay Dying*, p. 58). Faulkner has said that all his books originate in "a moment in experience—a thought—an incident—that's there," and that what he then does is to go back to that moment and lead his people up to it, and then work away from it and see how they act after it; he has also said that the origin of *The Sound and the Fury* was this image of the muddy bottom of a little girl's drawers seen in a tree by her brothers below, an image which he soon realized could become a symbol of "the lost Caddy."[1]

In Quentin's narrative, too, images of wetness and mud are constantly associated with Caddy and cause him as well as Benjy to recapture the past he had lived through with her. During the present (June 2, 1910, in this section) Quentin and the little girl he calls "sister" are walking by the river in Cambridge, when he feels "the sense of water mute and unseen." Abruptly he goes back to a rainy day in Mississippi when he ineptly tried to seduce a girl named Natalie, whom Caddy had pushed into some mud, thus enabling Quentin to associate her with his sister during his crude sexual overtures. He tried to brush off Natalie's dress with his hands, but she angrily—and perhaps even virtuously—repulsed him and walked off; alone, Quentin let himself wallow in the mud. "Hear them in swimming sister?" he asks the little girl back in the present. "I wouldn't mind doing that myself" (*The Sound and the Fury*, p. 155). But he immediately returns to the same day in the past, when shortly after the scene with Natalie he smeared Caddy herself with mud. Quentin, in this way, continually goes back and forth between present and past. Later, with Shreve, Gerald, and Mrs. Bland, he seems to lose all contact whatsoever with his actual surroundings as

---

[1] Cynthia Grenier, "The Art of Fiction: An Interview with William Faulkner—September, 1955," *Accent* 16 (Summer 1956):171; *Faulkner in the University*, p. 31. Faulkner is quoted as saying much the same thing about this image elsewhere: see Stein, "Faulkner," p. 130, and the "unpublished autobiographical piece" quoted in Michael Millgate, *The Achievement of William Faulkner*, p. 34.

And in *Faulkner at West Point*, p. 109, Faulkner cites this scene as an example of the artist's attempt "to condense all experiences onto the head of the pin." Cf. Malcolm Cowley, *The Faulkner-Cowley File*, p. 112, where Faulkner is quoted as saying that his ambition "is to put everything into one sentence—not only the present but the whole past on which it depends and which keeps overtaking the present, second by second."

he suddenly recaptures another incident that had taken place in the rain, when he found Caddy sitting in a brook after she had been making love with Dalton Ames—"she was lying in the water her head on the sand spit the water flowing about her hips there was a little more light in the water her skirt half saturated flopped along her flanks to the waters motion" :

> poor Quentin
> she leaned back on her arms her hands locked about her knees
> youve never done that have you
> what done what
> that what I have what I did
> yes yes lots of times with lots of girls
> then I was crying her hand touched me again and I was crying against her damp blouse then she lying on her back looking past my head into the sky I could see a rim of white under her irises I opened my knife
> do you remember the day damuddy died when you sat down in the water in your drawers
> yes
> I held the point of the knife at her throat. . . .
> Caddy do you remember how Dilsey fussed at you because your drawers were muddy
> dont cry
> Im not crying Caddy [Pp. 168, 170-71]

For partially obscure but powerful reasons, Quentin is no more able to rid himself of that strangely symbolic moment when Caddy had muddied her drawers than is Benjy.

There are a number of other similarities between Benjy's and Quentin's recaptures of the past. In particular, they serve essentially the same thematic and structural purposes, though these are inevitably modified in Quentin's less illogical narrative. For the sake of clarity, the sudden temporal shifts of both brothers are introduced by italics. Faulkner has explained that he uses this method to indicate that Benjy and Quentin have "no sense of time"; the device is less important here than "in Benjy's part, because Quentin was only half way between Benjy and Jason. Jason didn't need italics because he was quite sane" (*Faulkner in the University*, pp. 94-95).

Quentin's identification of the past with the present can never be so absolute as Benjy's; though it is true that he occasionally seems unaware of the actual present, as during his fight with Bland (as

Sartre points out, "Quentin is not even conscious of having insulted Bland, for he is reliving his quarrel with Dalton Ames" ["Time in Faulkner," p. 228]), it is also true that afterward he can realize what has happened to him. His consciousness thus provides new developments impossible in the artistic presentation of Benjy. Quentin is tormented by the duality of his condition: able to re-capture the past—in his case, actually unable and unwilling to rid himself of it—he is nevertheless intellectually aware of the fact that it is gone forever. Epiphanies in which it is momentarily brought to life again are not enough; and indeed one of the major reasons for Quentin's suicide is his dread that as time passes he will be less concerned about what his sister has done, less able to live in the past in which her sin seemed agonizing, important, even tragic. So he tries to contemplate "an apotheosis in which a temporary state of mind will become symmetrical above the flesh and aware both of itself and of the flesh it will not quite discard" (*The Sound and the Fury*, pp. 195-96). Throughout the day he attempts to escape from or prevent the inevitable passage of time and thereby prevent the past from disappearing. It is in vain that Mr. Compson has urged him not to fight time, not to waste his life by trying to hold on to the past or deny the present. That is exactly what Quentin does try to do, and of course he fails. Pathetically, he twists the hands off the watch; but time ticks on. So his only remaining choice seems to be to commit suicide, and his father proves to have been right: "One day you'd think misfortune would get tired, but then time is your misfortune" (p. 123).

In precisely the opposite way, it is also Jason's. Instead of stress-ing the past, which means nothing to him, Jason completely ignores it, never recapturing or even vividly remembering it. He is con-cerned only with the present and the future. "Whether or not she was in school today is already past," he tells his mother in a typical remark; "If you've got to worry about it, worry about next Mon-day" (p. 277). Thus Jason, no less than Quentin, distorts time—and is almost as frustrated by it. If it does not drive him to suicide too, it does make him nearly distraught. He never has enough of it: when his boss asks him if a telegram has been bad news, Jason tells him to find out in the telegraph office. "They'll have time to tell you. I haven't" (p. 252). Actually, he never does have the time to do all he tries to do; throughout the third section and much of the fourth he hurries from one place to another. Constantly on the

move, he lives primarily in the realm of space. It is in this fact that
we see one of the major reasons why the passages of the novel centering on Jason contain no epiphanies : he literally does not stay still
long enough to become fully aware of what is going on around him.
A number of other Faulkner characters share this trait, which is
related to a general tendency in his treatment of time and space
and their relationship to illumination that is worth a short digres-
sion here.

Many critics have noticed the great importance in Faulkner's
work of static images, scenes that seem frozen in time; Karl E. Zink
calls them *"tableaux vivants"* and makes clear their relevance to
epiphany, though he does not use that term : "The *tableau vivant*
is an image of stasis which betrays the desire to cherish memorable
experiences and, especially, to understand their significance. As a
narrative technique, the *tableau vivant* is a means of dramatizing
or heightening the significance of an event. . . . It is a moment of
insight into true meaning."[2] Yet I have come across no discussion
of the fact that Faulkner's *observers* are usually static at the
moment of insight, whether the scene perceived be frozen or not.
His characters are rarely able to undergo such an illumination as
long as they are moving in space, and he frequently seems to
associate motion with obliviousness, and stasis with sensitivity, or at
least with awareness.

An illustration of his treatment of this association is a scene that
occurs twice in *Sanctuary*, once from the viewpoint of a stationary
person and once from the viewpoint of two people in a fast-moving
car. In the first, we see Ruby's reaction as she stands by the road
and Temple and Popeye ride swiftly by; she is quiet but sentient,
and without knowing about Tommy's murder she perceives something is wrong and reflects that Temple's face is "like a small, dead-
colored mask drawn past her on a string and then away." In contrast, we later read that the two occupants of the speeding car see
nothing, do not even notice that Ruby is there :

. . . she looked at them quietly from beneath the faded sun-

[2] "Flux and the Frozen Moment: The Imagery of Stasis in Faulkner's
Prose," *PMLA* 71 (June 1956):299. For comments on the significance of
stasis and motion in Faulkner that in key ways run contrary to mine, see
Richard P. Adams, *Faulkner: Myth and Motion*, for example, pp. 11-13
and, especially, pp. 110-11.

bonnet, flicking swiftly in and out of Temple's vision without any motion, any sign.

When they reached the tree Popeye swung the car out of the road and drove it crashing into the undergrowth and through the prone tree-top and back into the road again in a running popping of cane-stalks like musketry along a trench, without any diminution of speed. Beside the tree Gowan's car lay on its side. Temple looked vaguely and stupidly at it as it too shot behind.

Popeye swung back into the sandy ruts. . . . Temple gazed dully forward as the road she had traversed yesterday began to flee backward under the wheels as onto a spool. . . . [Pp. 123, 162-63]

We frequently see the same sort of distinction made in regard to epiphanies. All of Ike McCaslin's, for instance, occur while he is static, as in "The Old People" when—in the still virgin Eden of the big woods—he has his vision of the old buck, and Sam Fathers raises his arm and says "Oleh, Chief . . . Grandfather" (*Go Down Moses,* p. 184). Elsewhere, we find out that at this moment Ike has "ceased to be a child"; that statement is made in "The Bear," when he has another, very similar moment of vision. Again he is not moving— with very good reason, for he has come across a snake : "he froze, immobile, one foot just taking his weight, the toe of the other just lifted behind him, not breathing. . . ." The snake—the serpent in the garden—is both compared and contrasted to the buck. It too is "the old one," but it is is also "the ancient and accursed about the earth, fatal and solitary . . . evocative of all knowledge and an old weariness and of pariah-hood and of death." Ike seems to have a vision of the same wild, natural force he had once seen in the form of the buck : apparently he now sees its malevolent, deathly side, rather than its benevolent, paternal one. Nevertheless, it is the same force, and so Ike repeats "without premeditation" Sam's old words, in the old tongue : " 'Chief,' he said : 'Grandfather.' " The negative, almost despairing note suggested in this scene is continued in the next, which ends "The Bear" with Ike serving as a strong contrast to both the chaos of the squirrels in the tree and Boon's wild and frantic movement as he shouts, "Dont touch them! Dont touch a one of them! They're mine!" (pp. 329-31).

In a number of ways this scene is extremely ambiguous, and whether it reveals anything to Ike is not clear, but for the reader it does at least serve as a symbolic manifestation of the theme of greed and possessiveness that pervades "The Bear," and in fact all of *Go Down, Moses*. In any case, not until Ike is in his eighties, in "Delta Autumn," does he fully realize why he has always hated possessions, especially the idea of owning land. Once more the moment of illumination occurs while he is motionless, this time lying on his bunk : "Then suddenly he knew why he had never wanted to own any of it, arrest at least that much of what people called progress. . . . He seemed to see the two of them—himself and the wilderness—as coevals . . . the two spans running out together, not toward oblivion, nothingness, but into a dimension free of both time and space . . ." (p. 354).

The passages describing Ike's epiphanies are not the only ones in *Go Down, Moses* to show an association between vision and stasis. In "Pantaloon in Black," Rider sees his dead wife Mannie only as long as he stays absolutely still; when he moves, she fades away. The same association is made in Faulkner's other works. Hightower sits at his window as he waits for the galloping horses. At one point in *Absalom, Absalom!* Rosa Coldfield must—even in the midst of motion—"stop dead" before she can realize the full impact of Clytie's trivial yet immensely significant act of touching her (p. 139). In *A Fable*, too, it is not enough for General Gragnon to be "immobile and calm in the moving car"; in order for him to experience his epiphany he must become for a moment completely still :

> So at first he did not realise what had startled, shocked him. He said sharply : 'Stop' and sat in the halted car in the ringing silence which he hadn't even heard yet because he had never heard anything here before but guns : no longer a starred, solitary man in a staff car behind a French battle-front, but a solitary boy lying on his stomach on a stone wall outside the Pyrenean village where, for all any records stated or knowledge remembered, he had been born an orphan; listening now to the same cicada chirring and buzzing in a tangle of cordite-blasted weeds beyond the escarpment landmarked since last winter by the skeleton tail of a crashed German aeroplane. Then he heard the lark too, high and invisible, almost liquid but not quite, like four small gold coins dropped without haste into a cup of soft silver, he and the driver staring at each other until he said, loud and harsh : 'Drive on !' . . . [Pp. 36-37]

This passage is an epiphany not only because Gragnon recaptures his past, but also because the incongruity of the sounds of a cicada and lark amid the devastation of war recall the world as it used to be and will someday be again. It recaptures not so much the world of Gragnon's youth as the world of peace.[3]

In *The Sound and the Fury*, another source of Jason's inability to experience any sudden spiritual illumination, besides his lack of interest in the past and his constant, furious movement, is his cold, rational way of looking at life in general and things in particular. As we have seen, epiphany is largely Romantic, intuitive, and irrational, perhaps even antirational—all of which are qualities important in Faulkner's general attitude toward experience. His most sympathetic characters all act as if they agree with McCaslin Edmonds and Ike that it is in the heart and not the head that we must find truth, that *"what the heart holds to becomes truth, as far as we know truth"* (*Go Down, Moses*, p. 297; cf. p. 260). Jason, however, is "logical rational contained . . . thinking nothing whatever of God one way or the other." He fears and respects only Dilsey, who has "divined" that he has been blackmailing Caddy—not discovered or suspected it, as if by logical deduction, but *divined* it "by simple clairvoyance" (*The Sound and the Fury*, p. 16). Certainly that quality of hers is one of the chief reasons for the fact that, though he is incapable of appreciating her, he knows enough to fear her. She is everything he is not; possessing what Quentin calls "white facts" (p. 189), and thus by his own standards knowing a great deal more than she, he actually understands much less.

Early in the novel, therefore, when Caddy wants to know, "When is the Lawd's own time, Dilsey" (p. 44), she clearly asks the right person. Dilsey is the only major character who does not distort time. Unlike the Compsons, she does not ignore or overemphasize either the past or the present, but accepts both of them for what they are. More than ever, this is so after the sermon by the preacher from St. Louis, during which, sitting absolutely still, she has the most encompassing revelation in *The Sound and the Fury*:

Dilsey sat bolt upright . . . crying rigidly and quietly in the

---

[3] In a curious parallel to this scene, young William Faulkner had quoted, thirty-four years earlier in 1920, some lines from a poem by W. A. Percy about hearing the "mystical and calm" song of "a simple bird/Alone, among dead trees" (*Early Prose and Poetry*, p. 72).

annealment and the blood of the remembered Lamb.

As they walked through the bright noon, up the sandy road with the dispersing congregation talking easily again group to group, she continued to weep, unmindful of the talk. . . .

"I've seed de first en de last," Dilsey said. . . .

"First en last whut?" Frony said.

"Never you mind," Dilsey said. "I seed de beginnin, en now I sees de endin." [P. 313]

Providing not so much an epiphany, perhaps, as a semimystical moment of enlightenment, the preacher's words give her a vision of the eternal God himself, the first and the last, the beginning and the ending, Alpha and Omega.

Readers of Faulkner's earlier novels must have felt unprepared for his huge leap forward in *The Sound and the Fury*. Little in his previous work could have led them to expect such boldness in attempt or such success in achievement; his new experiments with epiphany were only one example of his departures from traditional form and technique. Yet, with the twenty-twenty vision of hindsight, we can see that the few epiphanies which did appear in his early work were precisely the kind stressed in *The Sound and the Fury* : those that involve the recollection or recapture of the past.

For example, in "Home," one of the more baroque and sentimental of the New Orleans "Sketches," Faulkner describes how Jean-Baptiste, a stranger in the city, waits for accomplices who plan to take advantage of his knowledge of explosives in connection with some sort of crime. He is uneasy, for he does not really like the idea and is uncertain about what to do, when suddenly he hears a man begin to play a musical saw. "Jean-Baptiste paused, stricken, and about him rose the land he called his. . . . He saw the cottage where he was born, and ate and slept, sharp in the sun; he saw the wheeling candle light soft in a golden dusk beneath a single star like a yellow rose. He saw all this and knew that he had pursued a phantom into a far land. . . ." He makes his decision and leaves without keeping his appointment, while in the last words of the sketch we read, with some embarrassment, that the sky is "rumorous with dawn, a new day" (*New Orleans Sketches*, p. 79). In its own way, the snatch of music from a carpenter's saw and a violin bow has the same effect on Jean-Baptiste that the artistically sophisticated phrase from Vinteuil's sonata has on Swann : it provides a vision of the past and a revelation of the future.

G

In Faulkner's first novel, *Soldiers' Pay*, the nearest thing to an epiphany occurs when Donald Mahon, now able to remember almost nothing, nevertheless relives the moment when his plane crashed, "the one trophy he had reft from Time and Space" (p. 293). And the only evident sudden revelation in *Mosquitoes*—the scene where David feels as if "he had been in a dark room and all of a sudden the lights had come on : simple, like that"—is also associated with a similar experience in his past (p. 162).

In *Sartoris*, the past incident is once again a plane crash, this time the one that killed John Sartoris. It lives on in the mind of his brother Bayard, who "relived it again as you might run over a printed, oft-read tale, trying to remember, feel, a bullet going into his own body or head that might have slain him at the same instant" (p. 321). Earlier, he has had another epiphany, in which "for an instant" he sees before him "the recent months of his life coldly in all their headlong and heedless wastefulness," bringing to the surface for perhaps the first time his irrational but overwhelming sense of guilt for John's death (p. 311). Despite its epiphanies, however, the main interest of *Sartoris*, for my purposes, lies in the fact that it is the first of Faulkner's novels to focus the attention of the characters, as well as of the novel itself, on the relationship between past and present. The past important here is partially that of the South itself and of Southern Tradition as represented by the Sartoris family, but it is also that of the chief characters, who constantly reflect upon their own histories through both vivid memories and—in the case of young Bayard and Miss Jenny—Romantic imagination. Their general sense of the past and of its persistence in the present appears in all of Faulkner's later work, but especially in *The Sound and the Fury, Light in August, Absalom, Absalom!, Go Down, Moses*, and *Requiem for a Nun*, where Gavin Stevens speaks for many of Faulkner's characters when he says that "the past is never dead. It's not even past" (p. 92).

In Gavin, the realization of this fact is both a recognition of necessity and part of a healthy fascination or even enchantment with the past; but for other citizens of Jefferson this fascination can become a deadening obsession. In *Light in August*, it is just such an obsession that makes Gail Hightower decide to come to live in Jefferson, where during the Civil War his grandfather had ridden

in the raid that was so to distort the life of the grandson who had
not even been born yet. Hightower's preoccupation with the past—
to men like him, "this world is peopled principally by the dead"
(p. 459)—is directly related to his sensitivity to present moments of
intense illumination. As always in Faulkner, we can see in this novel
a general connection between the relationship of each character
toward time and space and whether or not he is sensitive enough to
experience epiphanies.

Like Joanna Burden, who also lives completely taken up with
time, Hightower is spatially immobile and sedentary. The elemental
but dense Lena Grove, on the other hand, lives in space, in slow but
constant movement; having come all the way from Alabama to
Mississippi at the beginning of the novel, by the end she finds herself already in Tennessee, not so much seeking Brown as "just
travelling" (p. 480). In these terms, her apparently imminent union
with Byron becomes a sort of Faulknerian metaphysical marriage,
and the last chapter a sort of Prophetic Book, for the sensitive Byron
lives his life very much in the realm of time. The contrast between
him and Lena is brought out during their first conversation, when
she cannot understand why he is so concerned with checking his
watch to see how long he is resting from his work. "A few minutes
wouldn't make no difference, would it?" she asks; " 'I reckon I
aint paid for setting down,' he says. 'So you come from Alabama' "
(p. 47). The major effect of their contact is to introduce Chaos into
Byron's previously placid and Beulah-like life, while Lena serenely
continues to seek his opposite, Brown. Even more insensitive than
Lena, Brown is like her a wanderer—though his movement is more
rapid and desperate—and he, too, has no concept of time : "How
do I know what time it was? Do you expect a man doing the work
of a nigger slave at a sawmill to be rich enough to own a watch?"
(p. 89).

In contrast, one of Christmas' first purchases with money of his
own from the sale of his heifer had been a watch, an act perhaps to
be expected of anyone so time-conscious as he. Even during his
flight after killing Joanna, when he feels that for the first time in
his life he is altogether outside of time, he is more concerned with
finding out the day of the week than with getting food. It is true
that Christmas is also a wanderer, "doomed with motion" (p. 213),
but to some extent his movement is deceptive, and Faulkner seems
to go to great lengths to give the impression that Christmas really

lives more in time than in space. We are told, for example, that from the night of the argument with McEachern and the beating by Bobbie's friends, "the thousand streets ran as one street"—and that street is measured not spatially but temporally, as "the street which was to run for fifteen years" (p. 210). Moreover, at the end of those fifteen years Christmas realizes that despite his travels the street "had made a circle and he is still inside of it" (p. 321). Except perhaps for Hightower, no one in the novel is so identified with time. No one, certainly, is given more epiphanies; like Hightower's, his frequently involve the past, and a number of them also serve to introduce flashbacks. The flashbacks really form the structural basis of *Light in August*, as they do in some of the other novels as well. In Faulkner, epiphanies—especially those that recall the past— serve not only to provide revelations for characters, but often also introduce vital scenes from their background or in some way supply the reader with important information about it, and even serve as a device to usher in lengthy episodes or narratives. But though the recapture of the past and the flashback are frequently used to- gether, they are of course not identical and may also appear in- dependently.

One of the most effective and revealing of Christmas' epiphanies, for instance, is one that takes him back to a period of his life which Faulkner has already described to us, and therefore it does not lead into a flashback. It does, however, serve another essential artistic function by relating some of the chief strains of the novel to one another. Christmas has slipped through Joanna's kitchen window for the first time; Faulkner wonders whether Christmas remembers how he used to sneak through the window of McEachern's house, but guesses that "very likely" he does not. Once in the kitchen, Christmas finds in the darkness some food, almost as if he knew beforehand it would be there :

> He ate something from an invisible dish, with invisible fingers : invisible food. He did not care what it would be. He did not know that he had even wondered or tasted until his jaw stopped suddenly in midchewing and thinking fled for twentyfive years back down the street . . . *I'll know it in a minute. I have eaten it before, somewhere. In a minute I will* memory clicking know- ing *I see I see I more than see hear I hear I see my head bent I hear the monotonous dogmatic voice which I believe will never cease going on and on forever and peeping I see the indomitable*

bullet head the clean blunt beard they too bent and I thinking
How can he be so nothungry and I smelling my mouth and
tongue weeping the hot salt of waiting my eyes tasting the hot
steam from the dish "It's peas," he said, aloud. "For sweet Jesus.
Field peas cooked with molasses." [Pp. 216-17]

A comparison of this scene with Proust's madeleine experience
could easily tempt one into a discussion of the wonders of the human
mind, which can enable a semitramp eating field peas in a rundown
kitchen in Mississippi to undergo a sensation identical with one felt
by Marcel in his mother's elegant Parisian home as he takes a cup
of tea. As a matter of fact, Christmas' sensation is in a very real way
the purer one, for at first he does not even know what he is eating
and his impression relies solely on his senses of taste and smell. And
though in this case the epiphany is not one that makes possible the
entire novel, as Marcel's does, it does illuminate one of the central
threads of the story, for it provides still another association between
Joanna and Christmas' life with the McEacherns. Later, this
association becomes especially significant when she, too, demands
that he kneel and pray, a demand that eventually drives him to kill
her, as he has probably already killed McEachern.

Not all of Christmas' epiphanies concentrate on the past, however,
and perhaps the most central of all is the one in which—having
exchanged shoes with a Negro woman in order to throw blood-
hounds off his trail—he finally feels himself irrevocably entrapped
by his blackness, "bearing now upon his ankles the definite and
ineradicable gauge of its upward moving" (p. 313). The power of
blackness is also important in the passage describing Christmas'
death, which provides for those who witness it the most apocalyptic
revelation in the novel :

For a long moment he looked up at them with peaceful and unfathomable and unbearable eyes. Then his face, body, all,
seemed to collapse, to fall in upon itself, and from out the
slashed garments about his hips and loins the pent black blood
seemed to rush like a released breath. It seemed to rush out of
his pale body like the rush of sparks from a rising rocket; upon
that black blast the man seemed to rise soaring into their
memories forever and ever. They are not to lose it, in whatever
peaceful valleys, beside whatever placid and reassuring streams
of old age, in the mirroring faces of whatever children they will

contemplate old disasters and newer hopes. It will be there, musing, quiet, steadfast, not fading and not particularly threatful, but of itself alone serene, of itself alone triumphant. [Pp. 439-40]

The man they are never to lose is partly a representation of Christ, and of their guilt and apparent redemption through him, and yet partly of the guilt which is theirs eternally and cannot be absolved, the "curse of the white race" of which Joanna's father had told her —the curse of "the black shadow in the shape of a cross" (pp. 239-40).

Hightower, too, occasionally has moments of vision that center on the present or the future—even while he may be sitting and waiting for his grandfather and the galloping horses. One such moment provides him with a manifold illumination : listening to the music from the nearby church, he first hears in it "the apotheosis of his own history, his own land, his own environed blood"; and he comes to a new awareness of the true nature of the people, the Protestant church-going people, from whom he comes and whom he had once meant to serve—their barrenness, and above all their glad willingness to let *their religion drive them to crucifixion of themselves and one another*" (p. 347). Lastly, he arrives at a realization of the fate that awaits Joe Christmas—to be crucified.

But for Hightower the most significant epiphanies are those that enable him to recapture the past rather than those that involve the present or the future. The flashback that tells us about what may very well have been the second most formative incident of his entire life is introduced when, a middle-aged man, he feels "that he can still smell the rain, the moist grieving of the October earth, and the musty yawn as the lid of the trunk went back" on the day when he was only eight years old and found the coat his father had worn during the Civil War, twenty-five years before. The day he now revives contained in itself an intense moment of illumination that "stopped his very heart" (pp. 443-44) : among the patches of Confederate gray on his father's coat he saw a dark Yankee blue patch that filled him with terror—though a terror he did not feel as he listened to the Negro Cinthy's violent tales of the exploits of his dead grandfather. Even as a child Hightower was a true Romantic, and his father was too much a part of his own life for the boy to be able to endow him with heroic glory, or to feel anything about his father's war but a sense of the horrors of the wars of real life. In contrast, the absence of the pressure of present reality allows the moment when his grandfather rode in a gallant cavalry raid (against a henhouse) to become the central event in Hightower's existence.

Thus, though Hightower's recapture of the moment when he had seen his father's coat is revealing and important in its own right, its primary function in the novel is to help us understand the most major of all his visions, the one that continues to be repeated every night of his life. It is an odd experience, in which he seems not so much to recapture an incident as to imagine it, to create rather than to recreate. But for all that it is no less real to Hightower, who realizes that for fifty years he has "not even been clay : I have been a single instant of darkness in which a horse galloped and a gun crashed" (p. 465). His only source for the story of what had occurred many years before he was even born is Cinthy, who is certainly not one to stress historical accuracy; yet he would believe her even if he knew she was not telling the truth, "because even fact cannot stand with it. . . . You can see it, hear it : the shouts, the shots . . . you can feel, hear in the darkness horses pulled short up, plunging. . . . That you must hear, feel : then you see. . . . All this you see before the crash of the shotgun comes : then blackness again" (pp. 458-59). Anyway, so Hightower by an act of will sees, hears, feels, and then comes again to blackness every evening at the same instant, when night falls.

In so far as the original incident actually did once occur, Hightower's epiphany is not complete fantasy and in a strange way "recaptures" a past, though a historical rather than a personal one. His attitude toward the moment of his grandfather's death is foreshadowed in *Sartoris* by Miss Jenny's attitude toward the moment of the first Bayard's similar death, the story of which she has so expanded upon and enriched that "what had been a hare-brained prank of two heedless and reckless boys wild with their own youth had become a gallant and finely tragical focal point to which the history of the race had been raised from out of the old miasmic swamps of spiritual sloth by two angels valiantly fallen and strayed, altering the course of human events and purging the souls of men" (p. 9).

The device of having a character imaginatively revive a past he has never personally known and which even antedates his own birth is important again in *Absalom, Absalom!* and in "The Jail" section of *Requiem for a Nun*. It is a much more frequent and significant technique in Faulkner than in any of the other novelists I have discussed, although there are a few vaguely similar scenes in some of their works too. The pivotal chapter of Mann's *The Magic Mountain*, "Snow," centers on such an experience during a vision of Hans Castorp's, as he "remembers" the world of the Mediterranean—of which he actually should know nothing. But the most extraordinarily comparable situation appears in poetry, in the work of T. S. Eliot. For the incident in the rose garden, apparently one of the most significant in the poet's life, is, like the most critical event in Hightower's, one he never actually experienced. Indeed, it never really occurred at all, to anyone. Yet "what did not happen is as true as what did happen" (*Complete Poems*, p. 277), so the poet constantly recalls it and strives to go back to it, to live through it at last. In a similar way, young Bayard Sartoris longs to go back to the moment of his brother's death and to believe that at that very same instant he died too, while Quentin Compson tries to convince not only his father but himself as well that he committed incest with Caddy. And Hightower, who feels that he lives through the past moment in all its sensual intensity, finally seems able to accept the paradox that he *is* his dead grandfather and thus died twenty years before his birth.

Toward the end of *Light in August*, the most climactic occurrence of Hightower's imagined historical epiphany is preceded by a sudden revelation that brings him as close to an understanding of the meaning—or meaninglessness—of his entire life as he ever comes. For the first time, he becomes fully aware of his own guilt toward his wife, and of himself as "the instrument of her despair and death." Although his immediate impulse is to repress this emerging self-knowledge, it forces itself upon him, and he goes on to grasp it and much more besides. "Out of the instant," a new light comes into "the lambent suspension of August," a light in the form of "a faint glow like a halo" in which he re-envisions "all the faces which he has ever seen." Although "they all look a little alike," Joe Christmas' face remains for a time the most confused and obscure, until Hightower realizes that it is merged with Percy Grimm's—in a unity suggestive of keys to the thematic significance of Grimm's role in the novel, to the import of the way in which Christmas is killed, and even to the meaning of his death. From this vision Hightower goes on to a realization that he too is dying; but he finds himself unable to pray, or even to try. And despite all the new understanding brought to him by his moment of revelation and the fact that for the first time in fifty years he has approached a full awareness of the implications of what he is doing, his weakness not merely endures, but prevails; for he still awaits his grandfather and the galloping horses. When they come, "borne now upon a cloud of phantom dust," it seems to him that they are all he has "left of honor and pride and life" (pp. 464-66)—his pathetic self-delusion and persistence in his vision revealing perhaps more than anything else the full depths of degradation and futility to which that vision has brought him.

Faulkner further pursues his interest in epiphanies that reveal a historical past in *Absalom, Absalom!*, where not just one but two characters share a desire—and for all we know the ability—to summon up a past they have never personally experienced, and where it is chiefly the past they thus recreate or create that is presented to the reader as the substance of the novel. Quentin and Shreve are not participants in the story of the Sutpens, but they are the two most important people who narrate it and speculate on it. In a major sense I really misrepresent their roles when I say that they are not "participants" in the events, for Faulkner tries to show that they not only imagine what must have happened long ago but actually live through it, act it, and become those who first lived through it and acted it.

For instance, they are so successful in sensing what it was like around the campfires in Carolina toward the end of the war that Faulkner tells us that "now both of them were Henry Sutpen and both of them were Bon, compounded each of both yet either neither, smelling the very smoke which had blown and faded away forty-six years ago . . ." (p. 351); and this scene is only one of many passages indicating the ability of the two boys to recapture an imagined past in all its fullness, an ability especially strong in Quentin, whose attachment to his own personal past we have already seen in *The Sound and the Fury*. Here, Faulkner's favorite phrases to describe Quentin's sensual participation in an imagined past are, "Quentin seemed to watch . . ." and, "It seemed to Quentin that he could actually see. . . ." At one point Faulkner even goes so far as to say that Quentin "could see it; he might even have been there. Then he thought *No. If I had been there I could not have seen it this plain*" (p. 190; see pp. 8, 21, 132, 189).

Real as such scenes may seem, however, they remain speculations; and inherent in any novel whose plot is based upon the imaginative musings of its own characters, of course, are many implications about the relativity of truth, about the facts of fiction and the fictions of fact. In *Absalom, Absalom!*, technique literally becomes discovery, and uncertainty about much of what we are told is essential to Faulkner's purposes. Shreve's and Quentin's revelations of the past actually give them information that is at best unsubstantiated and occasionally contrary to the reports of others and to apparent fact. Consequently, much of the narrative they end up with is put on a purely conjectural basis. In order to take it seriously, they and the reader must suspend disbelief and together assume that at least part of it reflects some sort of truth. And, indeed, it does, for as Rosa Coldfield says (and Hightower, for one, would wholeheartedly agree with her), "there is a might-have-been which is more true than truth" (p. 143). Shreve and Quentin may be wrong about facts, but nevertheless each moment in which they feel they recapture the past does seem to give them a glimpse of reality. To use Joseph Conrad's strange expression, they see "the truth disclosed in a moment of illusion" (*Lord Jim,* p. 323).

In order to accept the illusion (to "follow the dream," as Conrad's Stein claims one must), the destructive element to which Rosa must submit is the past, as it is for so many of Faulkner's people. And like them her ability to immerse herself in it is as sensually complete as it is mysterious; to her, "the substance of remembering" is "sense, sight, smell : the muscles with which we see and hear and feel—not mind, not thought : there is no such thing as memory : the brain recalls just what the muscles grope for : no more, no less . . ." (*Absalom, Absalom!*, p. 143). Yet though she is haunted by a world she refuses to give up for dead, the moment out of that world which most fascinates her is one in which she was given a revelation that concentrated on the present. Actually, much of the emphasis in *Absalom, Absalom!* is on a number of very significant present epiphanies which, if anything, incline to look toward the future rather than the past. Centering chiefly on Rosa, Bon, and Sutpen, they not only reveal to the reader a good deal about the characters who experience them, but they also become very important moments in these characters' lives, which they influence as greatly as they do the development of the narrative. They are moments which all three figures have waited for and have sooner or later undergone—what Rosa seems to be thinking of when she describes living as "one constant and perpetual instant when the arras-veil before what-is-to-be hangs docile and even glad to the lightest naked thrust if we had dared, were brave enough (not wise enough : no wisdom needed here) to make the rending gash" (pp. 142-43).

Rosa makes her own thrust at the arras-veil when she is only nineteen and has just heard that Henry has murdered Bon. This news comes as a shock, of course, but it is itself too important to produce an epiphany : that must wait for the relatively less significant moment when she enters the Sutpen house to see Judith but first encounters Clytie, Sutpen's part-Negro daughter. "Perhaps I knew already," she later reflects in retrospect, "on the instant I entered the house and saw that face which was at once both more and less than Sutpen, perhaps I knew even then what I could not, would not, must not believe" (p. 140). However, such knowledge of what she refuses to believe is initially unconscious if it exists at all, and it becomes conscious only when she experiences an epiphany consisting of several phases, all occurring within the space of a very few seconds and each providing a related yet almost distinct aspect of the complete revelation.

The first phase comes as Rosa starts to rush toward the steps to go up to Judith, and Clytie says, "Dont you go up there, Rosa"; and though words alone are not enough to stop her, it seems to Rosa as though it were not Clytie "who spoke but the house itself that said the words—the house which he had built. . . ." Rosa, in an anger both feigned (for she realizes that for the first time in her life someone is not treating her like a child) and real (the words have come, after all, from a Negro), keeps advancing toward the stairs; so the crisis is postponed for a fraction of a second until Clytie lightly touches her : ". . . and then I did stop dead. Possibly even then my body did not stop. . . . I knew only that my entire being seemed to run at blind full tilt into something monstrous and immobile, with a shocking impact too soon and too quick to be mere amazement and outrage at that black arresting and untimorous hand on my white woman's flesh." The impact is more than mere amazement and outrage because the contact of flesh with flesh also

provides a violent illumination of "the fall of all the eggshell shibboleth of caste and color too." Especially for a sheltered Southern
white woman of the nineteenth century, this upheaval of all assump-
tions and preconceptions about race and caste is even more out of
proportion to its cause than most epiphanies. Even the symbolic
relevance of this incident to the event of major importance that has
just occurred—Henry's killing Bon—is never disclosed to Rosa, and
to us only when we discover that Bon, like Clytie, was Sutpen's part-
Negro offspring. Henry has killed as a Negro a man he revered as a
brother, while in what may be regarded as the third phase of this
frozen moment of time, Rosa now recognizes—even as she says,
"Take your hand off me, nigger!"—that she and Clytie have been
"twin sistered" by their contact. "And you too?" she cries. "And
you too, sister, sister?" In the next phase she finds herself "waking
into the reality, the more than reality, not to the unchanged and
unaltered old time but into a time altered to fit the dream which,
conjunctive with the dreamer, becomes immolated and apotheo-
sized." For at last the seemingly endless moment ends when the two
women hear Judith speak: "the voice parted us, broke the spell. It
said one word: 'Clytie.' like that, that cold, that still: not Judith,
but the house itself speaking again, though it was Judith's voice"
(pp. 138-42). Rosa spends as many pages as she does analyzing her
reaction to this incident—while completely ignoring her reaction to
the news of the murder—because it has perhaps taught her more
than any other single event in her life.

But she experiences other moments of revelation as well—such as
the one she shares with Sutpen of his spontaneous decision to marry
her. It comes to him in "a sudden over-burst of light, illumination"
when he notices her in the garden, while she, in turn, when she sees
him looking at her, loses "all the shibboleth erupting of cannot, will
not, never will in one red instant's fierce obliteration" (p. 163). As
she fully realizes, he desires marriage simply as a means toward his
own end: the salvation of his grand "design," which must include
a son to inherit what is left of Sutpen's Hundred. The irony is that
Sutpen might still have had such an heir had he not refused to
grant even the slightest form of recognition to his only other son,
Charles Bon, whose own enlightenment centers on his discovery that
Sutpen is his father.

That epiphany comes during Bon's trip to the University of
Mississippi. His mother's lawyer, who knows that the two young

men are half brothers, has sent Henry an outwardly quite ordinary letter of introduction; but even before Bon finds out about that letter, he feels that he is on the verge of some major discovery, "the jigsaw puzzle picture integers of it waiting, almost lurking, just beyond his reach, inextricable, jumbled, and unrecognizable yet on the point of falling into pattern which would reveal to him at once, like a flash of light, the meaning of his whole life, past . . ." (p. 313). Despite his eager anticipation, however, the revelation of the meaning of his whole life never comes; we may say that for him, as for Virginia Woolf's Lily Briscoe, "the great revelation perhaps never did come. Instead there were little daily miracles, illuminations, matches struck unexpectedly in the dark . . ."[4]

But at times such little miracles provide enough new knowledge so that, even if they do not entirely illumine one's life, they can nevertheless entirely change it. For Bon, the match is unexpectedly struck by Henry, who one day shows him the lawyer's letter, which produces "no gentle spreading glow but a flash, a glare" (*Absalom, Absalom!*, p. 313), irrationally but correctly persuading him that Henry's father must be his as well. So he agrees to go home with Henry for Christmas, believing that when he and his father meet at last, "there would be that flash, that instant of indisputable recognition between them and he would know for sure and forever —thinking maybe *That's all I want. He need not even acknowledge me* . . ." (p. 319). But Sutpen makes no sign whatsoever, and the flash and the glare seen by Bon do not so much clarify or resolve anything as confirm a mystery and a dilemma all the more intensely —like, in the words of *Intruder in the Dust*, "the struck match which doesn't dispel the dark but only exposes its terror—one weak flash and glare revealing for a second the empty road's the dark and empty land's irrevocable immitigable negation."[5]

[4] *To the Lighthouse*, p. 249. Cf. Slatoff, *Quest for Failure*, p. 1: "The integers never do fall into place for Charles Bon. Much the same can be said about Benjy and Quentin Compson, Darl Bundren, Gail Hightower, Thomas Sutpen, and numerous other characters in Faulkner's novels."
[5] P. 95. The words "flash" and "glare" are favorites with Faulkner, who likes to use them with Mrs. Woolf's image of the match struck in the dark— with, of course, his own variations. One of these is his emphasis on the paradox that it is by virtue of its very evanescence that any experience is permanent. In "All the Dead Pilots," he says that "the instant of sublimation" is "too strong for steady diet. And if it were a steady diet, it would not be a flash, a glare. And so, being momentary, it can be preserved and prolonged only on paper: a picture, a few written words that any match,

Both Bon and Sutpen are concerned with the idea of heritage, but while in Bon this concern is reflected in a need to discover his own past heritage, Sutpen is possessed by a desire for a posterity, for descendants who would carry on the heritage he wants to create. Bon searches for a father, while Sutpen ends in seeking a son. Sutpen's obsession originated in an epiphany he had as a boy; because the revelation he then experienced continues to control his life, it is through that experience that the past persists in the present, though in effect it does so by making him most conscious of the future—his own and that of his descendants. As long as he is "the slave of his secret and furious impatience" for the future, as long as he retains his conviction of the "need for haste, of time fleeing beneath him" (p. 34), he remains strong. His decline after the war, Bon's death, and Henry's disappearance is best seen in his preoccupation—completely new to him—with his past, with the promising days that have gone rather than with the unpromising days to come. When he proposes marriage to Rosa, he gives her his dead wife's wedding ring "as though in the restoration of that ring to a living finger he had turned all time back twenty years and stopped it, froze it" (p. 165). This almost pitiable gesture shows that like, say, Quentin or Hightower, the more concerned Sutpen is with the past the more futile he becomes.

At first, when he is only a boy, Sutpen's desire is to escape from the past and the present, too, the present of his childhood and of the world he lives in, for he learns the utter insignificance of his place in that world in a moment of enlightenment while he is still very young : "He remembered when he found it out, because that was the same second when he discovered his innocence. It was not the second, the moment, that he was long about : it was the getting to it. . . ."[6] The very nature of the boy's new enlightenment will

---

a minute and harmless flame that any child can engender, can obliterate in an instant. A one-inch sliver of sulphur-tipped wood is longer than memory or grief; a flame no larger than a sixpence is fiercer than courage or despair" (*Collected Stories*, p. 531). (And thus it is for "a scrap of paper—something, anything" that Judith Sutpen longs, "something that might make a mark on something that *was* once for the reason that it can die someday, while the block of stone cant be *is* because it never can become *was* because it cant ever die or perish . . ." [*Absalom, Absalom!*, pp. 127-28].)

[6] P. 226. A very similar incident appears in Faulkner's unpublished story, "The Big Shot," where it is a key event in the boyhood of a racketeer, Dal Martin. See Millgate, *Achievement of William Faulkner*, pp. 159-60.

later make it impossible for the grown man to acknowledge a part-Negro as his son; for the epiphany occurs when the boy tries to deliver a message at the front door of a mansion but is told by the butler—a Negro—to go around to the back. Somehow, he now perceives for the first time the true role played in his world by Negroes : that it is not they whom he and the other poor whites hate or want to hurt, but rather the rich, inaccessible white man who owns the mansion and the Negro too, and beyond him something even more remote and more hateful and more difficult to understand.

This realization comes to the boy in the form of a sudden recollection of all that he has seen since he and his family came down from the mountains; he feels himself rushing "back through the two years they had lived there, like when you pass through a room fast and look at all the objects in it and you turn and go back through the room again and look at all the objects from the other side and you find out you had never seen them before, rushing back through those two years and seeing a dozen things that had happened and he hadn't even seen them before . . ." (p. 230). He sees at last the full significance of experiences which now take on the character of retrospective epiphanies : times when he would notice the antagonism of his sisters and other white women toward the Negro slaves who dressed better than they; a night when his father came home drunk after some other men and he had whipped "that goddam son of a bitch Pettibone's nigger"; an afternoon when he and his sister were walking along the road and she refused to make way for a carriage driven by a Negro and carrying two white ladies with parasols—he threw dirt after the carriage as it swept by, though he now knows "that it had not been the nigger coachman that he threw at at all, that it was the actual dust raised by the proud delicate wheels, and just that vain" (p. 231). But the result of these recollections of the past is a major revelation of his present state, a new perception of himself and his family "as the owner, the rich man (not the nigger) must have been seeing them all the time—as cattle, creatures heavy and without grace, brutely evacuated into a world without hope or purpose for them . . ." (pp. 234-35).

Finally, as he tries to plan some sort of revenge, the ultimate illumination hits him; the realization that, as things are and in his present condition, *"there aint any good or harm either in the living*

world that I can do to him. It was like that . . . like an explosion—
a bright glare that vanished and left nothing, no ashes nor refuse;
just a limitless flat plain with the severe shape of his intact innocence rising from it like a monument. . . ." Recognizing that he can
only injure such men with their own weapons, he determines to
accumulate "land and niggers and a fine house to combat them
with" (p. 238). Toward that end, he goes to the West Indies, where,
however, the whole fine structure of existence that Sutpen has
elaborately constructed collapses when he makes the ironic discovery that his wife, and therefore the son who would have carried
on his name, is part Negro, and that his new existence—like the
face of the Negro butler who had once barred his way—is a balloon
too easily burst.

His experience in front of the rich man's door had revealed to
him his innocence, but it had not caused him to lose it, so he follows
his dream once more, coming to Mississippi with some slaves and
just enough money to buy the tract of land he calls Sutpen's Hundred. He builds his mansion, remarries, and begets his second son,
always working toward the fulfillment of his grand design. Since
this whole design arises from the sudden and new self-awareness he
once had while he was still a boy, in a very real sense that single
epiphany brings about all the subsequent events of his life and thus
forms the basis of the entire novel—and, in turn, illuminates the
novel for the reader.

In a later book, Faulkner goes even further and explicitly tries to
furnish his readers with an illumination of his whole vision and
life's work, as revealed in his concentration on the history and
mythology of Yoknapatawpha. "The Jail," a section of *Requiem
for a Nun* in the form of a historical essay, attempts to evoke the
past of Jefferson, using the jail both as a point of departure and as
a symbol. Early in this section Faulkner mentions moments when
one recaptures the historical past, "as when you stand say alone in
a dim and empty room and believe, hypnotised beneath the vast
weight of man's incredible and enduring *Was*, that perhaps by
turning your head aside you will see from the corner of your eye
the turn of a moving limb—a gleam of crinoline, a laced wrist,
perhaps even a Cavalier plume—who knows?" (p. 215). The rest
of "The Jail" leads up to just such an experience in which, so to

speak, one senses the presence of the old people. First Faulkner sets the background by relating how, long ago, a jailor's sickly young daughter scratched her "fragile and indelible signature" on one of the windows of the jailhouse : *"Cecilia Farmer April 16th 1861"* (p. 229)—four days after the firing on Fort Sumter. Faulkner later conjectures how "you," the reader, "an outlander say from the East or the North or the Far West," might come to Jefferson today and wonder why in the world a friend (a man, let us say, very much like Faulkner) would "elect to live here—not specifically here, of course, not specifically Jefferson, but such as here, such as Jefferson . . ." (p. 252).

As it turns out, the answer to this question, which would obviously provide insight into all of Faulkner's own life and work, lies in the inscription in the window, which your friend would insist that you look at. You would do so impatiently, however, for it would seem rather a waste of time—"until suddenly . . . the faint frail illegible meaningless even inference-less scratching on the ancient poor-quality glass you stare at, has moved, under your eyes, even while you stared at it, coalesced, seeming actually to have entered into another sense than vision . . ." (p. 254). Such an experience would have a profound effect on you, for you would now know why your friend has chosen "such as Jefferson," because Jefferson would have briefly done for you what it has always done for him : evoked not only the past but, even more important, the sense of the past: "you know again now that there is no time : no space : no distance" (*Requiem for a Nun,* p. 261). A moment from the past can come alive because, as Gavin Stevens says, it is not even past.

When Ernest Hemingway died, Faulkner made a statement praising him for "his dedication to his craft; which is to arrest for a believable moment the antics of human beings involved in the comedy and tragedy of being alive." A few years before, Faulkner had made a similar remark—"the aim of every artist is to arrest motion, which is life, by artificial means and hold it fixed so that a hundred years later, when a stranger looks at it, it moves again since it is life"—and then he added that "this is the artist's way of scribbling 'Kilroy was here' on the wall of the final and irrevocable oblivion through which he must someday pass."[7] The moment preserved by the artist is like Judith Sutpen's scrap of paper that lives

[7] *New York Times,* 3 July 1961, p. 6; Stein, "Faulkner," p. 139.

and makes its mark for the reason that it can die someday. It is like an epiphany, like the flash and glare of a struck match : for, like Cecilia Farmer's inscription on the window, it is both "fragile and indelible."

7

Afterword: Contemporaries

Tenryu just lifted one of his fingers and said nothing.
This however was enough to open Gutei's mind at once
to the ultimate meaning of Zen, and it is said that ever
since Gutei did or said nothing but just hold up a finger
to all the questions that might be asked of him concerning Zen.

There was a boy in his temple, who seeing the master's
trick imitated him when the boy himself was asked about
what kind of preaching his master generally practised.
When the boy told the master about it showing his lifted
little finger, the master cut it right off with a knife. The
boy ran away screaming in pain, when Gutei called him
back. The boy turned back, the master lifted his own
finger, and the boy instantly realized the meaning of the
. . . Zen of Tenryu as well as Gutei.

Daisetz Teitaro Suzuki

But I've gotta use words when I talk to you.

Sweeney[1]

In recent years novelists have assimilated epiphany with many of the
other thematic and technical devices that have been discovered, re-
discovered, or newly emphasized by modern writers. And like those
techniques—the interior monologue and the stream of consciousness
are probably the most conspicuous—epiphany has already become
part of the literary tradition, although, again like those techniques,
it has become so only for novelists who have not disregarded or
reacted against "modernism" in modern fiction. The authors now
writing who have chosen not to ignore the existence of Joyce, Virginia Woolf, Faulkner, and all the other important pioneers of new
fictional techniques can be divided rather crudely into two groups:
one consisting of those who have consolidated the gains the earlier

---

[1] *Essays in Zen Buddhism* (First Series), p. 34; T. S. Eliot, "Fragment of an
Agon," *Complete Poems*, p. 83.

giants have made, who acknowledge their influence but do not feel it necessary to make additional sweeping experiments in technique; and the other consisting of writers who are trying to go even further in formal experimentation, who—however they may claim to be reacting against certain particular modernist aspects of Proust, say, or Joyce—are clearly continuing along the same roads. In the work of the novelists of the second group—people like Samuel Beckett, Lawrence Durrell, John Barth, Alain Robbe-Grillet, Nathalie Sarraute, and just about all the other writers associated with the *nouveau roman* in France—epiphany is often used almost as strikingly as in the major novels I have examined in this book.

In the novels of the consolidators—such as Bernard Malamud, William Golding, Saul Bellow, William Styron, Edward Lewis Wallant, and James Baldwin—the use of epiphany sometimes seems less elaborate, but it remains much more central than it had ever been in eighteenth- and nineteenth-century fiction. There is probably no need to discuss the ways in which all these writers have adapted epiphany to their own needs, but a few examples may indicate how, in their novels, the appearance of epiphany is not nearly so casual as one might assume. Baldwin's *Another Country*, for instance, does not let us forget that, as Leona puts it, "sometimes a minute can be a mighty powerful thing" (p. 11). Delicate moments of illumination provide essential connections between Rufus' present existence and his past life. Telling a homosexual who has bought him a sandwich, "I'm not the boy you want, mister," he "suddenly remembered having said exactly these words to Eric— long ago" (p. 44); the scene is moving because on earlier occasions, too, a "lover" has similarly reminded Rufus of the affair he once had with Eric. When he first met Leona, he told her, "You ain't got to be afraid"; almost like a forecast of the future, a sense of the past enveloped him in an experience of *déjà vu* : "He had said this before, years ago, to someone else" (p. 19). Only later do we learn that he had spoken these perhaps unconsciously deceptive words to the other lover from the deep South whom he almost destroys, Eric. And toward the end of the first section, just before Rufus kills himself, his alienation and loneliness are poignantly conveyed through an image frequent and powerful in Wolfe, Virginia Woolf, and Faulkner. Walking among the people in the streets, some of whom he recognizes, he feels

. . . as removed from them . . . as he might have felt from a fence, a farmhouse, a tree, seen from a train window : coming closer and closer, the details changing every instant as the eye picked them out; then pressing against the window with the urgency of a messenger or a child; then dropping away, diminishing, vanished, gone forever. . . . In an instant, gone in an instant—it was not his fence, his farmhouse, or his tree. As now, passing, he recognized faces, bodies, postures, and thought. *That's Ruth.* Or *There's old Lennie. Son of a bitch is stoned again.* [Pp. 83-84]

With the decline of the passenger train, the image of the train window will presumably become less common : even the train in which Léon rides in Michel Butor's *A Change of Heart* "won't be running next year, apparently" (p. 21). But the image still gets a prominent place in William Styron's opening evocation in *Lie Down in Darkness* of the railroad trip from the North to Virginia, each of the scenes glimpsed from the window forming a "sudden, swift tableau" (p. 10). Other images describing fleeting moments such as these are also frequent in Styron's work—indeed, few contemporary novelists include so *many* frozen moments of vision as Styron does— but he especially favors photographic imagery. With elaborations upon such imagery that occasionally make Thomas Wolfe's similar passages seem positively concise by comparison, Styron describes the freezing of time through the image of a snapshot, or that of the sudden stopping of a movie on the screen by a trick of the projector; he also likes to use movie parallels to produce what William Golding calls "trailers out of the past."[2]

Edward Lewis Wallant's novels are about "people sensitive to the subtle reverences due to certain resonant moments" (*The Tenants of Moonbloom,* p. 209). Occasionally in their lives, indeed, such "resonant moments" provide them with revelations less subtle than cosmic. Few novelists past or present depict a world so insistently harrowing and tortuous; each of Wallant's novels reveals a common pattern, in which we see the protagonist in his hell struggle against any denial of the total horror of human life. But in each case a sudden revelation brings him to a sense of reconciliation : not really a noble affirmation of life so much as a recognition of the value of

[2] *Pincher Martin,* p. 139. See Styron's *Lie Down in Darkness,* p. 118, and *Set This House on Fire,* pp. 148-49, 152-53.

merely living—although with hints of something deeper as well. The revelation thus achieved is never easy, however sudden, and certainly it is never oblivious of the ugliness out of which it must invariably come, but it is powerful and significant nevertheless.

In Wallant's first novel, *The Human Season*, the seed is sown for this new growth one day when, in the midst of his habitual curses against God, it suddenly occurs to Joe Berman "that no one heard him, that he was talking to himself. In absolute emptiness" (p. 165). Later, at the climax of the novel, this awareness comes to him even more powerfully by means of a literal shock treatment as he putters with his television set : "Suddenly ferocious life snaked up his arm and reached for his heart" (p. 171). Finally, he fully realizes that "what was out there in the dark," what he had hated so intensely, was not a bearded God out to get him but "nothing." Yet this new knowledge is not wholly negative :

> Answers come in little glimmers to your soul, most clearly in childhood, in the sounds of certain voices and faces and things, when you feel the miracle and the wonder; and he knew then that the Torahs and prayer shawls and churches and saints were just the art men tried to create to express the other, deeper feeling.
> "It's like a light that don't last long enough to recognize anything. But the light itself, just that you seen it . . . that's got to be enough. . . ." And then more emphatically, almost desperately, for it was his last hope : "It *is* enough!" [Pp. 191-92]

In *The Pawnbroker*, Sol Nazerman's rescue, too, comes, as he himself has said of all happiness, "in the *context* of sadness" (p. 145). It comes—like a "drowning man's cliché . . . some great distillation of everything" (p. 269)—when his assistant in the pawnshop, Jesus Ortiz, sacrifices his life to save Sol's, thereby saving his soul as well, and teaching him anew the healing power of love among men. Sammy Kahan, in *The Children at the Gate*, also recognizes that loneliness is the blackest ordeal, and that the loneliest man of all is he who seeks to avoid suffering, or to sever his involvement with the afflictions of mankind. Since everyone suffers, each of us *must*. This is a hard view, but the world is sometimes made less stark when one of us, out of love, makes the Christ-like sacrifice of suffering for the rest of us. Sammy goes to *his* crucifixion by falling down some steps and impaling himself on an iron spike. As Angelo De Marco watches the scene, he feels a strange desire :

He wanted Sammy to stay there, to stay and suffer that im-
molation over and over and over.

Oh, yeah, Sammy, I get it, I get it.

And Angelo began to laugh. [P. 173]

For the rest of his existence, Angelo knows, he will carry within him
the "mortal wound" created by Sammy's death—but he also knows
that, in the final words of the novel, "although the wound would
be the death of him, it would be the life of him too" (p. 184).

In Wallant's last novel and first comedy, *The Tenants of Moonbloom*, Norman Moonbloom's communion comes when he loses his
virginity with Sheryl Beeler, one of his tenants. The fact that she
puts out in order to hold out (on the rent) does not lessen for Moonbloom the spiritual significance of their love-making. It is at this
point that he undertakes to make repairs in all the apartments, to
clean them up and paint them—to put his houses in order. Although
he has to do the work himself, he succeeds remarkably; but always
hanging over him is the project he keeps putting off : repairing a
huge, ugly, swollen protrusion in the soft, damp wall behind
Basellecci's toilet. The possibilities for filth and corruption in
Basellecci's plumbing make Moonbloom gag, and upon it Basellecci
blames the tightness in his bowels as well as, by extension, all the
difficulties in his life. "And I begin and end with that . . . that *wall*,"
he tells Moonbloom; "It is the gateway to the ugliness for me . . ."
(p. 119).

Soon Basellecci discovers that his real problem is a fatal cancer,
and he becomes indifferent to the swollen wall. But Moonbloom
more and more realizes that he at any rate must confront it and all
that lies behind it : that indeed he must—if I may so paraphrase
Conrad—immerse himself in the disgusting element. And so at last,
with Basellecci helping him drink his way to the courage to follow
his dream, he chops away at the wall :

There came a rumbling, a choking, a gurgling. The wall ex-
ploded in a wet vomit of brown thick liquid. Norman was in-
undated. His eyes and mouth were clogged with a vile and
odorous viscosity, his clothes soaked. . . . He was a reeking, slimy
figure gleaming in the harsh light over the toilet. The world
waited for his outcry.

"*I'M BORN!*" he howled, with unimaginable ecstasy. "See,

Basellecci, I'm born to you. See, see, smell me, see me. You'll be healed. Everything will be all right!"

"But I'll die?" Basellecci squealed in terrible excitement.

"Yes, yes, you'll die," Norman screamed, laughing.

"In terrible pain?"

"In terrible pain."

"Alone?"

"All alone."

Basellecci began to laugh and cry at the same time. "I'm drunk," he wailed. "I'm so drunk that I'm happy."

"The wall will be new and clean and worthy of you," Norman said, wiping his filthy face and shaking with laughter. [Pp. 241-42]

Moonbloom has earned his laughter because he has confronted, recognized, and acknowledged the crap in Basellecci's wall. The obscenity of man's plight has been revealed—and thereby in a measure overcome.

For my present purposes, the writers devoted to new formal and thematic experiments—the more obviously "modernist" writers—are especially interesting, since their new theories about and attitudes toward their art usually go along with a fascination with epiphany, although sometimes, for all the value of their actual fiction, their critical originality is more imagined than real.

In Lawrence Durrell's *Alexandria Quartet*, the novelist Pursewarden says that the artist is one who "must catch every scrap of wind" (*Balthazar*, p. 114). Along the same lines, art, according to the novelist and narrator Darley, has its source in "the moments which possess the writer . . . and which live on perpetually . . . a fund upon which to build the part of one's life which is writing" (*Justine*, p. 25). At the start of his career, Durrell himself wrote Henry Miller that what he was trying to do was "to isolate . . . the exact moment of creation."[3] More recently, he has said that the novelist's art goes beyond recording such moments for the reader's observation; it "urges people to wake up" by giving them, too, "the vicarious feel of the poetic illumination."[4] Pursewarden's ideal, even

---

[3] Lawrence Durrell and Henry Miller, *A Private Correspondence*, p. 23.

[4] "The Kneller Tape (Hamburg)," in *The World of Lawrence Durrell*, p. 163.

more Romantically ambitious, is a reciprocal one : a "miracle" of mutual understanding and appreciation between artist and audience in a "great blinding second of illumination" (*Clea*, p. 140).

But the most famous and distinctive element of Durrell's aesthetics is his stress on the space-time continuum—another approach to fiction also expounded by Pursewarden. In *Time and Western Man* —a book that Durrell says has had a great influence upon him— Wyndham Lewis speaks of the absence of an "outstanding exponent in literature or art of einsteinian physics" to balance Proust's role as an exponent of Bergsonian duration.[5] Almost as a belated answer to this claim, Durrell says that in his art he has tried to "apply Einsteinian time instead of Bergsonian time."[6] It is not difficult to guess at the reasons for his preference. As obsessed as the "Bergsonian" writers ever were with "the nature of time, that ailment of the human psyche" (*Clea*, p. 12), Durrell feels a need for a fresher way of approaching it in fiction. But in literature it seems not to matter all that much, in actual artistic results, whether a writer's obsession with time is couched in Bergsonian or Einsteinian terms : according to Lewis, anyway, it is, for example, Bergson who must stand accused of having first "put the hyphen between Space and Time" (*Time and Western Man*, p. 419). And if for many intellectuals one of the fundamental attractions of Bergson's philosophy was its stress on intuition as a means of breaking the barrier between subject and object, for Durrell the distinction between the two can be "discarded in the light of Einstein's Relativity Theory" (*Key to Modern British Poetry*, p. 21). While still another appeal in Bergson's duration was the notion of the continuity and ultimate contemporaneity of all time, Durrell reminds us that "Einstein's time was not a past-present-future object. . . . It was a sort of time which contained all time in every moment of time" (pp. 28-29).

The "Einsteinian" concept that every moment contains in itself all time seems to be at the foundation of Durrell's application to literature of the space-time continuum in what he calls his "relativity poem" : so Pursewarden sees the "n-dimensional novel" as "a marriage of past and present with the flying multiplicity of the future racing towards one" (*Justine*, p. 248). The first three volumes

[5] P. 89. See Durrell, *A Key to Modern British Poetry*, p. xii.
[6] Quoted in Julian Mitchell and Gene Andrewski, " Lawrence Durrell," p. 278.

of the *Quartet* are meant to represent the dimensions of space, while only the fourth is to be associated with time, in "a continuum, forsooth, embodying not a *temps retrouvé* but a *temps délivré*" (*Clea*, p. 135)—a remark assuming differences between Durrell's and Proust's methods and goals much more sweeping than those that really exist. Some of Durrell's other analogical adaptations of the concept of "relativity" qualify even further our acceptance of his stress on the contradictions between his work and Proust's. "Our view of reality," says Pursewarden, "is conditioned by our position in space and time" (*Balthazar*, p. 14); from a notion of truth, then, kindred to that of *Remembrance of Things Past*—or *Absalom, Absalom!*—Durrell makes use of kindred narrative forms. Especially in *Justine* and *Balthazar*, Darley reconstructs a number of scenes out of his imagination, asking us, in effect, to suspend disbelief; and we do, proceeding with him under the assumption that, as Balthazar puts it, "to imagine is not necessarily to invent" (*Balthazar*, p. 98). "At every moment in Time the possibilities are endless in their multiplicity": out of this attitude toward reality arises "the intercalation of fact and fancy" (p. 226) that is the *Alexandria Quartet*.

In such a subjective world, the presentation of moments of illumination is inevitably ambiguous. Those recounted in *Mountolive*, however, would seem to be among the more dependable ones, since they appear within an "objective" narration, although even they are not fully reliable. One of the strangest and most moving provides a climax both for the novel and for Mountolive's life, and incidentally demonstrates how all time can be contained in each moment of time. Alone in a restaurant, Mountolive is approached by an old sheik who tells him, "*Effendi* mine. . . . What you seek will be revealed to you by me." His "romantic heart" beating with expectation—"was he now to be vouchsafed some mystical vision of religious truth?"—Mountolive is led to a house so dark that when light does come it gives him a "momentary illusion. . . . As if someone had opened and closed a furnace door in Heaven. It was only the spark of a match." But that spark is enough to reveal that he is in a house of child prostitutes. Horrified and dismayed, he tries to leave but is held back by the children, who fear the loss of a client. As their fingers rove "over him like ants," he has "a sudden memory, buried from somewhere back in his remembered reading, of a man staked down upon the burning sand over a nest of white ants which would soon pick the flesh from his very bones." Then follows another memory, this one so powerful that he loses all conscious contact with the actual present : ". . . suddenly everything cleared—as if a curtain had been drawn aside—to reveal him sitting beside his mother in front of a roaring fire with a picture book open on his knee"—open to a color plate showing a prone Lemuel Gulliver captive to the Lilliputians. This past scene is recaptured in abnormal detail, and Mountolive does not consciously return to the present until he has escaped to the street. In grotesque fashion, the promise of the sheik—"what you seek will be revealed"—has been inexplicably fulfilled : for Mountolive has "reached a new frontier in himself; life was going to be something completely different from now on. He had been in some sort of bondage all this time; now the links had snapped" (pp. 288-94).

General, structural use of epiphany is even more prominent in the three volumes narrated by Darley, which sometimes seem mere catalogues of the evanescent moments that have made their mark on his consciousness. What one character says about Justine seems true of all the other major characters as well, but especially of the Darley from whose perspectives we see them : "In a way she was not looking for life but for some integrating revelation which would give it point" (*Justine*, p. 70). Not surprisingly, the integrating revelation rarely if ever comes, but one of the striking things about the *Quartet* is the way Durrell consistently suggests that the most promising area in which to search for such revelation is in sex, which he often presents in terms of visionary experience. In an interview, Durrell has acknowledged that in his book "the sexual act becomes identified with all knowledge, all knowing . . . the awakening of the psychic forces latent in the human being . . . since I'm neither priest nor prophet I can only label this sort of awakening 'poetic illumination' "—an arresting phrase indeed when one considers that he then goes on to say that art "urges people to wake up by giving them the vicarious feel of the poetic illumination" ("Kneller Tape," pp. 161, 163). Within the novel itself one is made to feel that, in the world of Alexandria, if a perfect sexual orgasm were possible it would have to be equivalent to the apocalyptic vision.

Durrell's work, except for the major fact that it contains so many melodramatically exciting events—so much of what Nathalie Sarraute disdainfully calls "the superficial dramatic action constituted by plot" (*Tropisms*, p. 9)—has a great deal in common with the

French *nouveau roman*. Certainly Durrell shares important traits and critical precepts with his contemporaries in France who are associated with that "school." Their great reliance upon dubious, undependable narration comes immediately to mind, as does their almost total disruption of normal or actual chronology. Durrell and writers like Mme Sarraute, Alain Robbe-Grillet, Claude Simon, and Marguerite Duras are trying—with Pursewarden—"to escape from the absurd dictates of narrative form in prose" (*Balthazar*, p. 117). The same, to be sure, has also been rightly said of several novelists of earlier generations, including those I have already discussed. Nevertheless, the younger writers have made original contributions in their various new emphases. "For the writer," says Durrell's Arnauti, "people as psychologies are finished" (*Justine*, p. 113). The degree to which Durrell's own novels really follow from this attitude is, no doubt fortunately, limited, just as Robbe-Grillet can be taken only so seriously when he presses his similar critical "dismissal of the old myth of 'depth.' "[7] Yet this approach does produce in their work a valuable freshness.

The answer of the new French novelists to Arnauti's inescapable subsequent question—"What now remains to the writer?"—seems to lie in the world of external reality. Since nothing else exists, they say in effect, all significance must be attached to what can be seen, touched, materially perceived : thus the "school" of the *nouveau roman* is sometimes called *l'école de l'objet*, or *chosisme*, and its "members" display an urge to catalogue and describe material objects equaled only by the categorizing passions of characters out of Samuel Beckett. I have used the word "significance" in regard to the approach of these writers to the material world, but "importance" is probably more generally accurate, for some of them, like Robbe-Grillet, deprive objects of all objective meanings : to give a material thing "significance" is to humanize it—that is, to distort it. Probably no one surpasses Robbe-Grillet in the sheer concentration he exerts on simple objects themselves, or in his refusal (not shared by his characters) to go within or beyond them in explicit terms; but in varying degrees he is joined in this approach by

[7] "A Fresh Start for Fiction," trans. Richard Howard, *Evergreen Review* 1, 3 [1957]:103. Cf. Nathalie Sarraute's discussion of the contemporary novelist's discovery that " 'the psychological,' which had been the source of such great disappointment and sorrow, did not exist" (*Age of Suspicion*, p. 60).

his contemporaries. Not since Virginia Woolf's *Jacob's Room* and *The Waves*—books surely no less "anti-novels" than the works currently being given that title—have so much effort and space been devoted by important writers to describing material objects *as objects*. Aware of the dangers of this obsession, both Mrs. Woolf (in "Solid Objects") and Mme Sarraute (in tropism XXII) tell the stories of men who carry their fascination with such objects beyond the realms of sanity.

Mme Sarraute also shares with Mrs. Woolf a stress on the role in her art of something very much like epiphany, as in her concept of the "sub-conversation" (*sous-conversation*): the unuttered, indeed not fully conscious interplay between two people who, while they are talking aloud, are simultaneously carrying on a silent conversation—an "interior dialogue," as it were—that proceeds by an indefinite series of perceptions, "those illuminations . . . those sudden divinations, such as do occur."[8] These perceptions arise not directly, through "real words like the ones we articulate distinctly out loud or in our thoughts," but indirectly, through, as one of Mme Sarraute's narrators puts it, "signs so brief . . . that I could never succeed in really understanding or seizing them, I can only recover them in bits and snatches and translate them awkwardly by the words these signs represent, fleeting impressions, thoughts, feelings . . ." (*Martereau*, p. 25).

The connection between epiphany and Mme Sarraute's fiction is even more evident in her central theory of "tropisms"—in her actual artistic application of which, moreover, moments of vision are more effectively employed, since they can appear in less narrowly restricted contexts than the sub-conversation can supply. She first applied her concept in a volume called *Tropismes*, which appeared in 1939. This was a small book of eighteen (later twenty-four) brief, unconnected vignettes—Mme Sarraute speaks of it as "made up of a series of moments" (*Tropisms*, p. 9)—extraordinarily reminiscent of Stephen Dedalus' proposal for a volume of collected "epiphanies."

In the Foreword she wrote in 1962 for the English translation, Mme Sarraute reveals that she composed her first tropism in 1932 "under the impact of an emotion, of a very vivid impression" (p. 7);

[8] *Martereau*, p. 8. See "Conversation and Sub-Conversation," in *Age of Suspicion*.

its name derived from its "spontaneous, irresistible, instinctive nature, similar to that of the movements made by certain living organisms under the influence of outside stimuli" (p. 9). "Movement" seems the key word in understanding her concept : tropisms are "inner 'movements' . . . hidden under the commonplace, harmless appearances of every instant of our lives"; they "develop and pass through us very rapidly in the form of frequently very sharp, brief sensations, without our perceiving clearly what they are" :

> These movements, of which we are hardly cognizant, slip through us on the frontiers of consciousness in the form of undefinable, extremely rapid sensations. They hide behind our gestures, beneath the words we speak and the feelings we manifest, all of which we are aware of experiencing, and are able to define. They seemed, and still seem to me to constitute the secret source of our existence, in what might be called its nascent state. [Pp. 7-8]

So important are they, indeed, that in art they are not to be seen as a mere means of, say, displaying character or developing plot; rather, the reverse is true, and "the barely visible, anonymous character," for example, serves "as a mere prop for these movements." Perhaps inevitably, placing so great a value on tropisms in her fiction leads Mme Sarraute to an affective interpretation of art that sees it as seeking to produce tropisms in its audience : "it was not possible to communicate them to the reader otherwise than by means of equivalent images that would make him experience analogous sensations" (p. 8). This view helps to clarify what she means when she says elsewhere that the original promise of the *nouveau roman* was that it would provoke "a mysterious, salutary shock, a sort of emotional commotion" making it "possible to apprehend all at once, and as in a flash, an entire object with all its nuances, its possible complexities, and even—if, by chance, these existed—its unfathomable depths" (*Age of Suspicion*, p. 62). Mme Sarraute's view, in fact, seems essentially like one of the many critical postures she satirizes in *The Golden Fruits*, the one which claims that "it is moments like these, these flashes of truth, that make great books" (p. 50).

As one might suspect, however, the volume *Tropisms* itself has only qualified interest and illustrates the inherent limitations of a book consisting entirely of disconnected epiphany-like fragments.

Mme Sarraute handles the form about as well as can be expected, but it prevents her from *doing* anything with the tropisms she only permits herself to record : she cannot use them to enhance any general effect, to build up to anything, or to climax anything. They are just there. Presumably, these considerations explain why she has not written a second book like *Tropisms*. But, as she says, "this first book contains *in nuce* all the raw material that I have continued to develop in my later works," and "tropisms are still the living substance of all my books" (*Tropisms*, p. 9). Part of the fragmentary, unstructured effect remains too. As a result of her de-emphasis on plot, for example, only rarely are the illuminations that her novels record truly major or climactic, like the one experienced by the narrator in *Portrait of a Man Unknown* when confronted with the portrait for the first time. Rather, the dominant note is of an incessant stream of fleeting moments of awareness : of self, of others, above all of the relationships between oneself and others. In her world, life is a trauma, and few experiences are much more traumatic than other experiences : instead we have a continual sense of the excitement and terror that can be constantly aroused by the most banal trivia.

In a short book significantly titled *Instantanés*, Alain Robbe-Grillet has published a collection of sketches very like Mme Sarraute's *Tropisms*. As an independent work of art it is no more successful—but Robbe-Grillet has consistently had greater artistic success than Mme Sarraute in applying its method, the aesthetic views behind it, and epiphany to his longer works.

Robbe-Grillet's contribution to contemporary critical thinking in France lies in the freshness of his approach to the age-long dialogue on the relationship between perceiving subject and perceived object. Traditionally, Western aesthetics and philosophy have either sought ways to bridge the distance between subject and object, or despaired of being able to do so; Robbe-Grillet regards the gap as unbridgeable but sees nothing especially lamentable in that bare fact. "Things are things," he declares, "and man is only man." He realizes that to the "Humanists" he has committed a crime, "especially in recognizing this separation, this distance, without making any effort to transcend or to sublimate it,"[9] but for him the world

---

[9] "Old 'Values' and the New Novel," trans. Bruce Morrissette, *Evergreen Review* 3 (Summer 1959): 100.

is *objective* : something apart, other. Of course—although this is a point many readers have strangely missed—Robbe-Grillet does not mean to deny that every individual's perceptions of the external world are inescapably subjective, but rather that such responses are anything *more* than subjective. "Quite obviously there can never be anything except the world as seen from *my point of view*. . . . The relative subjectivity of my viewpoint serves, indeed, to define my situation in the world. I merely refrain from attempting, in my turn, to convert this situation into a form of servitude" (p. 117). To do otherwise is to indulge in dangerous and unhealthy delusions, as he feels even the Existentialists have done. When Camus, for example, sees the "absurd" as the impossibility of establishing between man and the world "any *rapport* other than 'strangeness,' " " 'absurdity' turns out to be a form of tragic Humanism" (p. 109). And for his part Robbe-Grillet claims to have no more use for tragedy than for Humanism : the world, he has said in one of his most frequently quoted remarks, "is neither significant nor absurd. It *is*, quite simply" ("Fresh Start," p. 100).

Whatever one may think of this approach epistemologically, in Robbe-Grillet's hands it yields fresh artistic results for fiction. It does so because, although Robbe-Grillet remains wary of "servitude" to his own peculiar point of view, his fictional characters are less cautious : and the consequent interplay between creator and creation is fascinating. While Robbe-Grillet remains behind or beyond his handiwork, his people often become pathologically obsessed with objects to which they attach sometimes unconscious but always emotionally explosive symbolic force. Moreover, the object with which a character is obsessed is never arbitrary, always ultimately revealing. In one case, that of Mathias, the maniacal murderer in *The Voyeur*, such objects are a piece of cord, a pack of cigarettes, a movie poster. Each, at first innocent of any special psychological coloration, becomes in the course of the novel horribly significant and illuminating : the poster depicts a man and woman in a scene suggestive of the murder or murders we discover Mathias has committed; the cord becomes his means of tying apart a young girl's legs; the cigarettes are the instruments he then uses to torture her. "In work like his," as in Robbe-Grillet's, too, there is "no such thing as a superfluous detail" (p. 23).

Similarly significant for Mathias—and therefore for the reader—are several scenes which he sees as *"instantanés,"* snapshots, tableaux, frozen moments in time. Mathias, indeed, is no less pre-occupied with time than with material objects in space, and often, as in the tableaux or some of his imaginings, the two obsessions be-come indistinguishable. His "work," fittingly, is selling watches door to door, peddling time in space. Even before he becomes primarily concerned with providing an alibi, he is extraordinarily precise in regard to the passage and measurement of time—which, neverthe-less, consistently confuse him.

His confusion is most vividly depicted through shifts within his consciousness from one period of time to another. Mathias often lives through, as if they were taking place here and now, experiences not actually of the present. Rather, in one way or another they come from outside it : from the past, from a projected future, or even from a realm within Mathias' unconscious that is wholly imagined and has no fixed time. Robbe-Grillet has remarked, in a discussion of the visual presentation of similar temporal shifts in *Last Year at Marienbad*, that "the total cinema of our mind admits both in alternation and to the same degree the present fragments of reality proposed by sight and hearing, and past fragments, or future frag-ments, or fragments that are completely phantasmagoric" (*Last Year at Marienbad*, p. 13). In the casualness and even unconscious-ness of such temporal displacements, *The Voyeur* is less reminiscent of Proust, in whom recaptures of the past are always announced and are dealt with far more elaborately, than of Faulkner, especially the Benjy and Quentin sections of *The Sound and the Fury*. And like Quentin's only more so, Mathias' associational journeys outside the present moment—particularly those involving a scene that has never really occurred, a mental subtlety of which Benjy is incap-able—contain strong undertones of insanity.

Mathias' recaptures of the past contribute invaluably to both our awareness and our understanding of his psychosis. The process by which this is accomplished can be suggested here by concentrating on only one of the persistently recurring scenes out of his past : the one in which he sees a room with an unmade bed. When we first hear of such a room, Mathias is on a boat docking at the island where the rest of the novel will take place. He recalls how earlier that morning, in an alley on the mainland, he had heard "a distinct moan" and looked through a nearby window. He could not dis-tinguish much besides an unmade bed, a masculine silhouette stand-ing near it, and under a lamp "a small blue rectangular object—

H

which must have been a pack of cigarettes." The sound of the moans made him guess that "the victim"—his own odd word—"must have been a very young woman, or a child. She was standing against one of the iron pillars that supported the deck . . ." (*The Voyeur*, pp. 19-20). After a moment's confusion, we realize that "she" now refers to a child he has been watching on the boat, and that we are back in the present.

The association and the temporal shift occur too early to be any more than vaguely ominous, but a number of the objects to which we have now been introduced serve as increasingly revealing leit-motifs throughout the rest of the novel. Thus later, when Mathias has "lost himself again among his specters" (one of Robbe-Grillet's rare explicit clues), he is standing by a door open just wide enough for him to see "a mistrustful face" and to "recognize" the "black and white tiles on the floor." The room is "not at all remarkable—except for an unmade bed with a red spread trailing on the floor." Why an unmade bed with a red spread is remarkable we are not informed; in any case, without transition we are belatedly told that Mathias is not really in such a room at all : "There was no red bed-spread, nor was there an unmade bed . . . there was no blue pack of cigarettes . . ." (pp. 58-59). We realize that he must have been recapturing a *past* scene. Soon he recaptures it again, on this occasion seeing "the girl with the timorous expression . . . sitting on the edge of the unmade bed." Again without transition we suddenly come back into the present as Mathias, now sitting on the rocks by the shore, takes out his wallet and removes a newspaper clipping about the brutal murder of a young girl (p. 61). Within a few pages, in still another recapture, we go farther into the past scene, which is narrated as usual in the present tense :

> The girl is sitting on the edge of the unmade bed. . . . Near her the red bedspread is trailing along the floor.
>   It is night. Only the little lamp on the night table is turned on. For a long moment the scene remains motionless and silent. . . . Mathias then notices, framed in the oval mirror above the dressing table, the man standing on the left side of the room. . . .
>   . . . the giant's fingers fall upon his prey who now lies at his feet—so small as to seem almost deformed.
>   His fingertips trail over the naked skin of her neck . . . finally forcing her to lift her head and expose the large dark eyes be-

tween their long doll's lashes.

A stronger wave broke against the rock with a slapping sound. . . . [Pp. 62-63]

With growing horror, we realize that the room which has by now become familiar was the scene of a murder: the killer was Mathias himself, a "giant" presumably because his victim—the girl with the timorous expression—was a mere child, "so small as to seem almost deformed." Mathias has already associated that girl with a barmaid on the island whom he has seen in one of his frozen tableaux, a girl with "a timorous face and the ill-assured manner of a dog that had been whipped" (p. 44). Shortly afterward, his inability to keep prolonged contact with present reality is displayed when he mistakes for that barmaid a very different woman in another café: "The girl behind the bar had a timorous face and the ill-assured manners of a dog that had been ill-assured manners of a dog that had been ill-assured manners of a girl who served behind the. . . . Behind the bar, a fat woman with a satisfied, jovial face . . . was pouring drinks . . ." (p. 89). On the evidence of the description of the earlier barmaid, the word Mathias cannot get to would seem to be "whipped." But his hesitation suggests something much worse: and as we are gradually discovering, he has just tortured and killed another little girl, during an hour we have not been told about.

He sees the room with the tiled floor once again that day, imagining it in the future rather than recapturing it out of the past. Having asked the first barmaid for a room to rent, he believes he is being taken to the same room—the bed, however, is now made—and observes it minutely until brought back into the present to realize that the girl has not yet answered him. All this occurs in his mind in the time it takes to pass "his hand in front of his eyes" (p. 147).

Robbe-Grillet has pursued the technique of unannounced temporal displacement in his subsequent novels, with some changes in emphasis arising from alterations in narrative point of view. In the unique approach of *Jealousy*, the character whose awareness and observations completely dominate the narrative is never referred too. We know of his existence because the information we are given could only pertain to such a perceiving consciousness, and because the shifts in space and time demand corresponding physical and mental movements by a man in a tropical country who must be observing his wife and their neighbor, and who must be jealous of them. Another peculiarity in the depiction of the temporal shifts in *Jealousy* is that—since the narration is limited by, but not identical with, the consciousness of the husband—there seems to be no chronological center, no temporal point of departure to which all other moments in time may be related : every scene is recounted in the present tense, and no period of time has a function corresponding to that of, say, April 7, 1928, in Benjy's section of *The Sound and the Fury*. Thus Robbe-Grillet is able to present temporal shifts in an even greater flux than would have been possible had he limited himself to the memories, recaptures, or illusions of a mind literally if not psychologically fixed in time and space.

Jealousy also differs from *The Voyeur* in the even greater stress it places on frequent repetitions of the same scene, not merely similar or mentally associated scenes. One key episode recounted again and again involves the husband's observations of how the neighbor, Franck, crushes on the wall of the dining-room a centipede "about as long as a finger; it has frightened A . . . the wife, whose hand "has clenched around the knife handle" (pp. 39-40). Despite its apparent triviality and the mere few moments it has taken, as this scene or the stain left on the wall by the centipede is repeatedly described, the reader's suspicions about its sexual significance for the husband increase. But they are given explicit support only when we are shown his lapse from reality one evening when A . . . and Franck fail to return from a trip into town. Without our being aware at first that the scene is not actually—objectively— occurring, the husband sees the centipede. Now "it is enormous : one of the largest to be found in this climate." Once again, Franck "squashes the creature against the wall"; but, this time not in the dining-room, he also "squashes it against the bedroom floor," while A . . .'s hand "has clenched into a fist on the white sheet" (pp. 111-13).

Robbe-Grillet's next novels, *In the Labyrinth* and *La Maison de Rendez-vous*, carry further the stress on totally imagined scenes. In *La Maison de Rendez-vous*, moreover, the fictional characters consciously create and aesthetically structure still other scenes for the perverse entertainment featured in Lady Ava's "sketches, or *tableaux vivants*" (p. 56). In *In the Labyrinth*—as in *Last Year at Marienbad*—almost everything hinges on a purely conjectured past, while within that past specific abrupt shifts in time are also important. In an unnamed city in a country losing a war, a doctor has cared for a dying soldier. After the soldier's death, the doctor, who is eventually revealed to be the narrator, sits in a room which he describes in great detail; one of the objects in it is a nineteenth-century etching of a tavern scene. Taking his cues from that picture and associating one of its figures with the soldier, he proceeds to provide, with many false starts along the way, an imaginary account of the last few days of the soldier's life. Within the picture (*"le tableau"*), as often within the narrative based on it, movements "are frozen . . . suspended, stopped short, which also makes their meaning uncertain" (p. 22). The entire novel—rich, forceful, real, and "uncertain" as it is—derives from that single captured and preserved moment of time.

As I hope this book has made evident, the role of epiphany in twentieth-century fiction has been as varied as the works of the highly individual writers in whom it has appeared. One is even tempted to say that the most comprehensive generalization one can make about it is that each of the writers I have considered has approached the experiences Joyce called epiphanies in his own unique way. Consequently, while it is useful to make comparisons among all or several of these novelists, we must also remain aware of important contrasts. If Joyce, Proust, and Mme Sarraute, to cite the most obvious examples, develop complex theories concerning certain moments of revelation, Wolfe and Faulkner attempt nothing of the sort, while someone like Virginia Woolf seems somewhere in the middle, intensely and intellectually curious about the true nature of her moments of being, yet just avoiding ever committing herself on what that nature might be like. Or if, for another example, in Wolfe, Joyce, and Proust the use of epiphany is closely connected with moments out of their own lives and those of their families, in Faulkner, Mrs. Woolf, and Durrell such connections, although apparently they exist, are rarer and not so significant. And, though all these writers are fascinated by epiphanies that recapture the past, in Joyce and even Mrs. Woolf—or, at least, in their art— this fascination is not quite so intense as it is in Proust, Wolfe, Faulkner, and Robbe-Grillet. And yet it is Mrs. Woolf, together with Faulkner, who takes special advantage of such moments, when she does depict them, to present flashbacks that provide the reader with important background. In others, such epiphanies serve this

purpose less frequently and seldom introduce long, independent
episodes from the past.

Another, perhaps less distinct, contrast involves the degree to
which novelists elucidate specific epiphanies. Joyce, gradually abandoning the clear-cut treatment of them employed in *Stephen Hero*
in favor of the bare handling in *Ulysses*, rarely even uses such labels
as "moment of vision" or "moment of revelation," while in Mrs.
Woolf few phrases are so common as these or their variants; she
too, however, does not "explain" particular episodes, but rather
leaves their significance and symbolic value to the imagination of
the reader. Faulkner is unusual in this respect; he occasionally
dwells on such moments with long analyses, but these analyses are
in themselves so complex and ambiguous that in the end he clarifies
very little. Both Wolfe and Proust, on the other hand, while
primarily using epiphany to *dramatize* meanings, also frequently
feel it necessary to explain, as much as possible, what those meanings are.

Nevertheless, despite all this diversity, the similarities we have
seen in the uses to which all these novelists put epiphany are much
more essential and revealing, and help to clarify why they, and not
all their contemporaries and very few of their predecessors, use
epiphany so often and in such basic ways. I have in this study
pointed out some qualities present in them that are difficult to define precisely, yet which they clearly share : their modernity, for
instance—the way they seem to exemplify many of the "advanced"
trends in twentieth-century literature; or their poetic vision—the
way they adopt techniques and emphases, including epiphany, that
for the most part had previously been found only in poetry. Other
qualities are less spectral and imponderable : their stress on intuition
and emotion, rather than reason; their hesitation, nonetheless, to
interpret epiphanies religiously; their highly subjective and personal
approach to experience and knowledge; the intense sensibility of
many of their characters, particularly to physical sensations; their
affinities with Romanticism. They share as well a common concern
with certain relevant themes and subject matter : the workings of
the mind and, especially, of the inner consciousness; the nature of
perception and knowledge; the sense of each man's isolation and
even alienation from the rest of humanity; the power of memory;
the nature of time—and, although their views toward time are far
from identical, they have parallel interests in the notion that all

time is psychologically coexistent, and an apparent reluctance to choose definitely between continuous or discontinuous temporal concepts.

More importantly, they all use epiphany to reveal and dramatize their own individual preoccupations, different as the attitudes they thus project may be. Perhaps no one's world view is more intimately related to epiphanies than Virginia Woolf's, with her acute sense of the mystery and magic of existence as revealed by her moments of being. But Thomas Wolfe's moments of illumination are also closely connected with his chief obsession—in his case, with what he called the escapes of Time and Memory. Faulkner's epiphanies, too, illumine all his central concerns : his awareness of the ambiguities of life, his Romantic, almost Gothic antirationalism, and his fascination with time—especially with the past, both personal and historic. And in Joyce, of course, epiphany is one of the primary bases of both his aesthetic theory and his practice—and therefore of his art and life.

In regard to epiphany, in fact, the most striking of the similarities among these writers is the degree to which it is related to their attitudes toward art and their conceptions of the role of the artist. To all of them, without exception, one of the major functions not only of the man of letters but of any artist is to record evanescent moments with extreme care—"to fix the most elusive of his moods" (*Stephen Hero*, p. 32). So, too, Pater's Marius wishes for the ability to arrest "certain clauses of experience" (*Marius the Epicurean*, p. 105). Virginia Woolf's Lily Briscoe tries in her painting to make "of the moment something permanent" (*To the Lighthouse*, p. 249), as Proust has Marcel praise the painter Elstir because "he had succeeded in transcribing, in fixing for all time . . . the throb of one happy moment" (*Within a Budding Grove*, 1 :676), or as Durrell in a poem praises the poet Cavafy because he attempts "always to preserve the adventive / Minute . . ." (*Collected Poems*, p. 157). And Faulkner believes that "the aim of every artist is to arrest motion" (Stein, "Faulkner," p. 139), while Wolfe's Eugene Gant sees in a "blaze of light" that "the reason why the artist works and lives and has his being" is his "intolerable desire to fix eternally in the patterns of an indestructible form a single moment of man's living" (*Of Time and the River*, pp. 550-51).

Implicit in all these remarks is the belief that the artist attempts not merely to record epiphanies but to produce or reproduce them, too— in James's phrase, to "render" them, "to produce the most momentary illusion" (*House of Fiction*, p. 33). Disillusioned with the capabilities of mere language and in despair at its limitations for any real communication with their audience, these writers nevertheless realize, with Sweeney, that they've got to use words when they talk to us. But they have tried through those words to bring about the effect not so much of communication as of revelation. The ultimate goal is always greatness: and "the experience of epiphany," Herbert Gold has also claimed, "is characteristic of great literature" (*The Age of Happy Problems*, p. 60). As Conrad says in the Preface to *The Nigger of the Narcissus*, "To snatch in a moment of courage, from the remorseless rush of time, a passing phase of life, is only the beginning of the task" (p. xiv); for the artist has accomplished his full task only when an epiphany in art produces a revelation of nature, when fiction illumines reality, when literature becomes experience.

Thus the epiphany, which may in a number of instances originate in life, appears in art and then, if the artist is successful, may become life once more. Wolfe therefore recognizes that the artist, in addition to striving to fix eternally a single moment, tries as well "to make live again" that "moment in lost time" (*Letters*, p. 322), just as Faulkner believes that the artist holds the moment fixed "so that a hundred years later, when a stranger looks at it, it moves again since it is life" (Stein, "Faulkner," p. 139). Virginia Woolf's aim is to startle her readers "into a flash of understanding" (*Moment*, p. 129); Durrell's is to produce in his readers "the vicarious feel of the poetic illumination" ("Kneller Tape," p. 163); and Nathalie Sarraute so values her tropisms that she seeks through her art to "communicate them to the reader" and "make him experience analogous sensations" (*Tropisms*, p. 8). Even Pater's Marius the Epicurean, though not an artist, wishes to be able to arrest his experiences "for others also" (p. 105).

Perhaps the classic fictional example of an epiphany arising from the apprehension or appreciation of a work of art is the one centering on Vinteuil's sonata, in Proust: it provides not merely a revelation of the work itself, but also a revelation for the listener of the world beyond the work of art, and of his own existence. Indeed, Vinteuil's music does this for two people, first for Swann and then for Marcel, who reflects upon the relationship between art and reality, and finds it difficult to distinguish between the privileged moments produced by each, since "nothing resembled more closely than some such phrase of Vinteuil the peculiar pleasure which I had felt at certain moments in my life, when gazing, for instance, at the steeples of Martinville, or at certain trees along a road near Balbec, or, more simply, in the first part of this book, when I tasted a certain cup of tea" (*Captive*, 2 :642).

These artistic qualities, hopes, and aspirations help account for the power of the literary epiphany, which is powerful because at its best it ceases to be simply literary. And when it does so it yields the kind of aesthetic sensation for which epiphanies are uniquely suited, and which now and then they do in fact provide for readers of modern fiction : the privileged moment, the sudden spiritual manifestation, the moment of being, the blaze of light, the flash, the glare that only great art can generate.

Abrams, M. H. *The Milk of Paradise*. Cambridge, Mass. : Harvard University Press, 1934.

———. *The Mirror and the Lamp: Romantic Theory and the Critical Tradition*. New York : Oxford University Press, 1953.

Adams, Richard P. *Faulkner: Myth and Motion*. Princeton, N.J. : Princeton University Press, 1968.

Adams, Robert M. *James Joyce: Common Sense and Beyond*. New York : Random House, 1966.

Aquinas, St. Thomas. *Basic Writings of Saint Thomas Aquinas*. Edited by Anton C. Pegis. New York : Random House, 1945.

Auerbach, Erich. *Mimesis: The Representation of Reality in Western Literature*. Translated by Willard R. Trask. Princeton, N.J. : Princeton University Press, 1953.

Augustine, St. *Confessions*. Translated by Edward B. Pusey. New York : Random House, 1949.

Baldwin, James. *Another Country*. New York : Dial Press, 1962.

Barnes, Djuna. *Nightwood*. New York : Harcourt, Brace, 1937.

Barth, John. *Lost in the Funhouse*. New York : Grosset & Dunlap, 1969.

Beckett, Samuel. *Molloy*. New York : Grove Press, 1955.

———. *Proust*. New York : Grove Press, n.d.

Beja, Morris. "The Wooden Sword : Threatener and Threatened in the Fiction of James Joyce." *James Joyce Quarterly* 2 (Fall 1964) :33-41.

Bell, Clive. *Art*. London : Chatto & Windus, 1924.

———. *Proust*. New York : Harcourt, Brace, 1929.

———. "Virginia Woolf." *Dial* 77 (December 1924) : 451-65.

Bentley, Phyllis. *Some Observations on the Art of Narrative*. London : Home & Van Thal, 1946.

Bergson, Henri. *An Introduction to Metaphysics*. Translated by T. E. Hulme. New York : Putnam, 1912.

———. *Matter and Memory*. Translated by Nancy Margaret Paul and W. Scott Palmer. London : G. Allen & Unwin, 1911.

———. *Time and Free Will: An Essay on the Immediate Data of Consciousness*. Translated by F. L. Pogson. London : S. Sonnenschein, 1910.

Blackstone, Bernard. *Virginia Woolf*. Writers and Their Work, no. 33. London : Longmans, Green, 1956.

Bowers, David. "Democratic Vistas." In *Literary History of the United States*, edited by Robert E. Spiller, Willard Thorp, Thomas H. Johnson, and Henry Seidel Canby. New York : Macmillan, 1948.

Budgen, Frank. *James Joyce and the Making of Ulysses*. Bloomington : Indiana University Press, 1960.

Butor, Michel. *A Change of Heart*. Translated by Jean Stewart. New York : Simon and Schuster, 1959.

Carlyle, Thomas. *Sartor Resartus and On Heroes and Hero Worship*. London : J. M. Dent & Sons, 1908.

Chapman, Emmanuel. "The Perennial Theme of Beauty and Art." In *Essays in Thomism*, edited by R. E. Brennan. New York : Sheed & Ward, 1942.

Chastaing, Maxime. *La Philosophie de Virginia Woolf*. Paris : Presses Universitaires de France, 1951.

[Chayes,] Irene Hendry. "Joyce's Epiphanies." *Sewanee Review* 54 (Summer 1946) :449-67.

Conrad, Joseph. *Lord Jim: A Romance*. New York : Doubleday, 1924.

————. *The Nigger of the Narcissus: A Tale of the Forecastle*. New York : Doubleday, 1924.

————. *Nostromo: A Tale of the Seaboard*. London : John Grant, 1925.

————. *A Personal Record*. New York : Doubleday, 1924.

————. *The Secret Agent*. New York : Doubleday, 1926.

————. *Typhoon*. New York : Doubleday, 1934.

————. *Youth and Two Other Stories*. New York : Doubleday, 1924.

Cornwell, Ethel F. *The "Still Point."* New Brunswick, N.J. : Rutgers University Press, 1962.

Cowley, Malcolm. *The Faulkner-Cowley File*. New York : Viking Press, 1966.

Daiches, David. *Virginia Woolf*. Rev. ed. Norfolk, Conn : New Directions, 1963.

Delakas, Daniel L. *Thomas Wolfe, la France et les romanciers français*. Paris : Jouve & Cie, 1950.

Delattre, Floris. *Le roman psychologique de Virginia Woolf*. Paris : Librairie Philosophique J. Vrin, 1932.

Dostoyevsky, Fyodor. *The Idiot*. Translated by Constance Garnett. New York : Modern Library, 1935.

———. *The Possessed*. Translated by Andrew R. MacAndrew. New York : New American Library, 1962.

Durrell, Lawrence. *Balthazar*. New York : E. P. Dutton, 1958.

———. *Clea*. New York : E. P. Dutton, 1960.

———. *Collected Poems*. New York : E. P. Dutton, 1960.

———. *Justine*. New York : E. P. Dutton, 1957.

———. *A Key to Modern British Poetry*. Norman, Okla. : University of Oklahoma Press, 1952.

———. "The Kneller Tape (Hamburg)." In *The World of Lawrence Durrell*, edited by Harry T. Moore. New York : E. P. Dutton, 1964.

———. *Mountolive*. New York : E. P. Dutton, 1959.

———, and Henry Miller. *A Private Correspondence*. Edited by George Wickes. New York : E. P. Dutton, 1963.

Edel, Leon. *The Modern Psychological Novel*. New York : Grosset & Dunlap, 1964.

Eliot, T. S. *The Complete Poems and Plays: 1909-1950*. New York : Harcourt, Brace, 1952.

———. "Introduction," in *Nightwood*, by Djuna Barnes. New York : Harcourt, Brace, 1937.

———. *Selected Essays*. New York : Harcourt, Brace, 1950.

Ellmann, Richard. *James Joyce*. New York : Oxford University Press, 1959.

Emerson, Ralph Waldo. *Essays: First and Second Series*. Boston : Houghton, Mifflin, 1883.

———. *Journals*, vol. 4. Edited by E. W. Emerson and W. E. Forbes. Boston : Houghton, Mifflin, 1910.

Faulkner, William. *Absalom, Absalom!* New York : Random House, 1936.

———. *Collected Stories*. New York : Random House, 1950.

———. *Early Prose and Poetry*. Edited by Carvel Collins. Boston : Little, Brown, 1962.

———. *A Fable*. New York : Random House, 1954.

———. *Faulkner at Nagano*. Edited by Robert A. Jelliffe. Tokyo : Kenkyusha, 1956.

———. *Faulkner at West Point*. Edited by Joseph L. Fant, III, and Robert Ashley. New York : Random House, 1964.

————. *Faulkner in the University: Class Conferences at the University of Virginia 1957-1958.* Edited by Frederick L. Gwynn and Joseph L. Blotner. Charlottesville : University of Virginia Press, 1959.

————. *Go Down, Moses.* New York : Random House, 1955.

————. *Intruder in the Dust.* New York : Random House, 1948.

————. *Light in August.* Norfolk, Conn. : New Directions, 1947.

————. *Mosquitoes.* New York : Liveright, 1927.

————. *New Orleans Sketches.* Edited by Carvel Collins. New Brunswick, N.J. : Rutgers University Press, 1958.

————. *Requiem for a Nun.* New York : Random House, 1951.

————. *Sanctuary.* New York : Random House, 1932.

————. *Sartoris.* New York : Harcourt, Brace, 1929.

————. *Soldiers' Pay.* New York : Liveright, 1926.

————. *The Sound and the Fury and As I Lay Dying.* New York : Random House, 1946.

————. *New York Times,* 3 July 1961, p. 6.

Feidelson, Charles, Jr. *Symbolism and American Literature.* Chicago : University of Chicago Press, 1953.

Fitzgerald, F. Scott. *The Letters of F. Scott Fitzgerald.* Edited by Andrew Turnbull. New York : Charles Scribner's Sons, 1963.

Forster, E. M. *Virginia Woolf.* New York : Harcourt, Brace, 1942.

Frank, Joseph. *The Widening Gyre.* New Brunswick, N. J. : Rutgers University Press, 1963.

Freedman, Ralph. *The Lyrical Novel.* Princeton, N.J. : Princeton University Press, 1963.

Freud, Sigmund. "Dostoevsky and Parricide." In *The Future of an Illusion . . . and Other Works.* The Standard Edition of the Complete Psychological Works, vol. 21. Edited and translated by James Strachey et al. London : Hogarth Press, 1961.

————. *Introductory Lectures on Psychoanalysis.* In *The Complete Introductory Lectures on Psychoanalysis.* Edited and translated by James Strachey. New York : W. W. Norton, 1966.

————. *The Psychopathology of Everyday Life.* The Standard Edition of the Complete Psychological Works, vol. 6. Edited and translated by James Strachey et al. London : Hogarth Press, 1960.

————. *The Unconscious.* The Standard Edition of the Complete Psychological Works, vol. 14. Edited and translated by James Strachey et al. London : Hogarth Press. 1957.

Frye, Northrop. *The Modern Century.* Toronto, Ont.: Oxford University Press, 1967.

Gardner, W. H. *Gerard Manley Hopkins (1844-1889).* New Haven, Conn.: Yale University Press, 1948.

Gilbert, Stuart. *James Joyce's Ulysses.* New York: Vintage, 1952.

Givens, Seon, ed. *James Joyce: Two Decades of Criticism.* New York: Vanguard Press, 1948.

Gogarty, Oliver St. John. *As I Was Going down Sackville Street.* London: Reynal and Hitchcock, 1937.

Gold, Herbert. *The Age of Happy Problems.* New York: Dial Press, 1962.

Golding, William. *Pincher Martin.* London: Faber and Faber, 1956.

Graham, J. W. "A Negative Note on Bergson and Virginia Woolf." *Essays in Criticism* 6 (January 1956):70-74.

Grenier, Cynthia. "The Art of Fiction: An Interview with William Faulkner—September, 1955." *Accent* 16 (Summer 1956): 167-77.

Guiguet, Jean. *Virginia Woolf and Her Works.* Translated by Jean Stewart. London: Hogarth Press, 1965.

Hafley, James. *The Glass Roof: Virginia Woolf as Novelist.* Berkeley: University of California Press, 1954.

Hardy, Thomas. *Collected Poems of Thomas Hardy.* New York: Macmillan, 1926.

——. *Jude the Obscure.* London: Macmillan, 1956.

Haugh, Robert F. *Joseph Conrad: Discovery in Design.* Norman: University of Oklahoma Press, 1957.

Havens, Raymond Dexter. *The Mind of a Poet.* Baltimore, Md.: Johns Hopkins Press, 1941.

Heller, Joseph. *Catch-22.* New York: Simon and Schuster, 1961.

Hemingway, Ernest. *In Our Time.* New York: Charles Scribner's Sons, 1958.

Hendry, Irene. See [Chayes,] Irene Hendry.

Hoffman, Frederick J., and Olga W. Vickery, eds. *William Faulkner: Three Decades of Criticism.* East Lansing, Mich.: Michigan State University Press, 1960.

Hopkins, Gerard Manley. *The Correspondence of Gerard Manley Hopkins and Richard Watson Dixon.* Edited by Claude Colleer Abbott. London: Oxford University Press, 1955.

——. *Further Letters of Gerard Manley Hopkins.* Edited by

Claude Colleer Abbott. London : Oxford University Press, 1956.

———. *The Journals and Papers*. Edited by Humphry House and Graham Storey. London : Oxford University Press, 1959.

———. *The Letters of Gerard Manley Hopkins to Robert Bridges*. Edited by Claude Colleer Abbott. London : Oxford University Press, 1955.

———. *The Note-Books and Papers*. Edited by Humphry House. London : Oxford University Press, 1937.

———. *The Poems and Prose of Gerard Manley Hopkins*. Edited by W. H. Gardner. London : Penguin, 1953.

Hulme, T. E. *Speculations*. Edited by Herbert Read. London : Kegan Paul, Trench, Trübner, 1936.

Huxley, Aldous. *The Doors of Perception*. New York : Harper and Brothers, 1954.

James, Henry. *The Altar of the Dead . . . and Other Tales*. New York : Charles Scribner's Sons, 1909.

———. *The Ambassadors*. New York : Charles Scribner's Sons, 1909.

———. *The American*. New York : Charles Scribner's Sons, 1907.

———. *The House of Fiction*. Edited by Leon Edel. London : Rupert Hart-Davis, 1957.

———. *The Sense of the Past*. New York : Charles Scribner's Sons, 1917.

James, William. *The Varieties of Religious Experience*. London : Longmans, Green, 1902.

Jones, Alun R. "Life Is the Story." *New York Times Book Review*, 27 May 1962, p. 6.

Joyce, James. *The Critical Writings*. Edited by Ellsworth Mason and Richard Ellmann. New York : Viking Press, 1959.

———. *Dubliners*. Edited by Robert Scholes and Richard Ellmann. New York : Viking Press, 1967.

———. "The Epiphanies." In *The Workshop of Daedalus*, q.v.

———. *Exiles*. New York : Viking Press, 1951.

———. *Finnegans Wake*. New York : Viking Press, 1958.

———. *Giacomo Joyce*. Edited by Richard Ellmann. New York : Viking Press, 1968.

———. *Letters of James Joyce*, vols. 2 and 3. Edited by Richard Ellmann. New York : Viking Press, 1966.

———. "A Portrait of the Artist." In *The Workshop of Daedalus*, q.v.

————. *A Portrait of the Artist as a Young Man*. Edited by Chester G. Anderson and Richard Ellmann. New York: Viking Press, 1964.

————. *Scribbledehobble: The Ur-Workbook for Finnegans Wake*. Edited by Thomas E. Connolly. Evanston, Ill.: Northwestern University Press, 1961.

————. *Stephen Hero*. Edited by Theodore Spencer, revised by John J. Slocum and Herbert Cahoon. Norfolk, Conn.: New Directions, 1963.

————. "The Trieste Notebook." In *The Workshop of Daedalus*, q.v.

————. *Ulysses*. New York: Random House, 1961/1934.

————. *The Workshop of Daedalus: James Joyce and the Raw Materials for A Portrait of the Artist as a Young Man*. Edited by Robert Scholes and Richard M. Kain. Evanston, Ill.: Northwestern University Press, 1965.

Joyce, Stanislaus. *The Dublin Diary of Stanislaus Joyce*. Edited by George Harris Healey. London: Faber & Faber, 1962.

————. *My Brother's Keeper: James Joyce's Early Years*. Edited by Richard Ellmann. New York, 1958.

Jung, C. G. *The Spirit in Man, Art, and Literature*. The Collected Works, vol. 15. Edited by Gerhard Adler et al., translated by R. F. C. Hull. New York: Pantheon Books, 1966.

Kafka, Franz. *The Castle*. Translated by Willa and Edwin Muir, with additional materials translated by Eithne Wilkins and Ernst Kaiser. New York: Alfred A. Knopf, 1954.

————. *Dearest Father*. Translated by Ernst Kaiser and Eithne Wilkins. New York: Schocken Books, 1954.

————. *The Diaries: 1914-1923*. Edited by Max Brod, translated by Martin Greenberg and Hannah Arendt. New York: Schocken Books, 1949.

————. *The Great Wall of China*. Translated by Willa and Edwin Muir. New York: Schocken Books, 1946.

————. *The Penal Colony*. Translated by Willa and Edwin Muir. New York: Schocken Books, 1948.

————. *The Trial*. Translated by Willa and Edwin Muir, with additional materials translated by E. M. Butler. New York: Random House, 1956.

Kennedy, Richard S. *The Window of Memory: The Literary Career of Thomas Wolfe*. Chapel Hill: University of North Carolina Press, 1962.

Kenner, Hugh. *Dublin's Joyce*. Bloomington : Indiana University Press, 1956.

———. "The Portrait in Perspective." In *James Joyce: Two Decades of Criticism*, edited by Seon Givens. New York : Vanguard Press, 1948.

———. *The Poetry of Ezra Pound*. Norfolk, Conn. : New Directions, [1951].

Keynes, John Maynard. *Two Memoirs*. London : Rupert Hart-Davis, 1949.

Kohler, Dayton. "Time in the Modern Novel." *College English* 10 (October 1948) : 15-24.

Kumar, Shiv K. *Bergson and the Stream of Consciousness Novel*. New York : New York University Press, 1963.

Langer, Susanne K. *Philosophy in a New Key: A Study in the Symbolism of Reason, Rite, and Art*. New York : New American Library, 1949.

Leaska, Mitchell A. *Virginia Woolf's Lighthouse: A Study in Critical Method*. London : Hogarth Press, 1970.

Levin, Harry. *James Joyce*. Norfolk, Conn. : New Directions, 1960.

Lewis, Wyndham. *Time and Western Man*. New York : Harcourt, Brace, 1928.

Litz, A. Walton. *The Art of James Joyce*. London : Oxford University Press, 1961.

McKillop, Alan Dugald. *The Early Masters of English Fiction*. Lawrence, Kan. : University of Kansas Press, 1956.

Magalaner, Marvin, ed. *A James Joyce Miscellany: Second Series*. Carbondale, Ill. : Southern Illinois University Press, 1959.

———. *Time of Apprenticeship: The Fiction of Young James Joyce*. London : Abelard-Schuman, 1959.

———, and Richard M. Kain. *Joyce: The Man, the Work, the Reputation*. New York : New York University Press, 1956.

Mann, Thomas. "Dostoyevsky—Within Limits." Translated by H. T. Lowe-Porter, in *The Thomas Mann Reader*, edited by Joseph Warner Angell. New York :Grosset & Dunlap, 1950.

———. *The Magic Mountain*. Translated by H. T. Lowe-Porter. New York : Alfred A. Knopf, 1958.

Matthiessen, F. O. *American Renaissance*. New York : Oxford University Press, 1941.

Mauron, Charles. *The Nature of Beauty in Art and Literature*. Translated by Roger Fry. London : Hogarth Press, 1927.

Mill, John Stuart. *Autobiography*. New York: H. Holt. 1874.

Millgate, Michael. *The Achievement of William Faulkner*. London: Constable, 1966.

Mitchell, Julian, and Gene Andrewski. "Lawrence Durrell." In *Writers at Work: The "Paris Review" Interviews: Second Series*. New York: Viking Press, 1963.

Moore, George Edward. *Principia Ethica*. Cambridge: Cambridge University Press, 1922.

Moore, Harry T., ed. *The World of Lawrence Durrell*. New York: E. P. Dutton, 1964.

Natanson, M. A. "Privileged Moment: A Study in the Rhetoric of Thomas Wolfe." *Quarterly Journal of Speech* 43 (April 1957):143-50.

Newman, John Henry. *Apologia pro Vita Sua*. Edited by Wilfrid Ward. London: Henry Frowde, 1913.

Noon, William T., S.J. *Joyce and Aquinas*. New Haven, Conn.: Yale University Press, 1957.

Ortega y Gasset, José. "Time, Distance, and Form in Proust." *Hudson Review* 11 (Winter 1958-59):504-13.

Pater, Walter. *Appreciations*. London: Macmillan, 1931.

———. *Marius the Epicurean: His Sensations and Ideas*. Edited by Joseph Sagmaster. New York: Doubleday, Doran, 1935.

———. *The Renaissance: Studies in Art and Poetry*. London: Macmillan, 1909.

Payne, Robert. *Dostoyevsky*. New York, 1961.

Peters, W. A. M., S.J. *Gerard Manley Hopkins: A Critical Essay towards the Understanding of His Poetry*. London: Oxford University Press, 1948.

Pippett, Aileen. *The Moth and the Star: A Biography of Virginia Woolf*. Boston: Little, Brown, 1953.

Poulet, Georges. *Studies in Human Time*. Translated by Elliott Coleman. Baltimore, Md.: Johns Hopkins Press, 1956.

Pound, Ezra. "A Few Dont's by an Imagiste." *Poetry* 1 (March 1913):200-6.

Proust, Marcel. *Jean Santeuil*. Translated by Gerard Hopkins. London: Weidenfeld & Nicolson, 1955.

———. *Letters*. Edited and translated by Mina Curtiss. New York: Random House, 1949.

———. *Remembrance of Things Past*. Translated by C. K. Scott Moncrieff and Frederick A. Blossom. New York: Random House,

1934.

Rank, Otto. *Beyond Psychology*. Camden, N.J. [privately published], 1941.

Richardson, Dorothy. *Pilgrimage*. New York: Alfred A. Knopf, 1967.

Robbe-Grillet, Alain. "A Fresh Start for Fiction." Translated by Richard Howard. *Evergreen Review* 1, 3 [1957]: 97-104.

———. *Instantanés*. Paris. Editions de minuit, 1962.

———. *In the Labyrinth*. Translated by Richard Howard. New York: Grove Press, 1960.

———. *Jealousy*. Translated by Richard Howard. New York: Grove Press, 1959.

———. *Last Year at Marienbad*. Translated by Richard Howard. New York: Grove Press, 1962.

———. *La Maison de Rendez-vous*. Translated by Richard Howard. New York: Grove Press, 1966.

———. "Old 'Values' and the New Novel." Translated by Bruce Morrissette. *Evergreen Review* 3 (Summer 1959):98-118.

———. *The Voyeur*. Translated by Richard Howard. New York: Grove Press, 1958.

Rousseau, Jean Jacques. *The Confessions*. Translated anonymously, revised by A. S. B. Glover. London: Nonesuch Press, 1938.

———. *The Reveries of a Solitary*. Translated by John Gould Fletcher. London: George Routledge & Sons, 1927.

Rubin, Louis D., Jr. *Thomas Wolfe: The Weather of His Youth*. Baton Rouge: Louisiana State University Press, 1955.

Sarraute, Nathalie. *The Golden Fruits*. Translated by Maria Jolas. New York: George Braziller, 1964.

———. *Martereau*. Translated by Maria Jolas. New York: George Braziller, 1959.

———. *Tropisms and The Age of Suspicion*. Translated by Maria Jolas. London: John Calder, 1963.

Sartre, Jean-Paul. "Time in Faulkner: *The Sound and the Fury*." Translated by Martine Darmon. In *William Faulkner: Three Decades of Criticism*, edited by Frederick J. Hoffman and Olga W. Vickery. East Lansing: Michigan State University Press, 1960.

Scholes, Robert. "Joyce and the Epiphany: The Key to the Labyrinth?" *Sewanee Review* 72 (Winter 1964):65-77.

———, and Richard M. Kain, eds. *The Workshop of Daedalus:*

James Joyce and the Raw Materials for A Portrait of the Artist as a Young Man. Evanston, Ill.: Northwestern University Press, 1965.

————, and Florence L. Walzl. "The Epiphanies of Joyce." *PMLA* 82 (March 1967): 152-54.

Schopenhauer, Arthur. *The World as Will and Idea.* Translated by R. B. Haldane and J. Kemp. London: Kegan Paul, Trench, Trübner, 1896.

Shelley, Percy Bysshe. *The Complete Poetical Works of Shelley.* Edited by George Edward Woodberry. Cambridge, Mass.: Houghton, Mifflin, 1901.

Slatoff, Walter J. *Quest for Failure: A Study of William Faulkner.* Ithaca, N.Y.: Cornell University Press, 1960.

Stein, Jean. "William Faulkner." In *Writers at Work: The "Paris Review" Interviews,* edited by Malcolm Cowley. New York: Viking Press, 1958.

Sterne, Laurence. *The Life and Opinions of Tristram Shandy, Gentleman.* Edited by James Aiken Work. New York: Odyssey Press, 1940.

Stevens, Wallace. *The Collected Poems.* New York: Alfred A. Knopf, 1954.

————. *The Necessary Angel: Essays on Reality and the Imagination.* New York: Alfred A. Knopf, 1951.

————. *Opus Posthumous.* Edited by Samuel French Morse. New York: Alfred A. Knopf, 1957.

Styron, William. *The Confessions of Nat Turner.* New York: Random House, 1967.

————. *Lie Down in Darkness.* New York: Bobbs-Merrill, 1951.

————. *Set This House on Fire.* New York: Random House, 1960.

Suzuki, D. T. *Essays in Zen Buddhism (First Series).* London: Rider, 1949.

————. *Zen Buddhism.* Edited by William Barrett. New York: Doubleday, 1956.

Trilling, Lionel. "Introduction." In *The Collected Stories,* by Isaac Babel, edited and translated by Walter Morison. New York: Meridian Books, 1955.

Turnbull, Andrew. *Scott Fitzgerald.* New York: Charles Scribner's Sons, 1962.

Turquet-Milnes, G. *From Pascal to Proust: Studies in the Genealogy of a Philosophy.* London: Jonathan Cape, 1926.

Unger, Leonard. "Ash Wednesday." In *T. S. Eliot: A Selected Critique*, edited by Leonard Unger. New York : Rinehart, 1948.

————. "T. S. Eliot's Rose Garden." In *T. S. Eliot: A Selected Critique*, edited by Leonard Unger. New York : Rinehart, 1948.

Von Phul, Ruth. "Joyce and the Strabismal Apologia." In *A James Joyce Miscellany: Second Series*, edited by Marvin Magalaner. Carbondale : Southern Illinois University Press, 1959.

Wallant, Edward Lewis. *The Children at the Gate*. New York : Harcourt, Brace & World, 1964.

————. *The Human Season*. New York : Berkley Medallion Books, 1960.

————. *The Pawnbroker*. New York : Harcourt, Brace & World, 1961.

————. *The Tenants of Moonbloom*. New York : Popular Library, 1963.

Walzl, Florence L. "The Liturgy of the Epiphany Season and the Epiphanies of Joyce." *PMLA* 80 (September 1965) :436-50.

Warfield, Benjamin B. "Augustine." In *Encyclopaedia of Religion and Ethics*, vol. 2, edited by James Hastings. New York : Charles Scribner's Sons, 1912.

Wilde, Oscar. *The Picture of Dorian Gray*. In *Complete Works of Oscar Wilde*, vol. 2, edited by Robert Ross. Boston : Wyman-Fogg, n.d.

Wolfe, Thomas. *From Death to Morning*. New York : Charles Scribner's Sons, 1935.

————. *The Hills Beyond*. New York : Harper & Brothers, 1941.

————. *Letters*. Edited by Elizabeth Nowell. New York : Charles Scribner's Sons, 1956.

————. *Letters to His Mother Julia Elizabeth Wolfe*. New York : Charles Scribner's Sons, 1943.

————. *Look Homeward, Angel*. New York : Charles Scribner's Sons, 1952.

————. *Mannerhouse*. New York : Harper & Brothers, 1948.

————. *Of Time and the River*. New York : Charles Scribner's Sons, 1935.

————. *The Story of a Novel*. New York : Charles Scribner's Sons, 1936.

————. *The Web and the Rock*. New York : Harper & Brothers, 1958.

———. *You Can't Go Home Again.* New York : Harper & Brothers, 1949.

Woolf, Leonard. *Beginning Again: An Autobiography of the Years 1911-1918.* London : Hogarth Press, 1964.

Woolf, Virginia. *Between the Acts.* London : Hogarth Press, 1941.

———. *The Captain's Death Bed and Other Essays.* New York : Harcourt, Brace, 1950.

———. *The Common Reader: First Series.* London : Hogarth Press, 1957.

———. *The Common Reader: Second Series.* London : Hogarth Press, 1953.

———. *A Haunted House and Other Short Stories.* London : Hogarth Press, 1953.

———. *Jacob's Room.* London : Hogarth Press, 1929.

———. "Lord Jim." *TLS*, no. 810 (26 July 1917) :355.

———. *The Moment and Other Essays.* London : Hogarth Press, 1952.

———. "Moments of Vision." *TLS*, no. 853 (23 May 1918) :243.

———. *Mrs. Dalloway.* London : Hogarth Press, 1958.

———. *Night and Day.* London : Hogarth Press, 1950.

———. *Orlando: A Biography.* New York : Harcourt, Brace, 1928.

———. *Roger Fry: A Biography.* New York : Harcourt, Brace, 1940.

———. *A Room of One's Own.* London : Hogarth Press, 1954.

———. *To the Lighthouse.* London : Hogarth Press, 1960.

———. *The Voyage Out.* London : Hogarth Press, 1957.

———. *The Waves.* London : Hogarth Press, 1955.

———. "The Waves." MS in the Berg Collection, New York Public Library.

———. *A Writer's Diary.* Edited by Leonard Woolf. London : Hogarth Press, 1954.

———. *The Years.* New York : Harcourt, Brace, 1937.

———, and Lytton Strachey. *Letters.* Edited by Leonard Woolf and James Strachey. London : Hogarth Press, 1956.

Wordsworth, William. *The Poetical Works of William Wordsworth.* Edited by E. de Selincourt and Helen Darbishire. Oxford : Clarendon Press, 1946.

Zink, Karl E. "Flux and the Frozen Moment : The Imagery of Stasis in Faulkner's Prose." *PMLA* 71 (June 1956) :285-301.

Index

Index